American Foreign Policy in a New Era

American Foreign Policy in a New Era

Robert Jervis

Routledge
Taylor & Francis Group

NEW YORK AND LONDON

Published in 2005 by
Routledge
Taylor & Francis Group
270 Madison Avenue
New York, NY 10016
www.routledge-ny.com

Published in Great Britain by
Routledge
Taylor & Francis Group
2 Park Square
Milton Park, Abingdon
Oxon OX14 4RN
www.routledge.co.uk

10 9 8 7 6 5 4 3 2 1

Library of Congress Cataloging-in-Publication Data

Jervis, Robert, 1940-
  American foreign policy in a new era / Robert Jervis.
    p. cm.
  Includes bibliographical references and index.
  ISBN 0-415-95100-3 (hardback : alk. paper) – ISBN 0-415-95101-1 (pbk. : alk. paper)
1. United States–Foreign relations–2001- 2. Bush, George W. (George Walker), 1946—Political and social views. 3. War on Terrorism, 2001- 4. Deterrence (Strategy) 5. Warfare. 6. World politics–21st century. 7. International relations. 8. Security, International. 9. Balance of power. I. Title.
  E902.J47 2005
  327.73–dc22

2004028638

Permissions

"Theories of war in an Era of Leading-Power Peace" originally appeared in *American Political Science Review* 96, no. 1 (March 2002): 1–14. Reprinted with the permission of Cambridge University Press.

A version of "September 11: How Has It Changed the World?" originally appeared in *Political Science Quarterly* 117, no. I (Spring 2002): 37–54. Reprinted by permission from *Political Science Quarterly*.

"The Confrontation between Iraq and the United States: Implications for the Theory and Practice of Deterrence" originally appeared in *European Journal of International Relations* 9, no. 2 (2003): 315–338. Reprinted by permission of Sage Publications Ltd. (© Sage Publications and ECPR [European Consortium for Political Research], 2003)

A version of "Understanding the Bush Doctrine" originally appeared in *Political Science Quarterly* 118, no. 3 (Fall 2003): 365–388. Reprinted by permission from *Political Science Quarterly*.

Dedication

To the memory of my parents, Dorothy and Herman Jervis, who tolerated and even encouraged my fascination with politics.

CONTENTS

ACKNOWLEDGMENTS

I am grateful for comments by Robert Art, Richard Betts, Demetrious James Caraley, Dale Copeland, Gregory Gause, Peter Gourevitch, Chaim Kaufmann, Deborah Larson, Robert Lieber, John Mueller, Barry Posen, Robert Schulzinger, Marc Trachtenberg, Kenneth Waltz, and Dessie Zagorcheva. As usual, the work-study staff of the Saltzman Institute of War and Peace Studies and its tireless administrator, Ingrid Gerstmann, provided quick assistance in tracking down all sorts of odd sources, and in a most congenial manner the members of the Institute and the faculty and students at Columbia gave me great intellectual stimulation and more challenges than I could meet.

INTRODUCTION

The first chapter of this book was sent to the publisher the morning that the planes struck the World Trade Center. I do not have to tell anyone how rapidly the world has changed in recent years, and while professors are supposed to concentrate on general theories and long-run trends, the temptation to try to understand our new world is hard to resist. Yielding to it, I hope, has value for both scholarship and the interested public. Our general theories about international politics inform—or should inform—our views about unfolding events, just as the latter probe, if not break, the former. Good social science theories are powerful tools to help make sense of the twists and turns of events that are themselves unpredictable.

Current world politics challenges many of our theories because it is new in fundamental ways. As I will discuss in chapter 1, the leading powers in the world no longer fear armed conflict with one another, a development we take for granted but that in fact is an enormous, indeed revolutionary, change from the past. A related change, which may be one of the main causes for peace among the leading powers, is unipolarity or American hegemony. With the disintegration of the Soviet Union and the failure of Europe to unite, no state is in a position to challenge the United States in terms of material power, widespread influence, ability to set the framework for debate, and the capability—although in many areas not a willingness—to provide public goods.

Whether or not this is beneficial to the United States or the rest of the world, the most important thing is that American power exists and is fantastically great, to paraphrase Bernard Brodie's famous statement about nuclear weapons.[1] I will argue, however, that while this degree of dominance is unprecedented in modern history, American behavior tracks in important ways with what very powerful states have done in the past, and that it is likely to prove self-defeating.

A third change, the rise of terrorism and the American response to it, may not prove to be as basic or lasting, but it now rivets our attention. To an extent that is impossible to determine with any precision, these phenomena are related to the first two changes. Whether the United States would have been the target of the attacks of September 11 if it were not so powerful is an open question, but the American response is clearly conditioned by the nation's great capabilities and the lack of challenges from peers. The attacks move us into new terrain where normal state-to-state relations offer relatively few guidelines. But even if established theories of international politics and foreign policy say little about the causes and consequences of terrorism, they tell us much more about how states are likely to respond, why the Bush administration has adopted the foreign policy that it has, whether there were viable alternatives for dealing with Iraq, and whether current policies can be sustained.

The chapters in this book discuss these topics and present snapshots of world politics over the past few years, taking up important questions as they became salient since 2001. I have made only minor changes in them to avoid awkwardness and to bring matters up to date. The collection as a whole makes no claim to be comprehensive. Most obviously, I focus on security issues. Globalization, the state of the world economy, and American foreign economic policy are also crucial, as are evolving conceptions and practices of sovereignty and human rights. Overhanging all of this is the possibility that human activities will fundamentally change our environment, most clearly by producing global climate change. These questions are beyond my expertise, but the fact that I do not discuss them does not mean that I think they are unimportant.

ANALYSIS AND PRESCRIPTION

This book explicates and explains more than evaluates and prescribes. Of course these tasks intertwine both logically and psychologically, but there is no incompatibility between trying to understand a policy and condemning it. Scholarship should start, if not end, with understanding, however, and a strong dose of humility, useful in trying to construct explanations, is even more appropriate for prescriptions.[2] But I should acknowledge at the start that I am deeply critical of most aspects of Bush's foreign policy. I believe that the overthrow of the

Saddam regime and the broader Bush Doctrine have diminished American security, not increased it.

Most obviously, while the Bush administration waged war in Iraq to reduce the long-term threat of terrorism, I believe it has had the opposite effect. Proof of course is impossible, but it is almost beyond doubt that the American policy has served to alienate much of the Arab world and recruit many terrorists to the cause. Indeed, those with conspiratorial minds might conclude that George Bush was a paid agent of Osama bin Laden: after the Madrid bombings of March 11, 2004, al-Qaeda said that it hoped for his reelection "because he acts with force rather then wisdom or shrewdness, and it is his religious fanaticism that will arouse our [Islamic] nation, as has been shown. Being targeted by an enemy is what will rouse us from our slumber."[3] The attack on Iraq, coupled with the almost unqualified support for Sharon, convinced many people that American policy is fundamentally anti-Islamic. Furthermore, the insurgency in Iraq has provided inspiration and a training ground for future terrorists. My guess is that the coming years will see any number of attacks by people who watched the carnage on Al-Jazeera or learned their craft in Iraq.

The administration's war aims ranged from making a democratic Iraq a model for the region, to furthering the war on terror, to gaining the support and participation of the international community.[4] They now make for dispiriting reading. Although the purpose of this book is not to give immediate policy advice, in part because by the time it appears the situation will have changed, I should state that ever since the political configuration appeared to be as difficult as I had expected and the insurgency grew more serious than I had anticipated (i.e., about a year after the invasion), I concluded that the best of the bad alternatives was for the United States to follow the strategy Senator Aiken urged in Vietnam: declare victory and leave. The problems facing Iraq cannot be solved by U.S. forces at the level we are willing to commit, staying longer will not improve the situation, and the constructive figures and factions in Iraq might be forced to cooperate when faced with the danger of civil war. Slogans that the United States must stay the course without wavering are a substitute for thought.

Condemning a policy can impede understanding it. This trap I believe I have avoided, although this is for the reader to judge. Indeed, although I see the particular outlook of Bush and his entourage as part of the explanation, I stress structural factors emanating from America's position in the international system. We often attribute failing policies to leaders' intellectual or moral shortcomings. Much as I think these are present in the Bush administration, we should overlook neither the sensible impulses behind the policy nor the degree to which it is a common response to the combination of great power and great fears.[5] It is particularly important not to jump to the conclusion that Bush and his colleagues are particularly limited and maladroit. The combination of the President's inarticulateness, the Secretary of Defense's apparently purposeless belligerence, and the Vice President's postmodern unwillingness to separate fact and fiction do point in this direction. Even though the leaders of the Bush administration, far from knowing things about Iraq that the rest of us did not, were blinded by what they wanted to see, it is readily apparent to anyone who has argued with Condoleezza Rice or Paul Wolfowitz that they know at least as much about international politics as do the critics. If the policy appears foolish in retrospect, and especially if the attempt to produce a stable, if not democratic, Iraq fails, however, people not only will search for culpability, but also will look for devious explanations, on the grounds that no sensible and well-motivated person would have acted in this way. Indeed, it is quite likely that failure will lead the most common explanation to be that the war was fought for oil and Israel. This would be most unfortunate.

There is some tension between explaining the policies largely as a response to the external environment, on the one hand, and claiming that they will end badly, on the other. If leaders are at all rational and if they seek to further the national interest, they should avoid patterns of behavior that have failed previously. But they do not. The pressures and temptations of great power produce recurrent pathologies. The United States may yet be able to resist these, but I believe that the behavior we have seen since September 11, 2001 is misguided but not unusual.

Most students of international politics, including those who see threats and the use of force as central, opposed the war in Iraq and many other aspects of Bush's policy. They believe that force should be a last resort, that diplomacy and conciliation are highly valued instruments, that alliances are of great value, and that foreign policies should not be overly ambitious. The fact that these general principles command approval across many divides in the scholarly community does not mean that they are correct or apply to this situation, however. Indeed, this general understanding of world politics led most of us to strongly oppose the expansion of NATO on the grounds that the countries being proposed as new members did not need security guarantees, that there were alternative ways to bring them into Europe, and that the cost in terms of friction with Russia would be very great.[6]

We were wrong, or at least our expectations about the effects on Russia were not borne out. Similarly, many of us, again including me, doubted that the Bush administration could successfully orchestrate six-party talks to deal with North Korea rather than having to engage in bilateral discussions. Of course at this point it is far from clear that the policy will succeed, but that the United States has gotten this far is a good reminder that we may be wrong, that we should be sensitive to evidence that indicates we are, and that we should eschew the ridicule and contempt that come so easily to experts whose advice is not heeded. But humility should not inhibit us from criticizing the policy as strongly as we think is merited.

American policy since 9/11 poses important questions for scholarship as well as for policy, and so this book is something of a hybrid. Although partially motivated by my opposition to American policy, it also seeks to understand what the events imply for our theories and what theories the actors seem to hold. As I will discuss in more detail in chapter 4, much of the American behavior conforms to the standard realist generalization that a state's definition of its interest will expand as its power does. More specifically, Offensive Realism perhaps provides the best explanation for what the United States is doing because it sees states as always wanting more power in order to try to gain more security for an uncertain future, although some of its proponents oppose these policies.[7]

This reminds us that many arguments about foreign policy are descriptive and explanatory, on the one hand, and prescriptive, on the other. When states behave "badly," theoretical claims may be embarrassed. Hans Morgenthau's assertions that states follow their objective national interests fit uneasily with his exhortations for them to do so, and claims that deterrent policies will produce certain effects run into difficulties when the actors do not agree, as I will discuss in chapter 3. We are theorizing about the behavior of actors who have their own theories, which may be different from ours, and we have a problem explaining behavior we consider foolish when our theories do not incorporate foolishness.[8] Models of strategic behavior do not do well when one or both of the players are incompetent, and sophisticated game theory arguments are problematic if they involve more complex and arcane calculations than people are likely to make.

Neorealism is not a theory of foreign policy and does not purport to explain or predict what individual states will do.[9] But it is not clear how many other theories can take the Fifth Amendment in this way. Individual scholars like myself who find American policy not only wrong but unusually misguided are hard pressed to come up with an account that is much more than ad hoc, or even ad hominem (which of course does not mean that such arguments are wrong). Nevertheless, realists of many kinds simultaneously believe that the desire for greater security, material benefits, and status will lead states to expand their influence when there are no immediate checks on their doing so, and that this behavior is self-defeating in the long run. Classical realists see the cause in human nature—modern realists, in the opportunities and temptations presented by the international environment. But if decision makers understood these patterns, they would presumably at least try to act differently. Perhaps a clue to some of the puzzles lies in the disorientation and fear produced by the terrorist attacks, as I will discuss in chapter 2.

The difficulties in coping with this fear may be one reason why the American debate over whether to go to war in Iraq was so feeble. Also important were the president's political skill, the Democrats' desire not to look weak, and—a factor often overlooked—the fact that the draft has been abolished. The immediate danger in the war was to other people and to other people's children. But in another way the debate was typical, in that both proponents and opponents of invading Iraq displayed irrational cognitive consistency, motivated bias, and the refusal to face value trade-offs.[10] Those who favored invasion rated the long-term prospects of deterring Saddam as low, the likelihood of a fairly easy military victory as high, the regional effects of overthrowing Saddam as favorable, and the prospects for constructing a stable and even democratic Iraq as bright. Opponents disagreed on all four points. Only a psychological explanation will account for this pattern, because the four factors being judged are logically independent from each other. A world in which allowing Saddam to build his weapons of mass destruction (WMD) would be very dangerous is not necessarily one in which overthrowing him would be relatively cheap. But people want to minimize the costs they perceive in their favored policy. In fact, many of the reasons they give are rationalizations, not rationales, and come to their minds only after they have reached their decisions.

INTELLIGENCE

Intelligence and intelligence failures loom large in the world we are trying to understand. It was ushered in by the most dramatic intelligence failure since Pearl Harbor and was followed by the gross overestimate of the vigor with which Saddam Hussein was pursuing WMDs, a striking misunderstanding of the postwar Iraqi landscape, and the prisoner abuse scandal. We may not think of the latter as an intelligence failure because what the leaders failed to understand was not what others were doing, but the actions taken within their own organization. But it was an intelligence failure in the broad sense, and it is often as difficult to know what one's own government is doing as it is to understand others, especially for naïve decision makers who think that their orders— or what they believe to be their orders—will be carried out to the letter. In this case, unlike many others, the failure is not made understandable or excusable by the lack of plausibility of the behavior. Far from it; abuses of prisoners are common in every country and every war, and although the full story is not available at this writing, it is clear that the Bush administration put pressure on the untrained and understaffed prison personnel to help produce valuable information. The fact that early warning signs from the Red Cross and others were disregarded cannot be explained by their seeming far-fetched. The blame for the error, therefore, must be a good deal greater than it is in the more familiar ones of 9/11 and Iraqi WMD.[11]

That most of the errors on Iraq were heavily driven by political preferences does not change the fact that future American foreign policy, especially if it follows the path laid down by President Bush, will require a good understanding of what motivates other countries, what they are likely to do in the future, and how they will respond to alternative American policies. We must therefore acknowledge the fact that intelligence, in both the narrow technical sense and the broader sense of understanding our environment, is very difficult, especially when we are dealing with a new political configuration and a wide variety of actors. The concluding chapter will discuss the intelligence failure in Iraq, but since the failure to anticipate the attacks of September 11, 2001 is so important and has received so much attention, I want to discuss it briefly here.

Many of the reasons for the failure are well known. The CIA was unable to gain sources within al-Qaeda's inner circle; the CIA and FBI did not share the information they did get; the incentives and organizational culture of the FBI were ill-suited to the task at hand; and the attacks themselves were audacious and were implicitly taken to be implausible by all but a handful of experts, which means that it would have required a great deal of unambiguous information for the preparations to have been detected.

I doubt if things would have been different with another president, but the Bush administration did suffer from four handicaps. First, it was new to the job, and no administration in modern history has been able to get off to a good start. The world and the government machinery are so complicated that the first year or two is essentially a period of transition in which mistakes are inevitable. Second, as Bush and his colleagues made clear in the presidential campaign and their first months in power, their focus was on great-power relations, particularly the potential menaces represented by China and Russia. Nation-states were the main actors in their worldview; terrorists not only were a second-order phenomenon but also gained their potency largely to the extent that they had state sponsorship. Third, even more than most administrations, this one was set on rejecting its predecessor's policies. The very fact that Clinton had said that terrorism was the greatest danger the United States was facing was reason for them to look elsewhere. Finally, these problems were compounded by Bush's lack of inquisitiveness. What is striking about his reaction to the August 6 Presidential Daily Brief (PDB) and other information about terrorism was not that he failed to see that al-Qaeda was about to fly airplanes into buildings but that he did not ask questions, probe more deeply, or call for follow-up reports.[12]

But hindsight misleads us twice over. First, pointing out how 9/11 could have been anticipated and avoided is not the same as showing that this really could have been done. This is especially true for the crucial matter of how the government was organized to deal with terrorism. The political and psychological obstacles to close cooperation between the CIA and FBI and more extensive intelligence-gathering powers were very great, and the opposition to them was rooted not only in deeply held preferences of the bureaucracy but also in good reasons of public policy and political philosophy. In fact, I think the measures needed to avoid September 11 could not have been taken without the shock of September 11.

Second, it is a fundamental misunderstanding to see the problem in terms of the failure to "connect the dots." There were countless dots—all of them, not only those whose significance is apparent in retrospect—and they could have been connected in a great many ways. I am sure that if we look back at all the information that was received, not only the bits that we now know could have led us to the plot, we will find a huge number of false alarms. These could have been significant, and at the time there was no reasonable way of deciding that they were not, and that it was the danger that turned out to be the real one that demanded our attention. For example, in retrospect the presence in flying schools of a handful of Arabs without obvious employment prospects called for immediate investigation, but if the attacks had been delivered by commercial gasoline or chemical trucks, we would now be bemoaning the failure to see the significance of the scattered warnings—which I am sure we could find—about Arabs who were enrolled in truck-driving schools. The same problem arises on a broader scale. If the crisis of late 2001 had turned out to be a PRC confrontation with Taiwan, which I think in the summer appeared no less likely than a terrorist attack, then we would be criticizing Bush for having been distracted by all sorts of minor threats and failing to focus on the main danger. Intelligence usually fails because information is very ambiguous and can be correctly interpreted only by the right theory, and this theory is not likely to be any more plausible than several competitors.[13] Indeed, as I will discuss more in the last chapter, what turns out to be the truth may be quite implausible not only given the evidence at the time, but in retrospect. Many things that happen simply do not make much sense, thereby presenting a nightmare for intelligence.

OUTLINE

The plan of the book is as follows. The first chapter discusses a change in world politics that is apparently unrelated to current pressing issues, but is fundamental and provides the context for much of what we are seeing. This is the fact that the leading countries of the world no longer contemplate war with each other. This is hardly a startling statement. Most of us take it for granted, and my undergraduate students are puzzled that I even bother asking them whether they think they will see a war between the United States and the countries of Europe or Japan in their lifetimes. But as those with longer memories know, the history of international politics is the history of war among the most powerful states. It is therefore crucial that we explore this change, understand its causes, and contemplate its implications. After that, I turn to the general impact of September 11 on world politics. Of course one must be tentative here, and in fact my own views have changed in response to events and further thought. Although change continues, we can nevertheless trace a number of issues, such as whether the struggles against terrorism should be considered a war, the relationship between terrorism and American support for illiberal foreign regimes, and the role of fear in the American response.

The invasion of Afghanistan was a widely approved measure to combat terrorism, even if its long-run effects remain uncertain. The invasion of Iraq was much more controversial, and the next chapter analyzes the crucial argument that Saddam posed such a threat to the United States that he had to be overthrown. More specifically, I evaluate the claim that if Saddam had gained nuclear weapons, he could have greatly expanded his influence in the Middle East and blackmailed the United States. The discussion here pivots on a counterfactual, since I argue that nuclear weapons would not have given Saddam the sort of influence that the proponents of the war believed. Even more than in many of the topics discussed in this book, proof is necessarily beyond us. Behavior of future "rogues," although relevant to my claim, could not prove or disprove it, because they will not be clones of Saddam and their behavior, for better or for worse, will have been influenced by his overthrow. The issue of whether rogues can be deterred, however, is a continuing one, and judgments about it drive many policy preferences (or perhaps these judgments are a product of preferences for regime change reached on other grounds). Deterrence theory is quite intricate, however, and readers who are not interested in its details may prefer to skip over the middle sections.

The next chapter looks at the broader approach that led to American policy on Iraq. Despite some tensions and inconsistencies, the Bush Doctrine is remarkably coherent and needs to be taken seriously. The fact that I and most experts think that it is badly flawed makes it particularly urgent that we understand it and consider that it may represent less a particularly American impulse than the response of an enormously powerful state without great rivals but with great fears.

Finally, I will pull some of these threads together and fill in some of the gaps in this tapestry—or patchwork quilt—by concentrating on the question of whether the Bush Doctrine can be sustained in the future and what the implications of its collapse might be. Although claims for the operation of "imperial overstretch" are common, the war on terrorism, even if carried out on a grand scale, need not undermine the American economy. It may well overtax the American political system and its ability to understand the world in which it is operating, however. And if the current policy falters or is renounced, as I believe will happen, the United States will not be able to restore the policies previously followed or those advocated by internationalist critics, because American actions have undermined the foundations on which they would need to rest. The future, then, is likely to fit an ancient Chinese curse: "May you live in interesting times."

1

THEORIES OF WAR IN AN ERA OF
LEADING-POWER PEACE

From the most remote ages onward, the peoples have perpetu-
ally assailed one another for the satisfaction of their appetites
and their egotistical interests [and their fears]. I have not made
this history, and neither have you. It is.
Georges Clemenceau, December 29, 1918[1]

[Although it was] quite right in the interests of peace to go on
talking about war with the United States being "unthinkable,"
everyone knows that this is not true.
Winston Churchill, July 20, 1927[2]

A new science of politics is needed for a new world.
Alexis de Tocqueville, 1835[3]

Throughout history, war and the possibility of war among the great
powers has been the motor of international politics, not only strongly
influencing the boundaries and distribution of values among them, but
also deeply affecting their internal arrangements and shaping the fates
of smaller states. Being seen as an ever-present possibility produced
by deeply rooted factors such as human nature and the lack of world

government, this force was expected to continue indefinitely. But I would argue that war among the leading great powers—the most developed states of the United States, western Europe, and Japan—will not occur in the future, and indeed is no longer a source of concern for them.[4] The absence of war among these states would itself be a development of enormous proportions, but the change goes even further because war is not even contemplated. During the Cold War peace was maintained, but this was due to the fear that if the superpowers did not take care, they would indeed fight.

Now, however, the leading states form what Karl Deutsch called a pluralistic security community, a group among whom war is literally unthinkable—that is, neither the publics nor the political elites nor even the military establishments expect war with each other.[5] No official in the community would advocate a policy on the grounds that it would improve the state's position in the event of war with other members. Although no state can move away from the reliance on war by itself, lest it become a victim, the collectivity can do so if each member forsakes the resort to force. Perhaps the best indicator of a security community is the lack of official war plans. Laymen might think this benchmark is easy to reach, but it is not, because militaries plan for almost everything, in part simply to hone their skills. Thus the absence of plans is rare and significant, as is indicated by the fact that in the 1920s one of Canada's top generals spent his spare time reconnoitering the routes by which American forces might invade.[6]

Security communities are not unprecedented. But what is unprecedented is that the states that constitute this one are the leading members of the international system, and so are natural rivals who in the past were central to the violent struggle for security, power, and contested values. Winston Churchill exaggerated only slightly when he declared that "people talked a lot of nonsense when they said nothing was ever settled by war. Nothing in history was ever settled except by wars."[7] Even cases of major change without war, such as Britain yielding hegemony in the Western Hemisphere to the United States at the turn of the twentieth century, were strongly influenced by security calculations. Threatening war, preparing for it, and trying to avoid it have permeated all aspects of politics, and so a world in which war among the most developed states is unthinkable will be a new one. The subsequent chapters will analyze the changes in world politics produced by the attack of September 11 and by the U.S. response to it. As important as these are, however, they are less of a shift than the establishment of the Security Community, which, as I will discuss in the final chapter, conditions current American policy. We—and especially the younger generations—take the Security Community for granted. This should not blind us to the importance of the change, however. To paraphrase and extend a claim made by Evan Luard, given the scale and frequency of war among the great powers in the preceding millennia, this is a change of spectacular proportions, perhaps the single most striking discontinuity that the history of international politics has anywhere provided.[8]

Two major states, Russia and China, might fight one another or a member of the Security Community.[9] But, as I will discuss below, such a conflict would be different from traditional wars between great powers. Furthermore, these countries lack many of the attributes of great powers: their internal regimes are shaky, they are not at the forefront of any advanced forms of technology or economic organization, they can pose challenges only regionally, and they have no attraction as models for others. They are not among the most developed states, and I think it would be fair to put them outside the ranks of the great powers as well. But their military potential, their possession of nuclear weapons, and the size of their economies render that judgment easily debatable. Thus I will not press it and, rather will argue that the set of states that form the Security Community are not all the great powers, but only the most developed ones.

CENTRAL QUESTIONS

Five questions arise. First, does the existence of the Security Community mean the end of security threats to its members, and more specifically to the United States? Second, will the Community endure? Third, what are the causes of its construction and maintenance? Fourth, what are the implications of this transformation for the conduct of international affairs? Finally, what does this say about theories of the causes of war?

Continued Threats

The fact that the United States is not menaced by the most developed countries obviously does not mean that it does not face any military threats at all. Indeed, even before September 11 some analysts saw the United States as no more secure than it was during the Cold War, being imperiled by terrorists and "rogue" states as well as by Russia and China. But I do not believe that even the war on terror has the potential to drive world politics the way that clashes among the leading powers did in the past. Neither this conflict nor the fear of war with Russia or China permeates all facets of international politics and structures state–society relations; they do not represent a struggle for dominance in the international system.

Even the fiercest foes of Russia, China, or the rogues do not see them as ready to launch unprovoked attacks against the United States or other members of the Security Community, let alone as out to control the world. Russia and China are not seeking to replace the United States; any clash will come out of these countries' desire for a sphere of influence and the American belief that such arrangements are inappropriate in today's world—at least for others. Thus, while there are reasons why the United States might fight with China to protect Taiwan or with Russia to protect the Baltic republics, these disputes are not like those that characterized great-power conflicts over the past three centuries. The United States is not defending traditional national interests, let alone vital ones, but is seeking what Arnold Wolfers called "milieu goals":[10] upholding values like democracy, self-determination, and rejection of coercion as a means of changing the status quo. These may be deeply held both for their intrinsic value and for their role in maintaining America's worldwide reach, but they are more akin to the concerns of imperial powers than to sources of conflict between equal major powers.

Will the Security Community Last?

Predictions about the maintenance of the Security Community are obviously disputable (indeed, limitations on people's ability to predict could undermine it), but nothing in the short period since the end of the Cold War points to an unraveling. Despite many disputes within the Community, even analysts who stress the continuation of the struggle for world primacy and great-power rivalries do not expect fighting.[11] If the United States is still concerned with maintaining its advantages over its allies, the reason is not that it believes that it may have to fight them, but that it worries that rivalry could make managing world problems more difficult.[12] The European efforts to establish an independent security force are aimed at permitting intervention when the United States chooses not to intervene (or, perhaps more likely, at threatening such action in order to trigger American intervention), not at fighting the United States.[13] Even in the unlikely event that Europe were to unite and the world were to become bipolar again, it is very doubtful that suspicions, fears for the future, and conflicts of interest would be severe enough to break the Community.

A greater threat would be the failure of Europe to unite coupled with an American withdrawal of forces, which could lead to security competition within Europe.[14] The fears would focus on Germany, but their magnitude is hard to gauge and it is difficult to estimate what external shocks or kinds of German behavior would activate them. The fact that Britain's Thatcher and France's Mitterrand opposed German unification is surely not forgotten in Germany, and is an indication that concerns remain. But this danger is likely to constitute a self-denying prophecy in two ways. First, many Germans are aware of the need not only to reassure others by tying themselves closely to Europe, but also to seek to make it unlikely that future generations of Germans would want to break these bonds even if they could. Second, Americans who worry about the residual danger will favor keeping some troops in Europe as the ultimate intra-European security guarantee.

Expectations of peace close off important routes to war. The main reason for Japanese aggression in the 1930s was the desire for a self-sufficient sphere of influence that would permit Japan to fight the war with the Western powers that was seen as inevitable, not because of particular conflicts but because it was believed that great powers always fight each other. By contrast, if states believe that a security community will last, they will not be hypersensitive to threats from within it and will not feel the need to undertake precautionary measures that could undermine the security of other members. Thus the United States is not disturbed that British and French nuclear missiles could destroy American cities, and while France objects to American missile defense, it does not feel the need to increase its forces in response. As long as peace is believed to be very likely, the chance of inadvertent spirals of tension and threat is low.

Nevertheless, the point with which I began this section is unavoidable. World politics can change rapidly, and saying that nothing foreseeable will dissolve the Security Community is not the same as saying that it will not dissolve.[15] To the extent that it rests on democracy and prosperity (see below), anything that would undermine these would also undermine the Community. Drastic climate change could also shake the foundations of much that we have come to take for granted. But it is hard to see how dynamics at the international level (i.e., the normal trajectory of fears, disputes, and rivalries) could produce war among the leading states. In other words, the Community does not have within it the seeds of its own destruction.

Our faith in the continuation of this peace is increased to the extent that we think we understand its causes and have reason to believe that they will continue. This is my next topic.

Explanations for the Security Community

There are social constructivist, liberal, and realist explanations for the Security Community that, although proceeding from different assumptions, invoke overlapping factors.[16]

Constructivism Constructivism points to the norm of nonviolence and the shared identities that have led the advanced democracies to assume the role of each other's friend through the interaction of behavior and expectations.[17] In contradistinction to the liberal and realist explanations, constructivism downplays the importance of material factors and elevates ideas, images of oneself and others, and conceptions of appropriate conduct. The roots of the changes that have produced this enormous shift in international politics among some countries but not others are not specified in detail, but the process is a self-reinforcing one—a benign cycle of behavior, beliefs, and expectations.

People become socialized into attitudes, beliefs, and values that are conducive to peace. Individuals in the Security Community may see their own country as strong and good—and even better than others—but they do not espouse the virulent nationalism that was common in the past. Before World War I, one German figure proclaimed that the Germans were "the greatest civilized people known to history," while another declared that the Germans were "the chosen people of this century," which explained "why other people hate us. They do not understand us but they fear our tremendous spiritual superiority." Thomas Macaulay similarly wrote that the British were "the greatest and most highly civilized people that ever the world saw" and were "the acknowledged leaders of the human race in the causes of political improvement." Senator Albert Beveridge proclaimed that "God has made us the master organizers of the world."[18] These sentiments are shocking today because they are so at variance with what we have been taught to think about others and ourselves. We could not adopt these views without rejecting a broad set of beliefs and values. An understanding of the effects of such conceptions led the Europeans, and to an unfortunately lesser extent the Japanese, to denationalize and harmonize their textbooks after World War II, and has similarly led countries with remaining enemies to follow a different path: the goals for the education of a twelve-year-old child in Pakistan include the "ability to know all about India's evil designs about Pakistan; acknowledge and identify forces that may be working against Pakistan; understand the Kashmir problem."[19]

For constructivists, the fact that all members of the Security Community are democracies is important, not so much for the reasons given by liberals (see below) as for the sense of common identity that the similarity in regime has generated.[20] The formation of common identities has been central to national integration, and it stands to reason that it plays a major role not only in keeping states at peace but also in making war unthinkable.[21] The evidence for shared identity within the Community is hard to find, however, or at least has not been produced.[22] Moreover, constructivists say little about when and why shared identities disintegrate, as they do when a country lapses into civil war.[23] Ironically, the spread of democracy might reduce the importance of democratic identity. The sense that being democratic is a vital part of one's self (as an individual or as a country) may diminish if it becomes less distinctive. Being democratic is highly salient when most others are not and when adversaries are hostile to democracy; in a world that is predominantly democratic, sources of identity may be different and more divisive.

The spread of democracy may be part of a general turn away from violence, conquest, honor, and glory, and the embracing of at least somewhat disinterested principles and laws.[24] The sort of nationalism mentioned in the previous paragraph went along with the idea that conquest was reasonable and legitimate—even praiseworthy and at times a duty. Although war is still seen as necessary when imposed on states by extreme circumstances, and some now argue that states not only should but must intervene to stop genocide, humanitarian disasters, and massive violations of human rights, no one talks about the importance of honor, which sparked many wars in the past, or sees wars as a way to satisfy national or individual quests for glory. States with these outlooks will not fight each other. Most, including all those in the Community, also apply these norms to others. In the summer of 1990 Saddam Hussein could have succeeded if he had limited his policy to coercing Kuwait, and would have met much less resistance if he had withdrawn his forces and established a puppet regime. It was the conquest of his neighbor that triggered the massive coalition against him. This conquest was unacceptable not only because it menaced others and showed that he could not be trusted, but also because it was illegitimate. Indeed, it was partly the illegitimacy that produced the perceptions that Saddam was a danger, literally an outlaw.

Learning is important here, as states and their leaders in the Security Community have come to see that war with each other is not a good way to solve their problems, that realist security policies can decrease security, and that more conciliatory and cooperative methods of behavior will serve them well.[25]

The obvious objection to constructivism is that it mistakes effect for cause: its description is correct, but the learning, identities, images, and self-images are superstructure, being the product of peace and of the material incentives discussed below. What is crucial is not people's thinking, but the factors that drive it.[26] The validity of this claim is beyond the reach of current evidence, but what is clear is that the constructivist belief that the Community will last places great faith in the power of socialization and the ability of ideas to replicate and sustain themselves. This conception may betray an excessive faith in the validity of ideas that seem self-evident today, but that our successors might reject. Constructivism may present us with actors who are "oversocialized"[27] and leave too little role for agency in the form of people who think differently, perhaps because their material conditions are different.

Liberalism The liberal explanation for the existence of the Security Community has received most attention. Although it comes in several variants, the central strands are the pacifying effects of democracy, economic interdependence, and joint membership in international organizations.[28] Interestingly enough, much of the Bush administration's post-9/11 policy implicitly or explicitly rests on liberal arguments like these, as I will discuss in chapters 4 and 5.

Democracy The members of the Security Community are democracies, and many scholars argue that democracies rarely, if ever, fight each other.[29] Although the statistical evidence is, as usual, subject to debate,[30] Jack Levy is correct that this claim is "as close as anything we have to an empirical law in international politics."[31]

Less secure, however, is our understanding of why this is the case. We have numerous explanations that can be seen as competing or complementary. Democracies are systems of dispersed power, and dispersed power means multiple veto points and groups that could block war. (This seems true almost by definition, but if the accounts of former Soviet leaders are to be trusted, Brezhnev was more constrained by his colleagues than was Nixon, at least where arms control was concerned.) Related are the norms of these regimes: democracies function through compromise, nonviolence, and respect for law. To the extent that these values and habits govern foreign policy, they are conducive to peace, especially in relations with other democracies that reciprocate.

Other scholars have argued that the key element lies in the realm of information. By having a relatively free flow of intelligence and encouraging debate, democracies are less likely to make egregious errors in estimating what courses of action will maintain the peace.[32] The other side of the informational coin is that democracies can more effectively telegraph their own intentions, and so can avoid not only unnecessary spirals of conflict but also wars that stem from others' incorrect beliefs that the democracy is bluffing (although an obvious cost is an inability to bluff).[33]

The two parts of the informational argument can reinforce or be in tension with each other. If one argues that democratic processes make democracies' behavior highly predictable, then even dictatorships should be able to estimate what they will do, thereby reducing the distinctiveness of interactions among democracies. In fact, this does not seem to be the case, as the misjudgments of Hitler, Stalin, and Saddam Hussein make clear. But if democratic processes do not provide totally unambiguous evidence, one can conclude that predictability will be high only when each side both sends and receives information clearly, thereby explaining the advantages of democratic dyads.

Finally, in a recasting of the traditional argument that democracies are less likely to go to war because those who hold ultimate authority (i.e., the general public) will pay the price for conflict, some argue that the electoral and coalitional nature of democratic regimes requires their leaders to pursue successful policies if they are to stay in office.[34] Thus democracies will put greater efforts into winning wars and be careful to choose to fight only wars they can win.[35] Autocracies have a narrower base and so can stay in power by buying off their supporters even if their foreign policies are unnecessarily costly. These arguments, while highly suggestive, share with earlier liberal thinking quite stylized assumptions about the preferences of societal actors and pay little attention to how each country anticipates the behavior of others and assesses how others expect it to behave.

The explanations for the democratic peace are thoughtful and often ingenious, but not conclusive. Many of them lead us to expect not only dyadic effects but monadic ones as well—that is, democracies should be generally peaceful, not peaceful only toward each other, a finding that most scholars deny.[36] They also imply that one democracy would not seek to overthrow another, a proposition that is contradicted by American behavior during the Cold War.[37] Versions that stress the role of dispersed power also would imply that countries that have this characteristic should be slow to fight even if they are not democratic. Furthermore, most of the arguments are built around dyads, but it is not entirely clear that the posited causes would apply as well to multilateral groupings like the Security Community.

The more recent arguments implicitly dispute rather than fully engage older ones that focused on the obstacles to effective foreign policies in democracies: the fickleness of public opinion, the incentives that leaders have to seek short-run success at the cost of investing for the long run, the recruitment of inexperienced leaders, and the parochialism that makes democracies self-righteous and prone to misunderstand others.[38] Because greater citizen participation can easily lead to emotional identification with the country, high levels of nationalism can be expected in democracies. Because public opinion has greater influence and pays only sporadic attention to foreign policy, consistency and commitments should be harder rather than easier for them. These once-familiar views may be incorrect, but they deserve careful attention.

The causal role of democracy is hard to establish because democracies have been relatively rare until recently, much of the democratic peace can be explained by the Soviet threat, and the same factors that lead countries to become democratic are conducive to peace between them (e.g., being relatively rich and secure, resolving regional disputes).[39] It is particularly important and difficult to control for the role of common interest, which loomed so large during the Cold War.[40] But interests are not objective, and may be strongly influenced by the country's internal regime. Thus the democracies may have made common cause during the Cold War in part because they were democracies; common interest may be as much a mechanism by which the democratic peace is sustained as it is a competing explanation for it.[41] Moreover, if democracies are more likely to become economically interdependent, additional common interest will be created. But to bring up the importance of interest is to highlight an ambiguity and raise a question. The ambiguity is whether the theory leads us to expect democracies *never* to fight each other or "merely" to fight *less* than do other dyads.[42] The related question is whether it is impossible for two democracies to have a conflict of interest so severe that it leads to war. This troubles the stronger version of the argument because it is hard to answer in the affirmative.

But would democracies let such a potent conflict of interest develop? At least as striking as the statistical data is the fact—or, rather, the judgment—that the regimes that most disturbed the international order in the twentieth century also devastated their own peoples: the USSR, Germany under the Nazis and, perhaps, under Kaiser Wilhelm. One reason for this connection may be the desire to remake the world (but because the international order was established by countries that were advanced democracies, it may not be surprising that those that opposed it were not). Not all murderous regimes are as ambitious as this (e.g., Idi Amin's Uganda), and others with both power and grand designs may remain restrained (e.g., Mao's China), but it is hard to understand the distinctive German and Soviet foreign policies without reference to their domestic regimes.

Interdependence The second leg of the liberal explanation for the Security Community is the high level of economic interdependence, which also could facilitate a common identity.[43] The basic argument was developed by Cobden, Bright, and the other nineteenth-century British liberals. As Cobden put it: "Free Trade is God's diplomacy and there is no other certain way of uniting people in bonds of peace."[44] Although the evidence for this proposition remains in dispute, the causal story is straightforward: "If goods cannot cross borders, armies will," in the words of the nineteenth-century French economist Frederick Bastiat, which were often repeated by Secretary of State Cordell Hull (perhaps excessively influenced by the experience of the 1930s).[45] William Clayton, Assistant Secretary of State after World War II, argued similarly that "Enemies in the market place cannot long be friends at the council table."[46] Extensive economic intercourse allows states to gain by trade the wealth that they would otherwise seek through fighting.[47] Relatedly, individuals and groups who conduct these economic relations develop a powerful stake in keeping the peace and maintaining good relations.[48] Thus it is particularly significant that many firms now have important ties abroad and that direct foreign investment ties the fates of important actors hostage to continued good relations.[49] There can be a benign cycle here as increasing levels of trade strengthen the political power of actors who have a stake in deepening these ties.[50]

The liberal view assumes that actors place a high priority on wealth, that trade is a better route to wealth than conquest, and that actors who gain economically from the exchange are politically powerful. These assumptions are often true, especially in the modern world, but are not without their vulnerabilities. At times honor and glory, in addition to more traditional forms of individual and national interest, can be more salient than economic gain. Thus, as the Moroccan crisis of 1911 came to a head, General von Moltke wrote to his wife: "If we again slip away from this affair with our tail between our legs. ... I shall despair of the future of the German Empire. I shall then retire. But before handing in my resignation I shall move to abolish the Army and to place ourselves under Japanese protectorate; we shall then be in a position to make money without interference and to develop into ninnies."[51] Traditional liberal thought understood this well and stressed that economic activity was so potent not only because it gave people an interest in maintaining peace, but also because it reconstructed social values to downgrade status and glory and elevate material well-being.[52] It follows that the stability of the Security Community rests in part on people giving priority to consumption. Critics may decry modern society's individualistic, material values, but one can easily imagine more noble ones that would generate greater international conflict.

Of course conquest can also bring wealth. The conventional wisdom that this is no longer true for modern economies, which depend less on agriculture and raw materials than on an intricate web of skilled tasks, has been challenged by Liberman's careful study of twentieth-century conquests.[53] But even if Liberman is correct, the net benefit from trade might have been even greater, especially when we consider the costs of arming and fighting. It also is not clear that conquered people will provide the innovation and ingenuity that produce wealth over the long run.

Here, as elsewhere, expectations are crucial, and this both strengthens and weakens the liberal argument. It strengthens it to the extent that most people believe that high levels of economic exchange strongly contribute to prosperity and expect that tensions, let alone wars, will decrease trade and prosperity. But it is also important that people expect good economic relations to continue as long as their country does not disturb them. Since people set their policies by the predicted future benefits, even high levels of beneficial exchange will be ineffective if a deterioration is foreseen.[54]

Interdependence will have its pacifying effect only if the actors who benefit from it are powerful. American social scientists often take for granted the model of contemporary American society in which this is the case, and overlook the fact it that is not universal. Thus Ripsman and Blanchard note that while leading businessmen in Britain and Germany opposed World War I, just as liberalism leads us to expect, they were not powerful enough to force their preferences on their governments.[55] Since elected leaders are now held accountable by their citizens for the condition of their economies, levels and kinds of interdependence that had little political effect in the past can now restrain countries.

There are four general arguments against the pacific influence of interdependence, however. First, if it is hard to go from the magnitude of economic flows to the costs that would be incurred if they were disrupted, it is even more difficult to estimate how much political impact these costs will have, since it depends on the other considerations at play and the political context. This means that we do not have a theory that tells us the magnitude of the effect. Second, even the sign of the effect can be disputed: interdependence can increase conflict as states gain bargaining leverage over each other, fear that others will exploit them, and face additional sources of disputes.[56] Third, it is clear that interdependence does not guarantee peace. High levels of economic integration did not prevent World War I, and nations that were much more unified than any security community have peacefully dissolved or fought civil wars. This does not mean that interdependence is not conducive to peace, but it does indicate that the effect can be overwhelmed by contrary forces.

Fourth, interdependence may be more an effect than a cause, more the product than a generator of expectations of peace and cooperation. Although Russett and Oneal try to meet this objection by correlating the level of trade in one year not with peace in that year but with peace in the following one, this does not get to the heart of the matter, since trade the year before could be a product of expectations of future good relations.[57] Short of onerous and subjective coding of large numbers of cases to establish expectations about future relations, it may not be possible to ascertain which way the causal arrow runs. Indeed, it probably runs in both directions, with magnitudes that vary with other factors. But the economic order in the current Security Community was premised on the belief that its members could, and had to, remain at peace. One part of the reason was the lessons of the 1930s and the belief that economic rivalries led to political divisions and wars. Another part was the perceived threat from the Soviet Union, which meant that the fear of relative economic gains was eased, if not reversed, because partners' economic growth brought with it positive security externalities.[58] This created a situation very different from that of the early twentieth century, when Britain and Germany, while heavily trading with one another, each feared that the other's prosperity would endanger it. As one British observer put it after a trip to Germany in 1909: "Every one of those new factory chimneys is a gun pointed at England."[59] Post-1945 European economic cooperation probably would not have occurred without American sponsorship, pressure, and security guarantees, and close American economic relations with Japan had similar political roots.[60]

International Organizations Even those who argue for the pacifying effect of common memberships in international organizations aver that the magnitude of this effect is relatively slight, at least in the short run, and so my discussion will be brief.[61] The causal mechanisms are believed to be several: enhanced information flows, greater ability to solve problems peacefully, increased stake in cooperative behavior linked to the risk of being excluded from the organization if the state behaves badly, and possibly a heightened sense of common identity.[62] Harder to pin down but perhaps more important are processes by which joint membership alters states' conceptions of their interests, leading them to see membership not only as calling for cooperative reciprocations but also as extending over a longer time horizon and including benefits to others.[63]

The obvious reasons to doubt the importance of shared institutional membership are that the incentives are not great enough to tame strong conflicts of interest and that membership may be endogenous to common interests and peaceful relations. States that expect war with each other are less likely to join the same international organizations, and political conflicts that are the precursors to war may destroy the institutions or drive some members out, as Japan and Germany withdrew from the League of Nations during the 1930s. Even with a strong correlation and reasonable control variables, the direction of causality is difficult to establish.

Realist Explanations The crudest realist explanation for the Security Community would focus on the rise of common external threats. But while the perceived menace of the USSR was central to the origins of the Community, it is hard to see the current threats from Russia or China as central. Such a claim would be hard to square with the views espoused by most elites in Japan and Europe, who are relatively unconcerned about these countries and believe that whatever dangers emanate from them would be magnified rather than decreased by a confrontational policy. Similarly, while all members of the Community may be menaced by terrorism, they disagree about how to deal with it.

American Hegemony Two other realist accounts are stronger. The first argues that the Security Community is largely the product of the other enormous change in world politics: the American dominance of world politics.[64] The United States now spends more on defense than all the other countries of the world combined, to take the most easily quantifiable indicator. Furthermore, thanks to the Japanese constitution and the integration of armed forces within NATO, America's allies do not have to fear attacks from each other: their militaries—especially Germany's—are so truncated that they could not fight a major war without American assistance or attack each other without undertaking a military buildup that would give a great deal of warning. American dominance also leads us to expect that key policies, from the expansion of NATO, to the American-led wars in Kosovo and the Persian Gulf, to the IMF bailouts of Turkey and Argentina in the spring of 2001, will conform to American preferences.

But closer examination reveals differences between current and past hegemonies. At least before George W. Bush came to power, the United States usually gave considerable weight to its partners' views; indeed, its own preferences were often influenced by theirs, as was true in Kosovo. For their parts, the other members of the Security Community seek to harness and constrain American power, not displace it, and increased European and Japanese strength need not lead to war, contrary to the expectations of standard theories of hegemony and great-power rivalry.[65] Unlike previous eras of hegemony, the current peace seems uncoerced and accepted by most states, which does not fit entirely well with realism.

Nuclear Weapons The second realist argument was familiar during the Cold War but receives less attention now.[66] This is the pacifying effect of nuclear weapons, which, if possessed in sufficient numbers and invulnerable configurations, make military victory impossible and war a feckless option. An immediate objection is that not all the major states in the Security Community have nuclear weapons. But this is only technically correct: Germany and Japan could produce nuclear weapons if a threat loomed, as their partners fully understand. The other factors discussed in the previous pages may or may not be important; the nuclear revolution by itself would be sufficient to keep the great powers at peace.

While there is a great deal to this argument, it is not without its problems. First, because this kind of deterrence rests on the perceived possibility of war, it may explain peace but not a security community. Second, mutual deterrence can be used as a platform for hostility, coercion, and even limited wars. In what Glenn Snyder calls the stability-instability paradox, the common realization that all-out war would be irrational provides a license for threats and lower levels of violence.[67]

Under some circumstances a state could use the shared fear of nuclear war to exploit others. If the state thinks that the other is preoccupied with the danger of war, it may expect the other to retreat, which means that the state can stand firm. In other words, the fact that war would be the worst possible outcome for both sides does not automatically lead to uncoerced peace, let alone to a security community.[68]

A Synthetic Interactive Explanation My explanation for the development and maintenance of the Security Community combines and reformulates several factors discussed previously. Even with the qualifications just discussed, a necessary condition is the belief that conquest is difficult and war is terribly costly. When conquest is easy, aggression is encouraged and the security dilemma operates with particular viciousness since even defensive states need to prepare to attack.[69] But when states have modern armies and, even more, nuclear weapons, it is hard for anyone to believe that war could make sense.

Of course statesmen must consider the gains that war might bring as well as its costs. Were the gains to be very high, they might outweigh the costs. But, if anything, the expected benefits of war within the Security Community have declined, in part because the developed countries, including those that lost World War II, are generally satisfied with the status quo.[70] Even when the strain is considerable, as in American relations with Japan in the early 1990s or with France in the run-up to the Iraq war, no one would think that a war could provide anyone much gross, let alone net, benefit: it is hard to locate a problem for which war among the Community members would provide a solution.

The other side of this coin is that, as liberals have stressed, peace within the Security Community brings many gains, especially economic. While some argue that the disruption caused by relatively free trade is excessive and urge greater national regulation, no one thinks that conquering others would bring more riches than trading with them. Despite concern for relative economic gain and the existence of economic disputes, people believe that their economic fates are linked more positively than negatively to the rest of the Community.[71]

Of course costs and benefits are subjective, depending as they do on what the actors value, and changes in values are the third leg of my explanation. Most political analysis takes the actors' values for granted because they tend to be widely shared and to change slowly. Their importance and variability become clear only when we confront a case like Nazi Germany, which, contrary to standard realist conceptions of national interest and security, put everything at risk in order to seek a dominant position for the Aryan race.

The changes over the past hundred years in what the leaders and publics in the developed states value are striking. To start with, war is no longer seen as good in itself;[72] no great-power leader today would agree with Theodore Roosevelt that "No triumph of peace is quite so great as the supreme triumph of war."[73] In earlier eras it was commonly believed that war brought out the best in individuals and nations, and that the virtues of discipline, risk-taking, and self-sacrifice that war required were central to civilization. Relatedly, as previously noted, honor and glory used to be central values. In a world so constituted, the material benefits of peace would be much less important; high levels of trade, the difficulty of making conquest pay, and even nuclear weapons might not produce peace.

Democracy and identity also operate through what actors value, and may in part be responsible for the decline in militarism. Compromise, consideration for the interests of others, respect for law, and shunning of violence all are values that underpin democracy and are cultivated by it. The Security Community also is relatively homogeneous in that its members are all democracies and have values that are compatibly similar. It is important that the values be compatible as well as similar: a system filled with states that all believed that war and domination were good would not be peaceful.[74] One impulse to war is the desire to change the other country, and this disappears if values are shared. The United States could conquer Canada, for example, but what would be the point when so much of what it wants to see there is already in place?

Central to the rise of the Security Community is the decline in territorial disputes. Territory has been the most common cause and object of conflicts in the past, and we have become so accustomed to the absence of conflicts within the Community that it is easy to lose sight of how drastic and consequential this change is.[75] Germans no longer care that Alsace and Lorraine are French; the French are not disturbed by the high level of German presence in these provinces. The French, furthermore, permitted the Saar to return to Germany and are not bothered by this loss—indeed, they do not feel it as a loss at all. Although for years the Germans refused to renounce their claims to the "lost territories" to the east, they did so upon unification and few voices were raised in protest. The Germans and French are not unique: the United Kingdom is ready to cede Northern Ireland to the Irish Republic if a referendum in the six counties were to favor it.

The causes of these changes in values in general, and in nationalism and concern with territory in particular, are subject to dispute, as are the developments that could reverse them. In particular, it is unclear how much they are rooted in material changes, most obviously the increased destructiveness of war and the unprecedented prosperity that is seen as linked to good political relations, and to what extent they are more autonomous, perhaps following a natural progression and building on each other. They may be linked (inextricably?) to high levels of consumption, faith in rationality, and the expectation of progress, although it would not be unreasonable to apply this description to Europe in 1914 as well. The decreased salience of territory is almost surely produced in part by the decoupling of territorial control and national prosperity, and most of the other relationships between material structures and ideational patterns are complex and reciprocal. Just as capitalism is built and sustained by precapitalist values and postmaterialism may grow from prosperity, so the values that sustain the Security Community can neither be separated nor deduced from changes in the means and levels of production and potential destruction.[76]

The obvious threat to these pacific values is an economic depression, which could also undermine democracy and weaken the links between good political relations and prosperity. If countries were to believe that the only way to improve their economic fortunes or halt a downslide was to disadvantage others, or even if they were to develop incompatible views about how to deal with dire economic circumstances, then not only would policies come into conflict but the values supporting peace might erode. It is also possible that these values could change by themselves as people become bored by the rich, peaceful world and come to desire glory, honor, and extreme nationalism once again. But some changes may be irreversible: just as it is hard to conceive of slavery, torture, or dueling coming back into fashion, so the current values may be highly stable, being sustained by constant socialization and supporting the peace and prosperity that serve the Security Community so well.[77]

The destructiveness of war, the benefits of peace, and the changes in values interact and reinforce each other. If war were not so dreadful, it could be considered useful for national enrichment; if peace did not seem to bring national well-being, violence would at least be contemplated; that military victory is no longer seen as a positive value both contributes to and is in part explained by the high perceived costs of war. In parallel, expectations of peace allow states to value each other's economic and political successes. Although these may incite envy, they no longer produce strong security fears, as was true in the past. The Security Community may then contain within it the seeds of its own growth through the feedbacks among its elements.[78]

Another dynamic element is crucial as well: the progress of the Community is path-dependent, in that without the Cold War it is unlikely that the factors we have discussed could have overcome traditional fears and rivalries. The conflict with the Soviet Union produced American security guarantees and an unprecedented sense of common purpose among the states that now form the Community. Since the coalition could be undermined by social unrest or political instability, each country sought to see that the others were well off and resisted the temptation to solve its own problems by exporting them to its neighbors. Since the coalition would have been disrupted had any country developed strong grievances against other members, each had reason to moderate its own demands and to mediate when conflicts developed between others. To ensure that relations would remain good in the future, leaders consciously portrayed the others as partners and sponsored the socialization practices discussed earlier. The American willingness to engage in extensive cooperation abroad, the European willingness to go far down the road of integration, and Japan's willingness to tie itself closely to the United States were improbable without the Cold War. But having been established, these forms of cooperation set off positive feedback and are now self-sustaining.

IMPLICATIONS

What are the implications of the existence of the Security Community for international politics in the rest of the world, for how the most developed states will carry out relations among themselves, and for general theories of war and peace?

International Politics in the Rest of the World

One obvious question is why the leading powers, but not others, have formed a security community. The preceding discussion implies that the outcome is overdetermined. As compared with others, the states in the Security Community are richer, more democratic, and more satisfied with the status quo; would lose more in a war; and have a more explicit American security guarantee. Furthermore, they were the core of the anti-Soviet coalition during the Cold War, which produced beneficial path-dependent results. This does not mean that other security communities will not form, but only that they are not likely to fit the pattern discussed here.

Despite the fact that war is thinkable outside the Security Community, it is striking that several other regions appear to be peaceful, most obviously South America.[79] The reasons remain unclear, but may include the role of the superpowers in controlling dangerous conflicts during the Cold War, American hegemony more recently, and the example of peace among the developed countries. Although war remains possible, even a pessimist would have to note that there is little evidence that the countries outside the Community will recapitulate Europe's bloody history. For these countries, the main security dangers stem from civil wars and insurgencies, either of which can lead to interstate war. These developments are beyond the scope of this chapter, but the obvious challenge would be to bring these countries and the Community into a common theory.

International Politics within the Community

In previous eras, no aspect of international politics and few aspects of domestic politics were untouched by the anticipation of future wars among the leading powers. As Charles Tilly put it: "Over the millennium as a whole, war has been the dominant activity of European states."[80] Much will then change in the Security Community. In the absence of these states amalgamating—a development that is out of the question outside of Europe and unlikely within it—they will neither consider using force against one another nor lose their sovereignty. There will then be significant conflicts of interest without clear means of resolving them. The states will continue to be rivals in some respects, and to bargain with each other. Indeed, the stability-instability paradox implies that the shared expectation that disputes will remain peaceful will remove some restraints on vituperation and competitive tactics. The dense network of institutions within the Community should serve to provide multiple means for controlling conflicts, but will also provide multiple ways for a dissatisfied country to threaten disruption. These effects came out in the intra-alliance politics surrounding the war in Iraq. Germany and France were free to actively oppose the United States without any fear that the American response would be so severe as to endanger the Community; the United States could respond polemically and with minor sanctions without concern that the tensions could get out of hand; neither side rushed to heal the breach in part because both understood the limits on the danger it posed.[81]

The fact that war is no longer an option within the Security Community poses challenges and opportunities for states. What goals will have highest priority? Will nonmilitary alliances be formed? How important will status be, and what will give it? Bargaining will continue, and this means that varieties of power, including the ability to help and hurt others, will still be relevant. Threats, bluffs, warnings, the mobilization of resources for future conflicts, intense diplomatic negotiations, and shifting patterns of working with and against others all will remain. But the content of these forms will differ from those of traditional international politics.

The question of whether (and how) states bandwagon with or balance against (or hide from, to use Paul Schroeder's useful category)[82] the most powerful state (i.e., the United States) will be central, but it too will not map on the classical form of the balance of power because this phenomenon was driven by the fear of war, and the ultimate sanction against a hegemon was the use of force. The other members of the Community do have reason to fear the United States, but not invasion from it, and they may want to oppose it, but force is not among the relevant tools. Their (well-grounded) worries include American economic and cultural domination, but in the wake of the invasion of Iraq, they center on how to restrain the United States, see that it does not precipitate a "clash of civilizations,"[83] and get it to contribute to public goods (to which the others can then perhaps reduce their payments). Thus leaders are searching for ways of containing American power without alienating the United States, methods of socializing or teaching it, and instruments that can entrap or coerce it and keep its behavior within acceptable bounds. In parallel, scholars are exploring new concepts of balancing.[84] What we will see in the future will undoubtedly have historical precedents and counterparts, but much will be different because the states will not be acting in the shadow of war and the task is more to guide the hegemon than to prevent it from attacking its peers and neighbors.

Politics within the Security Community may come to resemble in part the relations between the United States and Canada and Australia that Keohane and Nye described as complex interdependence: extensive transnational and transgovernmental relations, negotiations conducted across different issue areas, and bargaining power gained through asymmetric dependence but limited by overall common interests.[85] Despite this pathbreaking study, however, we know little about how this kind of politics will be carried out. As numerous commentators have noted, economic issues and economic resources will play large roles, but the changed context will matter. Relative economic advantage was sought in the past in part because it contributed to military security. This no longer being the case, the possibilities for cooperation are increased. States will still seek economic benefit but will care about whether others are gaining more than they are only if they believe that this can produce political leverage or future economic benefits. The range of cases in which the latter is true is now thought to be fairly small, however.[86]

Even though force will not be threatened within the Security Community, it will remain important in relations among its members. During the Cold War the protection the United States afforded to its allies gave it an added moral claim and significant bargaining leverage. Despite the decreased level of threat, this will be true for the indefinite future because militarily Japan and Europe need the United States more than it needs them. While the unique American ability to lead military operations like those in the Persian Gulf and Kosovo causes resentments and frictions, it also gives the United States a resource that is potent even—or especially—if it is never explicitly brought to the table.[87] The war on terror is likely to increase U.S. military leverage despite the widespread European opposition to American conduct as overmilitarized because it serves as a reminder that we still live in an era in which force is often deployed for good or for ill.

Four Possible Futures

Even within the contours of a security community, a significant range of patterns of relations is possible, four of which can be briefly sketched. All these should be seen against the background of the European and Japanese needs to restrain the United States and to keep close ties with it, and the American need for the active cooperation of the other Community members in maintaining an open economic system, containing proliferation and the growth of Chinese military power, and combating terrorism.

The greatest change would be a world in which national autonomy would be further diminished and the distinctions between domestic and foreign policy would continue to erode. This world could bear some resemblance to the United States before the Civil War or to medieval Europe, with its overlapping forms of sovereignty rather than compartmentalized nation-states, which might now dissolve because they are no longer needed to provide security and can no longer control their economies.[88] Although most scholars see the reduction of sovereignty and the growth of nongovernmental organizations as conducive to peace and harmony, one can readily imagine sharp conflicts (for example, among business interests, labor, and environmentalists; between those with different views of the good life; and between those calling for greater centralization to solve common problems and those advocating increased local control). But state power and interest would in any case greatly decrease, and the notion of "national interest," always contested, would become even more problematic.

A second world is a liberal internationalist one. Not completely incompatible with the first world, this would be one in which states in the Security Community continue to play a large role, but with more extensive and intensive cooperation, presumably produced and accompanied by the internalization of the interests of others and stronger institutions.[89] Relations would be increasingly governed by principles, laws, and persuasion rather than by more direct forms of power, a change that could benignly spill over into relations outside the Community. Although bargaining would not disappear, there would be more joint efforts to solve common problems, and the line between "high" and "low" politics would become even more blurred. The claim discussed in chapter 4 that Europe and the United States hold different values and worldviews would complicate but not preclude such arrangements. In this world the United States would share more power and responsibility with the rest of the Community than it does today.

While this world is popular with scholars,[90] at least as likely is a third model representing the continuation of the present trajectory, in which the United States maintains hegemony and rejects significant limitations on its freedom of action. Indeed, as I will discuss in the closing pages, even if the United States takes a more multilateral turn, presumably under a new president, recent events have shown not only scholars but also the other states in the Security Community that the United States can go off on its own if it chooses to do so, and this knowledge reduces the trust that is so important for the liberal international world. In this more realist world, national interests would remain distinct and the United States would follow the familiar pattern in which ambitions and perceived interests expand as power does (as I will discuss further in chapter 4). Consistent with the continuing concern with competitive advantages, both conflicts of interest and the belief that hegemony best produces collective goods would lead the United States to oppose the efforts of others to become a counterweight, if not a rival.[91] In effect, the United States would lead an empire, albeit a relatively benign one. But doing so would be complicated by the American self-image that precludes seeing the nation's role for what it is, in part because of the popularity of values of equality and supranationalism. Other members of the Community would resent having their interests overridden by the United States on some occasions, but exploitation would be limited by the Community states' bargaining power and the American realization that excessive discontent would have serious long-term consequences. Thus others might well accept these costs in return for American security guarantees and the ability to keep their own defense spending very low, especially because the alternative to American-dominated stability might be worse.

The fourth model also starts with the American attempt to maintain hegemony, but this time the burdens of American unilateralism become sufficient to produce a counterbalancing coalition, one that might include Russia and China as well.[92] Specific conflicts of interest on issues like trade (especially in agricultural goods), differences in outlook on the Third World (especially the Middle East), and the general divergence growing from the enormous disparities of power could lead to sharper clashes. Europe and Japan might also become more assertive because they fear not American domination but the withdrawal of the U.S. security guarantee. In this world, much that realism stresses—the egoism of national interests, unceasing concern for security, the weakness of international institutions, maneuvering for advantage, and the use of power and threats—would come to the fore, but with the vital difference that force would not be contemplated within the Security Community and the military balance would enter in only indirectly, as discussed above. This would be a strange mixture of the new and the familiar, and the central question will be what *ultima ratio* will replace cannons. What will be the final arbiter of disputes? What kinds of threats will be most potent? How fungible will the relevant forms of power be?

Outlining these possibilities raises three broad questions that I cannot answer. First, is the future essentially determined, as many structural theories would imply, or does it depend on national choices, perhaps strongly influenced by domestic politics, leaders, and accidents? Second, if the future is not determined, how much depends on choices the United States has yet to make, and what will most influence these choices? Third, will the course of the war on terror have a great impact on which world comes into being?

Implications for Theories of the Causes of War

Whatever its explanation, the very existence of a security community among the leading powers refutes many theories of the causes of war, or at least indicates that they are not universally valid. Thus human nature and the drive for dominance and glory may exist and contribute to much of the way we live, but they are not fated to lead to war.

The obvious rebuttal is that war still exists outside the Security Community and that civil wars continue unabated. But only wars fought by members of the Community have the potential to undermine the argument that, under some conditions, attributes of humans and societies which are often seen as inevitably producing wars in fact do not have to do so. One could point to the Gulf Wars and the operation in Kosovo, but they do not help these theories. These wars were provoked by others, gained little honor and glory for the Community, and were fought in a manner that minimized the loss of life on the other side. It would be hard to portray them as manifestations of brutal or evil human nature. Indeed, it is more plausible to see the Community's behavior as consistent with a general trend toward its becoming less violent generally: the abolition of official torture and the decreased appeal of capital punishment, to take the most salient examples.[93]

The existence of the Security Community also casts doubt on theories that argue that the leading powers are always willing to use force in a struggle for material gain, status, and dominance. Traditional Marxism claims that capitalists can never cooperate over a prolonged period; proponents of the law of uneven growth see changes in the relative power of major states as producing cycles of domination, stability, challenge, and war;[94] "power transitions" in which rising powers catch up with dominant ones are seen as very difficult to manage peacefully.[95] These theories, like the version of hegemonic stability discussed above, have yet to be tested because the United States has not yet declined. But if the arguments made here are correct, transitions will not have the same violent outcome that they had in the past, and this should lead us to pay greater attention to the conditions under which these theories do and do not hold.

For most scholars, the fundamental cause of war is international anarchy, compounded by the security dilemma. These forces press hardest on the leading powers because while they may be able to guarantee the security of others, no one can provide them with this escape from the state of nature. As we have seen, different schools of thought propose different explanations for the rise of the Security Community and so lead to somewhat different propositions about the conditions under which anarchy can be compatible with peace. But what is most important is that the Community constitutes a proof by existence of the possibility of uncoerced peace without central authority. Because these countries are the most powerful ones and particularly war-prone, the Community poses a fundamental challenge to our understanding of world politics and our expectations of future possibilities.

With terrorism, the aftermath of the war in Iraq, and the frictions within the Security Community now so salient, it is easy to lose sight of the significance for both policy and theory of the fact that the leading powers know that they will never fight each other. Nevertheless, this is the most important change in world politics since the beginning of international history. Furthermore, it provides the context for the dramatic events since September 11, to which we will now turn.

2

SEPTEMBER 11: HOW HAS IT CHANGED THE WORLD?

For many of us not a day will pass without thinking of the terrorist attacks of September 11, 2001. Nevertheless, I do not believe anyone has a full understanding of the causes and consequences of these awful events; I know that I do not. Our grasp of terrorism is even less secure than it is of other important social phenomena, such as poverty and ethnic conflict. Terrorism grounded in religion poses special problems for modern social science, which has paid little attention to religion, perhaps because most social scientists are not religious, shy away from deeply held beliefs, and find this subject unfathomable if not embarrassing. These obstacles help explain, if not excuse, why many of my arguments will be negative ones: the threat of terrorism is not as new as is often claimed; terrorism reinforces state power more than it either undermines it or exemplifies the diminished importance of states; claims for reducing terrorism by getting at its root causes are largely tendentious; viewing the struggle against terrorism as a war is problematic; and the world is not likely to unite against terrorism. But, contrary to what I believed at first, it is now clear that September 11 has led to major changes in Russian and, even more, U.S. foreign policy and has triggered assertive American hegemony.

WHAT IS NEW?

Although September 11 significantly altered world politics, many of the "lessons" espoused by academics and policy makers are those that the learner already believed. With the significant exception of many of the calls for increased domestic security and sacrifices of civil liberties, the measures that various groups advocate—from building missile defenses[1] to shunning them, from greater support of Sharon's policies to greater opposition to them, from greater multilateralism to increased economic assistance to the poor and to freer world trade, from shielding weak groups from the foreign competition to tax cuts—all correspond to what the advocates had wanted earlier.

As I will discuss below and in chapter 4, President Bush and some of his associates do appear to have been deeply changed by September 11. Since they are extraordinarily powerful, the impact of world politics has been great. But for many of the members of the Bush administration, the attacks permitted them to carry out policies they already favored, just as the Korean War allowed Secretary of State Acheson and his colleagues to implement the rearmament they had seen as needed, but previously out of reach. Although combating terrorism was not a central concern for them, many in the Bush administration had sought to overthrow Saddam Hussein, increase defense budgets, break free from confining bonds to European allies, ensure that no other state or grouping could rival the United States, and, as a means to those ends and a general guarantee of American interests and world stability, establish American dominance.[2] Many liberals in this country and Europe disagreed on all these points on September 10, and similarly found that the subsequent events only made more urgent their previous prescriptions of multilateral cooperation, greater respect for law, and sustained attention to global ills. Those farther to the left also see more confirmation of their views than cause for change, especially concerning their analysis of American society, politics, and foreign policy.[3]

Terrorism

When we are confronted with something as unsettling as the terrorist attacks, our first reaction is to see it as unprecedented, and indeed the world had never seen a terrorist attack that killed so many people. But terrorism itself is not new. A precise definition may be impossible, but some stab at one is unavoidable: the use of violence for political or social purposes that is directed primarily at civilians and that is not publicly authorized by leaders of recognized political units.

It is not surprising that terrorism is ancient, because individuals have never been fully bound to states and terror is needed by the weak, who lack other instruments. Although terrorism is not easy to mount, it is much easier than fielding a full-fledged military apparatus; a great deal of disruption is possible with relatively little force. Whether the goal is revenge, inflicting enough pain to get the adversary to change its behavior, or calling attention to one's cause, terror can be the only tool that might prove effective. Terrorism in general and suicide bombing in particular are not uniquely a tool of al-Qaeda or Islamic groups in general. The willingness to give up one's life for a cause or the welfare of a group or an ideology is widespread, and without it many cherished Western values might have been extinguished.

This is not to claim that September 11 represented nothing new, however. The form and scale of the attack obviously were enabled by modern technology. Large airplanes are a recent invention; since people now live and work packed together, many can be killed in one blow; since modern societies are highly interconnected, they can be disrupted by limited destruction. The advantages that medical science has given the world are matched by the speed with which infectious diseases can be spread through air travel.

Modern societies may also be uniquely vulnerable psychologically. The density of personal networks multiplies the number of people who lost a close friend or who know someone who did. Indeed, everyone I know in New York fits into the latter category if not the former. The rapid flow of information also means that everyone immediately learns about any terrorist attack, and because everyone gets this information, it dominates not only the thoughts of separated individuals but also social conversation, and so is incorporated into popular consciousness and culture. This effect is magnified by the availability of videos, which by their vividness make a deep and lasting impression.

Not only do terrorist attacks resonate more deeply through society than in the past, but they are more shocking because we are no longer accustomed to war, domestic riots, and raging epidemics. People in the advanced democracies now see themselves and their friends live long and relatively tranquil lives. Terrorism was less shocking when it was only one of many forms of violent death that could be expected. Now it stands out, which helps explain why people react so strongly. People cancel flights so that they can drive, at a greatly increased chance of dying; the fear of anthrax is much greater than concern about influenza, although the latter will kill thousands of times more Americans than the former and the chance of a massive anthrax attack is slight.

Similar processes explain the economic impact of September 11. The attacks came at a time when the U.S. economy was slipping, and the direct effect through damage to the airline and tourist industries was significant. But this cannot explain most of the subsequent economic downturn. Consumer confidence is crucial, and is susceptible to psychological magnification. Not only is confidence inherently subjective, being an estimate of how well the economy is likely to do in the future, but it is highly interdependent in the sense that each person's confidence is in part based on an estimate of how confident others are.[4] Positive feedbacks and bandwagon effects then are likely. These should not be dismissed as irrational: since the fate of the economy depends on how much people will buy, and this in turn is strongly influenced by their predictions of their future economic fortunes, I should be less confident if I think others are. So when shocks such as terrorism are widely felt and the level of consumer confidence is known to the general public, the economic health of the society is highly vulnerable. The chief economist of the International Monetary Fund noted that after September 11, most of the world economies suffered badly, not only because they reflected the downturn in the United States: "One reason we have become more synchronized is because we're all watching CNN."[5]

The obvious irony is that American society is now more vulnerable than its military. In the classical model, the armed forces literally stand between the population and the enemy. The development of airpower and, even more, nuclear weapons circumvented this barrier and replaced it with deterrence. Fulfilling this mission required retaliatory forces to be invulnerable, buried deep beneath the soil or the oceans, and standard academic conceptions of the stability of mutual deterrence called for the civilian population to be unprotected so that neither side would be tempted to attack. While no theories mandate civilian vulnerability to terrorism, civilian targets are easier to destroy than military ones and civilian life is easier to disrupt than the military. This might not be problematic if deterrence held, but terrorists have little to lose.[6]

We should remember, however, that short of an attack by a lethal and infectious disease such as smallpox, no terrorist can inflict nearly as much damage as standard, let alone nuclear, warfare. Even a mere fifteen years after the end of the Cold War, it is easy to forget that we used to live with the possibility of unimaginable devastation. Interestingly enough, in the earlier years of the Cold War, American leaders doubted that the country could live with such a prospect over a prolonged period of time.[7] In fact, the country did adjust without sacrificing many of its deepest values, and this gives some hope for our ability to cope with the psychological burdens imposed by the new threats.

The Decline of States?

At first glance, terrorism in general and September 11 in particular would seem to epitomize the declining relevance of states. These attacks are violence by private actors who are seeking public ends, which is just what states are supposed to stamp out, and represent the failure of states to protect their citizens, which is their primary purpose. A world characterized by extensive terrorism is one in which states are not the most important actors.

September 11 also represents the declining importance of states in two other ways. First, terrorist groups are transnational, united not by their national citizenship or even the desire to form a state, but by religious and ideological beliefs. Although most of the 9/11 hijackers were Saudis, letters found in al-Qaeda headquarters in Kabul tell us that its members came from at least twenty countries.[8] Were this a peaceful enterprise, we would celebrate it as showing the ability of people from different countries, social classes, and backgrounds to work together. Second, the attack demonstrates the importance of globalization. The hijackers traveled throughout the world and depended on the efficient movement of information and money. Their motives and goals also epitomize globalization in that they are seeking not the expansion or retraction of national power, let alone territory, but the stanching of the global flow of corrupting ideas and the protection, if not expansion, of the realm in which proper forms of Islam dominate.

There is something to these arguments, but in other ways September 11 and its sequelae show the crucial role of states. To start with, al-Qaeda gained many of its capabilities through its capture of the Afghan government. It could not have operated as it did without the acquiescence of the state. Extensive training of terrorists would have been impossible; semi-permanent headquarters could not have been established; the maintenance of a far-flung network would have been extremely difficult.[9] Furthermore, al-Qaeda and related groups seek to take over states in order to establish the desired forms of Islam within them. For its part, the United States has ratified and reinforced the links between terrorists and states by making it clear that it will hold the latter accountable for any acts of terror emanating from their territory.[10]

The targets of September 11 also included major elements of state power. The Pentagon was attacked, and the White House may have been the target of the plane that crashed in Pennsylvania. The response further showed the continued centrality of states. American public opinion and even traditionally antistate conservatives immediately looked to the government for order and protection. The National Guard was sent to New York City and airports; federal moneys poured into affected (and unaffected) locales; the airport security personnel system was federalized; the government was granted greatly increased powers of investigation and prosecution, despite the doubts of civil libertarians. In a time of crisis, Americans turned not to their churches, multinational corporations, or the United Nations, but to the national government. For better or for worse, one of the long-run consequences of September 11 is a larger and more powerful state apparatus.

Internationally as well, states were the dominant actors in the response. The United States put together a coalition of states, and when dealing with countries like Pakistan, Uzbekistan, and Tajikistan, did so in a way that increased the power of those states over their own societies by providing resources and expertise. Although the coalition was more ad hoc than the alliances to which we had become accustomed during the Cold War, an alliance of states it nevertheless is. It also used traditional diplomatic, economic, and military instruments. The technology is modern and the intelligence network represents a form of globalization, but there is little in the fundamental nature of the activities that would surprise an observer of past centuries.

WE MUST GET AT THE ROOT CAUSES OF TERRORISM

It has become a truism, especially among liberals, that while attacking al-Qaeda is necessary, it is not sufficient. Even if the campaign is successful, terrorism will recur unless we deal with the conditions that produce it. Central among these are grinding poverty in the Third World, great and increasing inequality within and among nations, corrupt and unresponsive governments, and American policies that range the United States alongside the forces of injustice and oppression, especially in the Middle East. This argument is deeply attractive. We all want to make this a better world, and few would disagree with the proposition that poverty and oppression cause enormous misery around the world.

This perspective is misleading as an explanation for terrorism or a prescription for dealing with it, however. It is difficult to say exactly what the "root causes" of terrorism are. Poverty and lack of liberties do not appear on the list of grievances articulated by terrorists, and neither the al-Qaeda leadership nor the hijackers were poor. Of course leaders of almost all political causes are drawn from the upper and middle classes, and perhaps the terrorists would not have chosen their cause had their societies been richer and more egalitarian. But rich societies produce their own terrorists, and many poor societies do not.

To see the absence of liberal arrangements as the root cause of terrorism is even more perverse. Tolerance for diversity, respect for human rights as the West defines them, free and diverse mass media, vigorous political competition, and equality for women do not constitute the vision of the good society held by al-Qaeda and its supporters. The very notion of elevating the rights of individuals and the ability to choose one's way of life is anathema to them. Traditions real or imagined, community values as they interpret them, and life regulated by Muslim clerics who read the Koran the way Taliban leaders did are their avowed objectives. Perhaps if their countries were remodeled along Western lines, terrorism would eventually subside. But resistance, including terrorism, would increase during the transition, which could last for generations.[11]

Even if poverty, inequality, and oppression were the root causes of terrorism, there is little reason to think that we could deal with them effectively. Many of us believe that the United States should provide higher levels of economic assistance to Third World nations and lower barriers to their goods, but we cannot point to solid evidence that doing so would make much difference. For all our studies, we are far from understanding what produces democracy, a well-functioning civil society, and respect for human rights. It is even less clear that the relevant variables can be much affected by outside interventions. It can be argued that one of the main barriers to democracy in Islamic countries is the lack of a separation between church and state, but it is hard to see what outsiders could do here. There is one specific thing that the United States could do that in all probability would have a good effect, however: it could provide funds for education and press host governments to do likewise, because as it stands now, many parents send their children to madrasas because no other education is available.

Of course the United States has not been passive, and the terrorists see a number of horrific policies. Foremost among them is the stationing of troops in Saudi Arabia and the support for a corrupt Saudi regime. Thus it is no accident that most of the September 11 hijackers were Saudis. The grievance that was second in prominence was the

American sanctions against, and the later attack on, Iraq. But it is not clear whether this position was much more than an attempt to cater to the beliefs of the followers; Saddam Hussein's regime, although repressive, opposed fundamentalist Islam. Bin Laden also berates the United States for its support of Israel, although this position received stress only after September 11 and may be designed to garner support from the widest possible Arab audience. Furthermore, bin Laden's opposition is to the existence of Israel and the American support for the Jewish state, not to the settlements or Israeli sovereignty over parts of Jerusalem. What this means is that there are no conceivable changes in the United States and in American policy that could reduce al-Qaeda's hatred. Even withdrawing U.S. troops from Saudi Arabia, as largely happened in the wake of Saddam's overthrow, is not likely to have much effect, although it might have done some good had it occurred before al-Qaeda became established.

The much larger group throughout the Islamic world that has some sympathy for the September 11 attacks, sees bin Laden as at least in part a hero, and is glad to see the United States humbled by the attacks, is harder to analyze, being much more disparate. Much of the rage is attributable to the members' own governments, which are unable to provide a decent life for their people while sponsoring mass media that blame most of their ills on the United States. Democracy and reform might have good effect here, especially if they were coupled with economic growth that led to improved lives for society's lower strata. But whether such an outcome could be produced by any U.S. policy is questionable.

American support for Israel in general, and the Sharon government in particular, is perhaps highest on the list of grievances in the Muslim world. Over the long run the Arab–Israeli dispute and the American role in it probably will play a large role in cultivating the next generation of terrorists, even if it is not responsible for the current one. But in the short run it is hard to tell how much of a difference a different U.S. policy would make, and the United States was not without enemies when it was actively promoting a settlement that would have given the Palestinians a state, most of the West Bank, and much of East Jerusalem. It is interesting that those who believe that the United States could diminish Arab hatred by pressing for an Israeli withdrawal also believe that this policy is moral and would bring peace between Israel and its neighbors. Those who call for a tougher stance toward Israel (or, conversely, toward the Palestinians) held these views on September 10. It would be more impressive if those who argue that new circumstances call for a new American policy in the Middle East had argued that the old policy was politically and morally appropriate at the time. (I also think that if the shoe were on the other foot, and circumstances had arisen which could lead people to believe that greater American support for an unyielding Israeli policy was expedient, liberals would object, arguing that it would be wrong to make the Palestinians pay for a policy that served only American interests.)

The call to understand why people hate us, then, while intellectually sound, is largely motivated by political agendas unrelated to September 11. There are many reasons to object to the Bush administration's policy in the Middle East—and I, for one, think it has been terrible—but it is disingenuous to claim that such a conclusion follows from an understanding of the motives of the terrorists or of why the United States is hated in the Islamic world. Indeed, almost any course of action can be rationalized on the grounds that it will increase approval of the United States and reduce terrorism. Thus a member of the Kuwaiti parliament urged that his country adopt sharia on the grounds that if this were done, "there would be no terrorism."[12]

The arguments by the Bush administration about how to deal with the causes of terrorism are at least as flawed. The main claim is for close links between terrorism and dictatorial regimes, which in fact is uncertain and variable. Some such regimes do sponsor terrorism, particularly in the Middle East. But some dictatorships, such as North Korea and Libya, seem to have gotten out of the business, and others never entered it. This is not surprising. Dictators usually seek predictability and tight control. Terrorist groups are loose cannons not only in the sense of moving about in ways that are difficult to predict, let alone control, but also in being prone to shoot in several directions. Terrorists may serve the narrow interests or broad ideologies of some dictators, but the connection is likely to be highly contingent rather than a powerful generalization. Al-Qaeda grew strong in Afghanistan, but rather than being a tool of the Taliban, it had sufficient strength to be an equal, if not a dominant, partner with that government; and the importance of this case for recent history should not lead us to see it as usual. As I will discuss in the next chapter, there was no reason to believe that Saddam Hussein would have allied himself with al-Qaeda or turned over WMD to it.

Conversely, democracies may harbor and sponsor terrorists. I suspect these cases are relatively uncommon, but they are certainly not unknown. A democratic India harbored Tamil terrorists; a democratic Ireland and the United States gave cover and financial support to the IRA; in the nineteenth century, immigrants from Ireland used American territory as a springboard against the British in Canada, and many filibustering expeditions were launched against Central American countries. If we expand our focus to include state-sponsored terrorists, many would indict the United States for a long list of covert actions (sometimes against democratically elected regimes), supporting the slaughter of innocent people who were believed to stand in the way of American-backed regimes, and sponsoring guerrilla groups that sought to destabilize regimes believed to be unfriendly. Indeed, although Bush declared that "democratic governments do not shelter terrorist camps," the United States decided not to prosecute the People's Mujahadeen of Iraq, which was based in Iraq when the United States took control of that country.[13]

Epitomizing its beliefs about the roots of terrorism was the Bush administration's overthrow of Saddam's regime in Iraq. Bush and his colleagues constantly repeated and apparently believed the argument that in a variety of ways tyrants produce and support terrorism, and so overthrowing the former is a way to attack the latter. Whatever the merits of this as an abstract theory, the application to Iraq appears to have been badly flawed. As noted in the introduction, the result in all probability has been to greatly increase rather than decrease the number of anti-American terrorists around the world. If this is correct, we will be paying the price for years to come for this attempt to deal with the supposed root causes of terrorism.

IT'S A WAR

In his speech to a joint session of Congress nine days after the 9/11 attack, President Bush declared that the United States would wage war against terrorism, accepting the formulation used by Secretary of Defense Rumsfeld just hours after the planes struck.[14] Consistent with this, the United States used military force to overthrow the governments of Afghanistan and Iraq. But the war in Afghanistan was not a normal war, and the very label is contentious and questionable, although it does have some value.[15] To start with, the oddity of the situation is indicated by the fact that the removal of the Taliban regime was not the ultimate goal of the effort, but only a means to combat terrorism. Afghanistan was attacked in order to install a new government that would eliminate the terrorists; had it been possible to attack the terrorists directly, this would have been done and the Afghan authorities would have been left in place even though they were repellent to American values.

If we are at war with terrorism, the obvious question is: what are our objectives. The normal answer would be to get the adversary to withdraw from disputed territory, to change its objectionable policies, or to replace a government that was deemed a menace by its very existence. But these conceptions of victory are inappropriate here, and there are no clear substitutes. So it is not surprising that the Bush administration has never issued a definitive statement of its war aims. Soon after the war was declared, Secretaries Powell and Rumsfeld said that it would be won when Americans felt secure again, an objective that sounds more like psychotherapy than international politics. This is not to say that it is an inappropriate goal when dealing with terrorism, however. By its nature, terror seeks to utilize political and psychological leverage in order to produce political effects that are disproportionate to the military force deployed. To the extent that it is more than mere revenge (a motive not to be underestimated, as I will discuss below), it seeks change through inducing fear, generally to a degree that is a magnification rather than a true reflection of what else could follow. So reducing fear and making Americans feel secure should be a crucial focus of American policy. But it is an unusual reason to wage a war.

The label "war" implies the primacy of military force. Other instruments, such as diplomacy and intelligence, may be used, but they are in service of the deployment of armed force. This conceptual frame is unfortunate when it comes to dealing with terrorism. Here diplomacy, the international criminal justice system, and especially intelligence are primary. With good information, terrorism is easy to attack; without it, very little is possible. Force and the threat of force play a vital role in generating information and attacking terrorist targets, but intelligence and international information-sharing are central. If they are sacrificed in order to gain military advantage, the policy will suffer. Conceiving of military action aimed at terrorists as war, then, gets us thinking in the wrong terms.

Others have seen the advantages of taking the United States at its word and justifying their behavior in terms of fighting terrorism. In addition to the Russian rhetoric in its conflict in Chechnya, a leader of Hamas said that no one expected the United States to refrain from violence in response to the September 11 attack, "so why do you expect me to react peacefully to occupation?"[16] In parallel, Sharon argues: "You in America are in a war against terror. We in Israel are in a war against terror. It's the same war."[17] One of Sharon's advisers explained that "the Palestinian Authority has an obligation to no longer harbor or give shelter to international terrorist organizations like Hamas."[18]

The Indians have equated December 13, 2001 (the date of the attack on their parliament), with September 11, an interpretation the United States has largely endorsed. All sorts of domestic oppression are also being claimed as counterterrorism. Thus the Mugabe government in Zimbabwe claimed that critical reporters "are assisting terrorists. ... We would like them to know that we agree with President Bush that anyone who in any way finances, harbors or defends terrorists is himself a terrorist. We, too, will not make any difference between terrorists and their friends or supporters."[19]

The United States initially responded that war was not against terrorism in general, but only against "terrorism with a global reach," as Bush put it in his speech of September 20. This modifier nicely got the United States out of one dilemma, but opened the door to several others, and soon was dropped. To say that America is fighting only a subset of terrorists raised the question of in whose interest the war is being waged. The United States seeks worldwide support on the grounds that al-Qaeda and related groups are seeking weapons of mass destruction that "would be a threat to every nation and, eventually, to civilization itself."[20] But terrorists, even with nuclear weapons, do not target the entire globe; they attack sites in and representatives of particular states. As a Russian diplomat said to me shortly after Bush's speech, "Ah, a global reach—that means terrorists who can attack America."

Partly because of the need for a justification that could attract wider support, partly because of the belief that terrorism itself really is a common enemy, and perhaps partly because of the power of rhetoric to persuade its users, Bush dropped the "global reach" modifier.[21] Important here were the events of December 2001, which saw bloody suicide attacks against Israel and the Indian parliament. These led the United States to broaden its definition and to push Arafat and Musharraf to eliminate the groups responsible, eventually leading to the unrelenting opposition to Arafat when Bush concluded that he supported terrorism and to greater support for Musharraf when he turned against the terrorists. But the exact scope of the American policy remains unclear. Terrorists in Sri Lanka, for example, do not seem to qualify even though they have cells in Canada. Neither is it clear whether the IRA would if it were to resume violence in Northern Ireland, which is fortunate, because an attack on areas supporting these terrorists would require military action in several American cities.

The expanded enemies list and increased consistency come at a price. A war against all terrorism seems to me to be one that cannot be won and that will cause much collateral damage. Even on the unreasonable assumption that such an effort would receive widespread support abroad, it would engender enormous opposition as well. It is worth remembering that many national leaders had previous careers as terrorists. Even if it is true that terrorism is now uniquely dangerous because modern societies are so vulnerable and terrorists could employ WMD, there is no reason to expect that even the best-designed and best-executed strategy could eradicate terrorism. Despite its danger, terror remains a tactic, not an enemy. Tactics of course can be driven out, but it is not clear how they can be defeated. At times, the Bush administration seems to recognize this when it argues that some of the path to eradication lies through changing worldwide norms and completely delegitimating terrorism, just as slavery was delegitimated in the nineteenth century.[22] Such trends might be possible: one can argue that part of the reason for the decline of warfare among developed countries is that it is no longer seen as a legitimate tool of statecraft for anything other than self-defense, at least when employed against other developed countries.[23] But this process is likely to be as prolonged as the delegitimation of slavery was. Furthermore, this sort of argument does not fit well with an administration that derides most notions of international legitimacy.

Framing the conflict as war also implies that we must be prepared to sacrifice many values in order to prevail. In a normal war, this would mean that citizens would be called to the colors, and those at home would expect to endure economic privation and even enemy bombardment. But none of this is part of American policy. In the immediate wake of the September 11 attacks, Bush urged people to fly and shop, and further tax cuts followed rather than programs to make the nation less dependent on oil and pleas for citizens to conserve energy and shun SUVs.[24] The policy may be correct, but it sits oddly with the idea of being at war.

Greater sacrifices are being required in the area of civil liberties. The claim that the American people must accept intrusions and restrictions that were previously intolerable is justified not by detailed claims that the value of the information produced will outweigh the cost to our privacy and liberty, but rather by blanket assertions that war requires these measures. Similarly, careful arguments for bringing terrorists before military tribunals are short-circuited by statements that this is what is done during wartime. As Bush declared: "The United States is under attack. And at war, the president needs to have the capacity to protect the national security interests and the safety of the American people."[25] Here it is especially troubling that the war will be prolonged, if not indefinite, since this means that suspects, including American citizens, may be incarcerated for life without a trial.[26]

Foreign policy sacrifices are common in war as well, since the state is willing to put aside other goals that conflict with victory and to work with any actor that is undermining its enemy. To some extent the United States has done the latter by supporting dictatorial regimes in return for their assistance against al-Qaeda although its continuing hostility toward Syria and Iran are important and telling exceptions. The willingness to give up other objectives is less clear, in part because Bush and his colleagues, like most of us, feel psychological pressures to deny painful value trade-offs. To critics, the overthrow of Saddam and the unilateral nature of many American policies are striking examples of the unwillingness to forego other goals that interfere with the war on terror; to the Bush administration, they are crucial means in waging the war.

Saying that the struggle against terrorism is a war has three beneficial effects, however. First, it reminds us that military victory does not automatically produce political victory—that is, it does not always reach the desired goals at a reasonable price. Critics believe that Bush fails to appreciate this crucial point, but the war terminology should make it harder to miss over the long run, although of course it does not tell us what should be done. Second, the idea of war brings urgency to the American response. As numerous officials have testified, despite the statements of CIA director George Tenet that al-Qaeda was the most pressing security threat to the United States, before September 11 this view did not resonate throughout the government, let alone the wider society. The political leaders were unwilling to pay the high price required to change priorities and shake up the bureaucracies, particularly by forcing the CIA and the FBI to work closely together. Since the attacks, however, officials constantly refer to the government being on "war footing," and while the phrase rings strangely to those outside Washington, it is part of the effort to change deeply ingrained ways of proceeding. Third and relatedly, choosing the metaphor of war rather than law enforcement was part of removing some of the constraints that restricted American counterterrorism to activities that could pass muster in civilian courts. Once the struggle was seen as warfare, the option of killing terrorists rather than having to capture them is not only permissible but obvious. Nevertheless, I am not convinced that the gains outweigh the costs or that the necessary changes required framing the struggle as a war. We should remember that while the United States has won most of the wars it has fought against other countries, the declarations of war against cancer, drugs, and poverty have led to disappointment, failure, and bitterness. As the great British statesman Lord Salisbury said when he tried to bring some perspective to the Eastern Crisis of 1877–1878: "It has generally been acknowledged to be madness to go to war for an idea, but if anything is more unsatisfactory, it is to go to war against a nightmare."[27]

TERRORISM IS SENSELESS

The attacks of September 11 seem not only inhumane but senseless. Despite the fact that terrorism often is an effective tactic,[28] it is hard to see what objective bin Laden thought he could reach. I doubt that he expected to change American support for Saudi Arabia and Israel or its opposition to Iraq. His actions also seem self-defeating because they endangered the Taliban regime, his life, and al-Qaeda.

But horrible actions are not necessarily irrational. Bin Laden and his colleagues may have been motivated, first of all, by the desire for revenge and justice. The United States had committed great crimes and had to be punished. Even if the attacks could not set the world aright, they would at least make the United States pay a price for its awful deeds. We—or at least we liberals—often underestimate the importance of revenge. Emotional, primitive, unamenable to analysis, it does not seem to belong in a civilized country. But it does. In everyday life we often try to punish people who have harmed us, not because we think it will change them but because we think this is appropriate; and these nonrational, if not irrational, impulses facilitate cooperation because they increase the likelihood that cheaters will be deterred. On a larger scale, the centerpiece of American strategic policy during the Cold War was the threat of massive retaliation against a Soviet attack on the United States, an attack that would have utterly destroyed the USSR. Retaliation could have reached no meaningful goal and would have been motivated entirely by revenge. No one doubted the credibility of this threat, however.

Bin Laden may also have had an instrumental purpose. His focus may have been less on the United States and the short run than on the Islamic world over a longer period. He could have reasoned that a dramatic action would put his movement and ideology at the center of attention, and that it would multiply the strength of his cause even if he died in the effort. As E.E. Schattschneider showed, the outcome of a conflict is often determined by the number of people who are mobilized to join in it.[29] Bin Laden may also have expected the attack to serve as a provocation that would lead the United States to strike out in a way that would rally support for him. Although September 11 was not a "clash of civilizations," he may have hoped to generate one, and in precipitating the attack on Iraq, may have succeeded.

A NEW WORLD?

American officials and commentators declare that "everything has changed after September 11," "this is the end of the post-Cold War era," and "the world will never be the same." While I remain skeptical that the world will unite against terrorism, the changes indeed are great, due to the fundamental shift in U.S. foreign policy.[30]

Uniting against Terrorism?

Is terrorism such a scourge that all countries will unite against it, just as most nations pull together if they are attacked? The Bush administration argues that this is what should happen, seeing the conflict as one of civilization against evil that must trump all differences. This expectation is not entirely unreasonable. In the past, states put aside old conflicts when faced by an even more pressing common enemy, as Britain and the USSR finally did in their struggle against Nazi Germany. But I doubt that most countries see terrorism as posing a threat of this magnitude, although a serious biological or nuclear attack might change this. At this point, however, it is hard to argue that most countries in the world are more concerned about al- Qaeda than they are about local threats. Indeed the U.N. was not able to adopt a strong antiterrorist resolution because of disagreements about how terrorism is to be defined.[31]

Many countries have taken advantage of the new opportunities offered by September 11, however. Sudan accepted the American "get out of jail free" card by offering intelligence cooperation in return for being removed from the list of countries that sponsor terrorism. Pakistan was transformed from a nuclear-powered troublemaker to a pillar of stability meriting extensive aid and a forgiveness of past sins, which with the revelation of A.Q. Kahn's extensive nuclear sales have turned out to be greater than previously believed. Uzbekistan's lack of democracy and violations of human rights were put aside to gain necessary bases.

Russia and China

More important, the changes in Russian foreign policy and Russian–American relations since September 11 have been dramatic and unexpected by many analysts as Russia embraced a high degree of cooperation with the United States, largely on American terms.[32] It not only endorsed the American response in Afghanistan, but facilitated it by not opposing an American military presence in Central Asia, an area previously seen as a Russian sphere of influence. Even more startling, Putin accepted the American renunciation of the ABM treaty and an arms reduction agreement that closely followed American preferences. In return for a greater role in NATO, Putin has muted his opposition to farther eastward expansion of this organization, although he still objects to it.[33] While points of friction remain, most obviously over Iran and Iraq, Putin has chosen to bandwagon with the United States rather than balance against it. The latter policy might have succeeded, because on many issues Russia was not isolated. Had Putin maintained his opposition to the American renunciation of the ABM agreement, he could have recruited many European countries to his side. But he apparently calculated that even if others joined him, the chances of success were not great and opposition had only limited value. What he needed was American support for his regime, acceptance into the ranks of Western countries, and help in rebuilding the Russian economy. For these goals, American support was essential.

This choice has significantly altered world politics. Although it would go too far to say that Russia will now be treated like any other European country or to be certain that the new course will be maintained, especially if it does not yield visible benefits, Russian–American cooperation has greatly increased and the prospects for the integration of Russia into Western projects has brightened. What cannot be readily determined, however, is the role that the common interest in fighting terrorism has played in bringing about this change. While Putin's desire for American support in Chechnya cannot be ignored, he probably saw antiterrorism as a convenient opportunity for a general reorientation of Russian policy. Granting the United States dominance was a significant price, but one worth paying to gain American acceptance and economic assistance.

Even greater, but probably more temporary, is the change in U.S.–PRC relations.[34] Before September 11, the Bush administration said that China was the greatest menace to world peace. In the aftermath of the attacks, this rhetoric ceased, relations were repaired, and during the 2004 Taiwan elections the United States took a position favorable to the People's Republic that would have been unthinkable for Bush and his colleagues before the attacks. For its part, the PRC has been quick to point out that it staunchly opposes terrorism throughout the world, and especially in the Muslim province of Xinjiang. But I doubt that this common interest will prove sufficient to permanently override the conflict over Taiwan, the South China Sea, and general influence in East Asia.

American Stance toward the World

The most important change has been in American foreign policy, which is now on a different course not only from what it was under Clinton but also from the direction that had been established by Bush before September 11. Although Clinton's foreign policy was far from consistent, it displayed a serious degree of multilateralism, meaningful consultation with allies, concern with preventing humanitarian disasters, and support for peacekeeping operations. Bush took a different stance in his campaign and his first eight months in office. He and his colleagues argued that the United States often had to act on its own, that military force should be used only to protect vital interests, that the United States should concentrate on the threats from China and perhaps Russia, and that the burden of humanitarian interventions should be left to others. The Defense Department and its ideological allies were pushing to withdraw American peacekeepers from Bosnia, Kosovo, and Sinai, and no one in the government thought the United States should engage in nation building.[35]

Policy after September 11 continued and extended some of these elements, but altered several others. As I will discuss in more detail in chapter 4, while unilateralism continued, abandoned were the focus on potentially hostile great powers and the restriction of American efforts, especially the use of force, to a narrow set of vital interests. Now Bush argues that if the United States is to be secure, it must spread both its influence and its values around the world.

American goals have grown steadily since September 11. The United States has a mission to crush terrorism, which is seen as a menace to civilization and as "the new totalitarian threat."[36] Furthermore, since terrorism and tyrants are linked, the latter not only are menaces on their own terms, but also must be combated lest they give terrorists weapons of mass destruction. The only sure route to safety is, then, to establish democracies around the world, even—or especially—in areas that have not seen them before. While this position was developed as part of the justification for the overthrow of Saddam Hussein, it seems to be meant more broadly and implies that the United States has little choice but to become not only the world's policeman but also its tutor.

These tasks should be undertaken with the help of others if possible, but without them if necessary.

As early as the morning after the September 11 attack, Bush declared that the United States was engaged "in a monumental struggle of good versus evil," and in his memorial remarks at the National Cathedral two days later, he said that "our responsibility to history is … clear: to answer these attacks and rid the world of evil."[37] While such a world-view is consistent with the American political tradition,[38] it also owes something to Bush's outlook as a born-again Christian. There is reason to believe that just as his coming to Christ gave meaning to his previously aimless and dissolute personal life, so the war on terrorism has become not only the defining characteristic of his foreign policy but also his sacred mission. As an associate of the President reports: "I believe the president was sincere, after 9/11, thinking 'This is what I was put on this earth for.'"[39]

Fear

Part of the reason for the new American foreign policy and the war in Iraq is that September 11 produced great fear and undermined many people's sense of what dangers were remote enough to be dismissed. I do not think it is an accident that one of the few lines that brought applause in Bush's brilliantly crafted Cincinnati speech of October 7, 2002, justifying the drive to depose Saddam, was "We will not live in fear." Taken literally, this makes no sense. Unfortunately, fear is often well founded. What it indicates is an understandable desire for a safer world, despite the fact that the United States did live in fear throughout the Cold War and survived quite well. But if the sentence has little logical meaning, the emotion it embodies is an understandable fear of fear, a drive to gain certainty, an impulse to assert control by acting.[40]

This reading of Bush's statement is consistent with the fact that his speeches are filled with the language of menace and fear, and with my impression that many people who opposed invading Iraq before September 11 but altered their positions afterward had not taken terrorism terribly seriously before 9/11—a category that includes George Bush.[41] Those who had studied the subject were surprised by the timing and method of the attacks, but not that they took place, and so they changed their beliefs only incrementally. But as Bush frequently acknowledges—indeed stresses—he was shocked by the assault, which greatly increased his feelings of danger and led him to drastically different policies. As he put it in a paragraph in his Cincinnati speech that came between two paragraphs about the need to disarm

Iraq: "On September 11th, 2001, America felt its vulnerability." Three months later, in response to an accusation that he had always wanted to invade Iraq, Bush replied: "Prior to September 11, we were discussing smart sanctions. ... After September 11, the doctrine of containment just doesn't hold any water. ... My vision shifted dramatically after September 11, because I now realize the stakes, I realize the world has changed."[42] Secretary of Defense Rumsfeld similarly explained that the United States "did not act in Iraq because we had discovered dramatic new evidence of Iraq's pursuit of weapons of mass murder. We acted because we saw the existing evidence in a new light, through the prism of our experience on September 11."[43]

Preliminary analyses of the 2004 election also indicate the strong influence of fear. The Bush campaign emphasized the reasons to fear terrorist attacks, and it appears that he owed his victory in significant measure to people feeling safer with him than with Kerry. The facts that the gender gap was less than usual and that married women, unlike their single counterparts, favored Bush are probably best explained by fear. Bush supporters were also remarkably ill-informed in believing that Saddam's Iraq had been developing weapons of mass destruction, misperceptions that may be both caused and been caused by their fears.[44]

The claim that some eventualities are unlikely enough to be put aside lost plausibility in face of the obvious retort: "What could be less likely than terrorists flying airplanes into the World Trade Center and the Pentagon?" During the Cold War, Bernard Brodie expressed his exasperation with wild suggestions about military actions the USSR might undertake: "All sorts of notions and propositions are churned out, and often presented for consideration with the prefatory words: 'It is conceivable that. ...' Such words establish their own truth, for the fact that someone has conceived of whatever proposition follows is enough to establish that it is conceivable. Whether it is worth a second thought, however, is another matter."[45] It is now hard to say this about anything; worst-case analysis is hard to dismiss. When a disturbing and unexpected event occurs, it is of course rational to change one's estimates of the likelihood of similar or related events. Thus when Chile's Pinochet took the unprecedented step of assassinating a leading adversary who had fled to the United States to organize opposition to the regime, the United States quickly gave credence to the previously dismissed reports that the Uruguayan dictatorship might try to kill a congressman who had sponsored a bill to cut off aid to that repressive regime.[46] It did not increase its worry about Soviet adventures or a PRC attack on Taiwan, however. It is much harder to say exactly what kinds of events the terrorist attacks should lead us now to see as more likely and what estimates we should leave unrevised. Thus when they were making the case for war against Iraq, Bush in his 2003 State of the Union Address mentioned the 9/11 attacks and said: "Imagine those 19 hijackers with other weapons and other planes—this time armed by Saddam Hussein," and Donald Rumsfeld similarly asked us to "imagine a September 11 with weapons of mass destruction."[47]

This helps explain how the option of preventive attack became psychologically as well as politically available after September 11. There was more evidence that bin Laden was a deadly menace to the United States before that date than there was that Saddam was a menace after it, but it would have been much harder to convince policy makers or the general public to take military action in the former case than it was in the latter, and the reason is the changes produced by the terrorist attacks. So when Tim Russert asked Bush to respond to the charge that he "brought the nation to war under false pretenses," Bush replied: "I expected to find [WMD]. ... And I made the decision based upon that intelligence in the context of the war against terror. In other words, we were attacked, and therefore every threat had to be reanalyzed. ... Every potential harm to America had to be judged in the context of this war on terror."[48] During the first presidential debate, Bush similarly responded to a question about Iraq by explaining that "when we had the debate in 2000 [I] never dreamt to be [committing troops to combat], but the enemy attacked us." This gave Kerry the opportunity to say that the president's answer was "extraordinarily revealing" because ... Saddam Hussein didn't attack us, Osama bin Laden attacked us."[49] But what Bush's comment really revealed was not that he believed that Iraq was behind the September 11 attacks, but that this terrorist strike had fundamentally changed how he thought about risk and dangers.

The fact that no one can guarantee that an adversary with WMD will not use them means that fear cannot be banished. Although administration officials exaggerated the danger that Saddam posed, they also revealed their true fears when they talked about the *possibility* that he could use WMD against the United States or its allies. At least some of them may have been insensitive to the magnitude of this possibility; what mattered was its very existence. Even the postwar revelations that Saddam had no serious WMD programs made little difference to them, because the intention was present and it was only a matter of time before Saddam acted on it.[50] As Bush explained to Diane Sawyer, what led him to go to war was "the possibility that [Saddam] could acquire [nuclear] weapons. If he were to acquire [nuclear] weapons, he would be a danger. ... A gathering threat, after 9/11, is a threat that needed to be dealt with."[51] The risk may have been slight, but this was not reassuring—it still existed. Psychology plays an important role here because people value certainty and are willing to pay a high price to decrease the probability of a danger from slight to none.[52] Bush's choice of words when declaring a formal end to the organized combat in Iraq was telling: "This much is *certain*: No terrorist network will gain weapons of mass destruction from the Iraqi regime."[53] Fear, justified or not, is a potent driver of people and policies. It is even more so when it is coupled with great power.[54]

CONCLUSION

Although for some government officials the war on terrorism permitted the sort of highly assertive American foreign policy that they had favored from the start, for others, including Bush, it represented a great change. The structural conditions for American hegemony were produced by the size and vitality of the American economy, the lack of political unity within Europe, and the collapse of the Soviet Union. But it took both September 11 and the particular outlook of the Bush administration to put the United States on its current path, which I will analyze more fully in the next two chapters. Although I do not think this course can be maintained (see chapter 5), it will take us into new and dangerous territory.

3

THE CONFRONTATION BETWEEN IRAQ AND THE UNITED STATES: IMPLICATIONS FOR THE THEORY AND PRACTICE OF DETERRENCE

As it became clear that Iraq lacked not only weapons of mass destruction (WMD) but also serious WMD programs, attention shifted to the intelligence failure, the general rationale for preventive war, and the misery of the occupation and attempted democratic transition. I will discuss these in the next two chapters, but here I want to return to the premises and implications of American policy in the run-up to the overthrow of Saddam, concentrating on deterrence, which was the centerpiece of American policy and theorizing during the Cold War but now seems contradicted and denied.[1] I will focus both on the actual deterrent relationship between the United States and Iraq was and on what Bush and his colleagues apparently believed. The divergence between the two, and the ways in which the actors' beliefs affect the use and impact of threats, raise questions of how we theorize about actors who are themselves thinking about deterrence. The Bush administration's main fear was that if Saddam gained nuclear weapons,[2] he would have been able to do great mischief in the region if not in the entire world. The implication is that the United States could not have deterred Saddam and, to turn this around, that the United States itself would have been deterred. The latter concern is linked to Bush's ambitious foreign policy goals, discussed further in chapter 4.

These beliefs and goals in part explain the war. But I admit that they are not a complete explanation of it, and in the end I still find the war hard to understand. Determining which beliefs drove the conclusion is difficult because proponents of the war (and opponents as well) displayed irrational cognitive consistency, motivated bias, and the refusal to face value trade-offs.[3] That is, the administration and its supporters rated the long-term prospects of deterring Saddam as low, the likelihood of a fairly easy military victory as high, the regional effects of overthrowing Saddam as favorable, and the prospects for constructing a stable and even democratic Iraq as bright. Opponents disagree on all four points. Only a psychological explanation will account for this pattern because the four factors being judged are logically independent from each other, as became clear in the aftermath of the war. A world in which allowing Saddam to build his WMD would be very dangerous is not necessarily one in which overthrowing him would be relatively cheap. But people want to minimize the costs they perceive in their favored policy. In fact, many of the reasons they give are rationalizations, not rationales, and come to their minds only after they have reached their decisions. I suspect that fear played a major role, as noted in the previous chapter, and that the feeling that the war was necessary produced the belief that its consequences would be benign. We will also see in the next chapter that expansion is the normal path of a state with the ability to do so, an argument that implies the irrelevance of most expressions of belief.

Nevertheless, the war seems particularly puzzling not only because it turned out so badly, but because this seemed the likely outcome to many of us. Indeed, when Richard Haass, head of the state Department Policy Planning Staff during the run-up to the war, was asked why Bush went to war, he replied: "I will go to my grave not knowing that. I can't answer it."[4] As noted in the introduction, theories that assume basic rationality are troubled by such events. So at this point in substitute for a fully satisfying account of why the Bush administration behaved as it did I can only look at its conception of why Iraq could not have been deterred because this was central to several of its rationales, can be linked to the changes induced by September 11, and had roots in the officials' earlier views.

COMMON ASSUMPTIONS

Before turning to deterrence, I want to flag three questions whose answers were generally taken for granted before the war but should not have been.

First, should the United States or other countries have been disturbed by Iraq's WMD programs? How did they menace American interests? Even those who opposed the Bush administration's policy wanted to see these programs, if not Saddam himself, eliminated, but we should remember Waltz's argument that the spread of nuclear weapons will bring stability, regardless of the characteristics of the regime and its leader.[5] The issue is too large to be fully addressed here, but it clearly is a mistake to jump from the fact that Saddam was evil to the conclusion that his possession of WMD would have threatened the United States and world peace. Would Saddam's nuclear weapons have given him greater influence in the region? Could these weapons have done anything other than deter an unprovoked attack on him? In back of many of the disagreements about the consequences of Iraqi nuclear weapons lay undebated differences in beliefs about how nuclear weapons change foreign policies.

Second, the focus on whether Saddam could have been contained should not have obscured the more fundamental question of whether threats needed to be primary. Might conciliation have been possible? After all, many bitter disputes have ended with some sort of rapprochement, and interrogations of leaders of the regime indicate that Saddam was open to this possibility, in part because he thought his main enemy was Iran, not the United States[6] Condoleezza Rice said that the problem was with "the ambition and behavior of Saddam Hussein, because sooner or later, the ambitions of Saddam Hussein and the interests of the United States are going to clash."[7] But does this mean that diplomacy, inducements, and compromises, all coupled with threats, necessarily would have been ineffective? The clash of interests is constant in international politics; war is not. Saddam presumably wanted to dominate the region, but he was hardly alone in this ambition. He supported terrorism against Israel, but so do countries with which the United States maintains tolerable relations. He murdered, tortured, and used poison gas against his own people, but this repulsive behavior was not seen as an insurmountable barrier to cooperation in the 1980s. This is not to deny that Saddam may have been beyond the reach of anything other than threats and force, but just to argue that this should be the conclusion of analysis, not its starting point.[8]

Third, even if the world would not have been safe if Saddam Hussein acquired nuclear weapons, he was years from that goal. So why did Bush seek an immediate resolution of the problem? He may have believed that only a rapid pace could garner the domestic support that was required. An alternative but not incompatible argument would point to the American election calendar. But what is clear is that both the timing and the content of the policy need to be explained, although the two enterprises might employ different approaches.

In hindsight, the most obvious assumption was that Saddam had active and advanced WMD programs. In the closing chapter I will discuss the reasons for this intelligence failure, but the fact that this belief was wrong should not blind us to the fact that it was quite reasonable and was held almost universally, including by opponents of the war. Even in retrospect it is hard to explain Saddam's behavior that led observers to be certain that he had active programs of prohibited weapons, if not the weapons themselves.

COERCION AND DETERRENCE

When discussing the utility and validity of arguments about deterrence, we need to distinguish between deterrence as an explanation for any individual state's behavior and deterrence as a theory of international outcomes, which depends on the interaction of two or more adversaries. The question of whether deterrence does or does not accurately describe how one state thinks or acts is different from the question of whether threats of deterrence have the influence that the theory posits. Deterrence thus could be flawed in the sense of providing bad guidance to decision makers and simultaneously be good as an explanation of their behavior. Indeed, many critics of American policy during the Cold War said that by following the prescriptions of deterrence, the United States heightened Soviet–American conflicts and made war more likely.

Further analysis requires a reminder that while we often talk of the distinction between deterrence and defense, the fundamental contrast is between coercion and brute force, each of which has two branches (deterrence and compellence for coercion, defense and offense for brute force).[9] Brute force, dominant in the prenuclear age,[10] is the ability of a state to take and hold what it wants by physically defeating the other's army. Coercion, by contrast, works on the adversary's will and intentions by inflicting pain and holding at risk what the other side values—that is, by threatening or carrying out punishment. Thus, during the Cold War neither side could prevent the other from destroying it, but each could deter attack by threatening retaliation. This does not mean that threats are necessarily absent from brute force, but here what is being threatened is that if the other does not comply peacefully, the state will physically defend itself or take what is desired. Although U.S. policy toward Iraq was often referred to as being coercive, this was true only in the colloquial and not the technical sense of the term, because Bush both threatened and used brute force.

Indeed, the nub of the Bush administration's argument was that disarmament, if not regime change, was needed because an Iraq with robust WMD could not have been contained by American coercion, especially deterrence. But we need to refine the question from "Could the United States have deterred Saddam Hussein if he gained a robust WMD capability?" to "What acts on Saddam's part could the United States not have deterred him from?" The more differentiated question is necessary because some actions are harder to deter than others and the United States was more worried about some actions than about others. Even proponents of overthrow did not say that Saddam would have used WMD to strike the American homeland. Absent an attack on America, the United States clearly could have been able to protect itself by the combination of the credibility of its threat to retaliate and Saddam's relatively low motivation to strike (although if he was as evil as the Bush administration believed, perhaps this is too optimistic).

Rather, the main American concern was with extended deterrence—its ability to deter Saddam from coercing his neighbors, especially Kuwait and Saudi Arabia. The problem arises from what Glenn Snyder called the stability-instability paradox.[11] This concept, developed in the context of the Cold War, starts with the common observation that under conditions of mutual second-strike capability, neither side can launch an all-out nuclear war because doing so would result in its own devastation. Although this stability is desirable, it permits either side to engage in adventures for lower stakes and at lower levels of violence, such as threatening or even attacking allies with conventional weapons. Whether the stability at the highest levels of violence actually gave many opportunities for mischief during the Cold War is hotly debated, but the fear that it would do so drove a great deal of American security policy. So it is not entirely surprising that the Bush administration worried that even a small Iraqi nuclear force would have undermined American extended deterrence, although it is worth noting that this judgment was apparently reached on the basis of instinct rather than analysis: it appears that the administration never asked for an intelligence assessment of Saddam's threat to the region.[12]

Put another way, Bush's stance showed not a lack of faith in the basic idea of deterrence but rather a healthy—or perhaps unhealthy—respect for Iraq's ability to deter the United States from protecting its allies or from rolling back any Iraqi attack on them.[13] Bush believed that Saddam (and America's friends in the region) would have thought that

U.S. power could not shield them. Deterrence, then, was operating, but it was not Iraq but the United States that would have been deterred.[14] Indeed, the administration's policy implied that the United States is easy to deter. Bush and his colleagues implicitly accepted Waltz's argument that nuclear proliferation will spread deterrence and bring about nuclear stability while rejecting his claim that nuclear weapons will moderate behavior.

The impediment to extended deterrence was believed to lie in the lack of credibility of American threats to destroy or defeat Iraq. But this is odd for three reasons. First, threats do not have to be 100 percent credible; effectiveness is a combination of credibility and the consequences that are expected if the threat is carried out, which are weighed against what the challenger will gain if the adventure succeeds. Saddam did not have to be certain that the United States would carry out its threat in order to be deterred. Indeed, because the consequence of a war with the United States would have been the destruction of his regime, even a little credibility would have gone a long way. Second, during the Cold War, both sides knew that Soviet conventional superiority meant that the United States could thwart a Soviet invasion of Europe only by resorting to nuclear weapons; by contrast, even if the Iraqis could have repeated their conquest of Kuwait, the United States could have evicted them without escalating to nuclear weapons, just as it did in 1991. Third, in the Cold War, American threats were inhibited by the danger that stopping a Soviet adventure could have led to a world war. Here, too, the situation with Iraq was more favorable to the United States because of its enormous predominance on all dimensions of military power. The United States could have conquered Iraq, as it did in 2003, and even if Iraq were armed with nuclear weapons, the harm that it could have inflicted on the United States would have been much less than the United States could exact, and much less than the USSR could have done. Indeed, if Iraq had moved against its neighbors, the United States would have had incentives to block and roll back the aggression even if it had not staked its word on doing so.[15]

A reply is that American resolve would not have been clear because others would have doubted that the interests at stake were important enough to justify the costs the United States would have paid. The relevant comparison for the United States was not between its war costs and Iraq's but between its costs and those of permitting Iraq a peaceful victory, and the former could have been seen as greater than the latter. The price of an American effort could be high despite the U.S. ability to prevail, because a conventional victory could have taken a significant toll and Iraq might have been able to attack the U.S. homeland with WMD. Even (or especially) without ICBMs, nuclear weapons could be smuggled into American cities; canisters of gas could be placed in subways; and biological agents are even more frightening to contemplate. These dangers are not insubstantial, but doubt is cast on the claim that a well-armed Iraq could have deterred the United States by the fact that the Bush administration proceeded with its attack despite its belief that Saddam had stockpiles of chemical and biological weapons. Furthermore, in the hypothetical future scenarios we are contemplating, Iraq would have had to bear the onus of escalating when it had everything to lose if the United States retaliated in kind, and only if Iraq did choose escalation (and probable death) would the United States have had to pay a high price.

The other part of the calculation was what the United States would have lost by not opposing Iraq, and this is more speculative. During the Cold War the American stakes in even a minor war in Europe were great, thus bolstering the credibility of its threat to respond with force even if this could lead to world war; today the United States can more readily afford to lose in most contested areas.[16] But to have permitted Iraq to use nuclear weapons to bully its neighbors would have been to advertise to other states that the United States could not protect them against a nuclear foe, which would have translated into a great loss.[17] Furthermore, the Middle East, while not Europe, is very valuable due to oil, Israel, and its potential for harboring terrorists. These American interests presumably are great; otherwise Bush would not have been willing to go to war. The Arabs' propensity to exaggerate the American ties to Israel and the U.S. greed for oil, while generally a handicap to U.S. diplomacy, may help here by magnifying the perception of U.S. interests.

Defenders of the administration policy could argue that the previous analysis is flawed by being overly abstract and ignoring the fact that the United States was dealing with a particular individual, Saddam Hussein. It does no good to show that by the logic of deterrence, American threats should have been credible. If the target does not see them as credible or is willing to fight anyway, then the threat will not deter. It is not our, but the other's, preferences, beliefs, and theories that determine his behavior. Unfortunately, it was argued, Saddam was like Hitler, a sociopath who could not be deterred, who discounted the American military superiority and ran unreasonable risks in order to gain even a small chance at domination. But the analogy does not hold, even leaving aside the counterfactual of whether Hitler would have challenged a nuclear-armed adversary. The Allies did not make a serious attempt to deter Hitler until he was so strong that it was far from clear that he could be defeated, and this emboldened him, in part because he knew it made it less likely that the Allies would fight.

An alternative claim is that Saddam could have been deterred if he had had the appropriate information, but because he killed anyone who disagreed or brought him bad news, he lived in a dream world, making him "accident prone."[18] But was he more of a menace than was the USSR, against which extended deterrence was quite effective despite the fact that it was much stronger than Iraq and a war would have destroyed the United States? Deterrence is most likely to fail when the challenger's motivation to change the status quo is extraordinarily strong, which leads both to the calculation that the attempt to do so is worth the chance of defeat and to an exaggeration of the likelihood of success. But it is not convincing to claim that Saddam's past behavior fit this description or for any other reason showed that he could not be restrained.[19] The attacks against Iran and Kuwait are not evidence of Saddam's undeterrability. The United States acquiesced in the former and refrained from trying to deter the latter. Not only is it likely that these acts appeared quite safe to Saddam, but they appeared so to many observers.[20] His use of poison gas against Iran and the Kurds also involved little risk and, in the former case, was driven by military necessity and tacitly approved by the United States. By contrast, Saddam refrained from using gas against the United States or Israel during the Gulf War when he confronted adversaries who could retaliate. Furthermore, he was quiescent after that, with the not-so-minor exception of the attempt to assassinate George H. W. Bush after he left office.

If Saddam's initial belief that he could conquer Kuwait was reasonable, it made less sense for him to expect American acquiescence at later stages, once the United States put a large force on Kuwait's borders. As the assumption that Saudi Arabia would not provide bases for U.S. forces became falsified, Saddam seems to have replaced it with the belief that he could inflict intolerably high casualties on the United States. This is a familiar if disturbing case of motivated bias, in that commitment to a policy produced intellectual and policy rigidity, although this case is different from many others in that Saddam could have retreated without endangering his power.[21] Indeed, he did display a willingness to make concessions at the last minute, but was diplomatically maladroit because his offers were slow and insufficient. Nevertheless, although this behavior was certainly unfortunate, for two reasons it did not mean that Saddam could not have been deterred in the future. First, this was not a failure of American deterrence but of compellence, since the United States was seeking not to block Iraq, but to force it to disgorge what it had taken, which is a more difficult task.[22] Second, in the weeks if not months before the war started, the United States, far from seeking an agreement by which Iraq would withdraw peacefully, wanted to use force because only that instrument could smash Saddam's army, thereby reducing his power and perhaps leading the officers to overthrow him. Had the United States limited its objective to liberating Kuwait, coercion probably would have succeeded.

Although the administration consistently stressed that it was the unique characteristics of Saddam's regime that made deterrence unreliable and preventive war necessary, its stiffened attitude toward Iran in the fall of 2004 implicitly calls these arguments into question. Iran had not attacked its neighbors, used chemical weapons, or massacred unusually large numbers of its own citizens, yet the administration did not appear any more willing to allow it to develop nuclear weapons than did to allow Iraq to proceed with a robust WMD program. This stance is certainly defensible, in part because if Iran gains nuclear weapons it will menace Israel and its neighbors, with the result that the United States might find itself either having to permit Iraq to get nuclear weapons or to pledge itself to Iraq's defense. But the argument that Iran's nuclear arsenal would be a deadly menace does not sit well with the claim that Iraq could not have been deterred for reasons that were unique to Saddam's regime.

In summary, even if Saddam had gained nuclear weapons, it is hard to believe that the stability-instability paradox would have strongly inhibited the United States, but not Iraq, especially since stability at the highest levels of violence would have been limited because the United States could have either destroyed or conquered Iraq, while Iraq could have done neither to the United States. At the worst, mutual deterrence at the level of WMD would have prevailed, and while this might have permitted an initial Iraqi adventure, it would have equally permitted an American conventional response with little fear that Iraq would escalate. This is not to say that Iraqi nuclear weapons would have made no difference at all: realism argues that the distribution of material power is a central determinant of international outcomes, and Saddam would not have tried to acquire nuclear weapons if he had not believed that they would have done him some good. They would have made an unprovoked American invasion unlikely, and the United States probably would have thought long and hard before moving to overthrow him even if he had undertaken major provocations, including invading his neighbors. Nuclear weapons would not have allowed such moves to succeed, however.

But even if I believe that deterrence would have been effective against a nuclear-armed Iraq, Bush and his colleagues did not. Can deterrence work, and can deterrence theory be applicable, when the United States rejects it? There could be a self-fulfilling prophecy here. If the Bush administration were to have pulled back without disarming Iraq, Saddam might have concluded that the United States was paralyzed and that he could expand with impunity. A United States that thinks it can be deterred is likely to behave in ways that invite challenges. Furthermore, the rejection of many arguments about deterrence by the Bush administration means that there will be much of its behavior that deterrence theory cannot explain.

The administration's doubt that Saddam could be deterred is in part a reflection of a general skepticism about deterrence, especially pronounced among conservatives. During the Cold War such an outlook produced the search for multiple nuclear options; the goal of equaling, if not surpassing, the USSR at every level of violence (what was known as escalation dominance); and the desire for defense in many forms, most obviously against missiles. It also reflects the legacy of September 11 in the form of a heightened sense of vulnerability and the associated feeling that nothing can be ruled out as totally implausible, as I discussed in chapter 2. Deterrence can fail; therefore it cannot be relied upon. As Bush put it when telling the press why he responded to the terrorist attacks by overthrowing Saddam: "After September 11, the doctrine of containment just doesn't hold any water."[23]

REMAINING FORMS OF DETERRENCE AND COMPELLENCE

It is hard to deny one of the main logical, as opposed to empirical, claims of deterrence, however: once Saddam believed that the United States was bent on overthrowing him, there would be no reason for him to be restrained because he had nothing more to lose. Furthermore, sometime in 2002–2003 Saddam probably became convinced (as I was) that Bush would try to overthrow him even if shown that Saddam had no WMD programs. So even if both he and Bush would have preferred the outcome of his being disarmed and remaining in power to fighting a war, this goal may have been put beyond reach. The Bush administration seemed to have trouble with Schelling's basic point that if the other is to be influenced, threats to act if it refuses to comply must be paired with promises not to take the action if the other does cooperate. Credible threats can fail because the other side believes the acts will be taken in any event. Thus American threats may have been undercut by the refusal to promise that Saddam could stay in power if he gave up the forbidden programs. Indeed, soon after the Security Council adopted Resolution 1441, a senior administration official said that Saddam might be tried for war crimes even if he disarmed, and shortly before the start of the war the White House returned to the theme it had dropped in the fall and declared that regime change was necessary if war was to be avoided.[24]

This is not to rule out the possibility that making the threat more credible could have led to compliance. Several senators justified their votes in favor of a muscular congressional resolution by saying that its passage made war less likely; a diplomat reported that Chirac won Syrian support for the U.N. resolution by arguing that "war is much less likely if you support the resolution than if you don't"; and an administration official said that "we had to make the case that the stronger the resolution was, the more likely a war could be avoided."[25] But shouldn't those who believed that these threats could compel Saddam to give up his WMD also have believed that he could have been deterred from adventures even if he had nuclear weapons? A reply would have to rest on the special value of even a few nuclear weapons in undermining extended deterrence and on the difficulty of sustaining a credible threat over a prolonged period.

It remains unclear if the United States did as much as possible to persuade Saddam that the only way to save his regime was by complete and convincing compliance. Although the threats were clear to most observers, he may have clung to the comforting illusion that it was a bluff. It is hard to see how massing more force, sending more diplomatic notes, or even securing a second Security Council resolution would have made much difference. Indeed given Saddam's isolation, his refusal to accept new information, his views of the world, and the unacceptable nature of the situation he was in, it was probably impossible to influence him. One bit of secret diplomacy might have been useful, however: France and Russia, opponents of the war who had decent relations with Saddam, might have told him that while they thought a war was not needed, they were convinced that Bush would wage it if Saddam did not comply. Although he could have discounted these warnings as either ill-informed or part of an American plot, they might have carried significant weight. If the United States did not urge France and Russia to convey this message, it committed a diplomatic blunder; if France and Russia thought about this possibility but rejected it (perhaps because they did not want the United States to gain the fruits of successful coercion), they bear some responsibility for the war.[26] Probably more minor, but perhaps still significant, was the American decision to deploy its forces to Kuwait in a series of surges or "spikes" that were designed to confuse and deceive Saddam. Although General Franks' "idea was to play with Saddam's head—to raise and lower his expectations of an attack," the inadvertent effect may have been to lead him to think that Bush was bluffing.[27]

To have maximized the credibility of the threat to invade unless Saddam disarmed, the United States might have had to do all the things that Bush did, and perhaps only a president who was willing to carry out the threat could have made the prewar effort that he did. Hindsight points up a real irony here. It now appears that Saddam could not have rebuilt his WMD programs if sanctions and inspections had remained in place. Before September 11, the allies and Russia were unenthusiastic about maintaining restraints like this, but they were even more opposed to a military invasion. Having made the threat to take this action quite credible, Bush then almost surely could have secured their consent to maintaining inspections and related import restraints in return for agreeing not to invade, which would have been in everyone's interest. But the same commitment on Bush's part to overthrowing Saddam that made the allies willing to pay a price in order to avoid this meant that such a bargain was unacceptable to him.

The knowledge that the president would attack if Saddam did not back down created a dilemma for critics who wanted him to give up his WMD but preferred leaving him in power, even if he did not disarm, to waging war: the only way to have gotten much chance of their first choice (disarming) was to follow a course of action that could lead to their third choice (war). This is an instance of the general characteristic that threats work by foreclosing the actor's own options, by making it more difficult and costly for him to retreat, and by increasing the likelihood that the outcome will be mutually undesired if the other does not comply. Threats, unlike warnings, are gambles that the chance of their convincing the other side to comply makes up for their having changed the state's interest so that the state may now have to take a costly action that it would not have had to take if it had not made the recent commitment.

Perhaps some domestic and foreign actors believed that while Bush was bluffing, their support for him would persuade Iraq to comply, thereby gaining their first choice of a peaceful solution that left Iraq without WMD. (The other side of this coin is that there was some validity to Bush's claim that those who urged the United States not to go to war were encouraging Saddam to think that the United States would not fight, and so were making war more likely.) But it is more likely that many supporters believed that Bush was bent on war and would go ahead without them, if necessary. At least in the porous American system, it is hard for a leader who is not committed to attacking to give extensive evidence of his willingness to fight.[28] Bluffing is difficult not only because of the costs of being caught out, but also because getting ready for a war entails such extensive military, political, and psychological mobilization that only a leader committed to carrying out the threat is likely to be willing to muster the necessary effort.[29] It is also possible that a leader who thought that he would pull back if need be could find himself politically and psychologically trapped by the process he set in motion, and end up believing that war was necessary.[30]

It would have made more sense for Saddam, rather than Bush, to have been the bluffer. That he was not is a puzzle to which I will return in the concluding chapter. He was bluffing in terms of acting as though he had WMD, but did not retreat at the last minute as many theories of rational behavior would have led us to expect. The United States had the ability to overthrow Saddam and the threat was believed by most observers—indeed, it is hard to imagine a much more credible one. Ironically, Saddam may have not only believed that the United States feared suffering casualties, but also have concluded that it had no reason to attack "because it had already achieved its objectives of establishing a military presence in the region."[31] The U.S. effort was further complicated by the fact that it was engaged not in deterrence, but in compellence, which is more difficult. Nevertheless, Saddam's intransigence was the strongest evidence that extended deterrence might not have held in the future.

Saddam may have thought that his WMD deterred the United States from marching to Baghdad in 1991 and the fear of them would do so again in 2003. The implications of such a belief for U.S. extended deterrence are not clear. Saddam could have concluded that a more robust arsenal would allow regional coercion, or could have believed more conservatively that it would have merely reinforced his ability to deter an unprovoked American attack without being useful to change the status quo.

Despite Iraq's willingness to fight, the Bush administration did seem to think that its coercion would work in some ways. American leaders appear to have been relatively unworried about Saddam's launching a WMD attack against the American homeland in the event of war, despite the belief that he had such weapons and had no compunction against using all forms of violence.[32] It also appears that many American leaders believed that overthrowing Saddam would establish a reputation for taking bold moves, and that this would have a favorable impact on the behavior of many other countries.[33] This is a form of compellence, and a very strong one.

During the war, how could the United States seek to deter Iraq from using what it believed were its chemical, if not its biological, weapons on the battlefield or against its allies (what is known as intra-war deterrence)? It apparently threatened the Iraqi generals and colonels that if they obeyed orders to use these weapons, then the United States would do (unspecified) harm to them, linked to the (sometimes implicit) promise to reward them if they refused those orders.[34] In a general statement of policy, the White House declared that "the United States will continue to make clear that it reserves the right to respond with massive force—including through resort to all our options—to the use of WMD against the United States, our forces abroad, and friends and allies."[35] Although clearly aimed at Iraq's top leaders, it is hard to see how deterrence could have applied here. During the Gulf War the United States sought to deter WMD use by threatening retaliation, which presumably would have led to or been accompanied by the replacement of the regime.[36] But intra-war deterrence requires that goals as well as means would be kept limited, and since the United States sought regime change, it had few coercive tools at its disposal. If the Bush administration believed that Saddam was such a monster, why should it have thought that he would care what would happen to his country if he was going to die? And if the United States could deter his WMD use in a war, why would extended deterrence have failed in peacetime even if Saddam had acquired nuclear weapons?

In fact, I doubt that the United States would have responded in kind to a chemical attack against its troops, partly because such an assault probably would not have done much damage. An attack against Saudi Arabia and Kuwait might have been more deterrable, in part because by killing many Arab civilians, it would likely have triggered the sort of world outrage that would not have been forthcoming from battlefield use. (Israel could deter a chemical attack against itself, or at least could do so better than the United States could, although there was a danger that Saddam would have sought to provoke Israeli retaliation, even with WMD, in order to rally the Arabs to his side.) But as long as

Saddam believed that he would be overthrown unless he could change the course of the war, deterrence would be crippled. This was especially true because the United States would have been inhibited by the political costs of using nuclear weapons (although it can also be argued that the gains in terms of future credibility would have more than compensated). Alternatively, the United States could have threatened to destroy oil facilities, but this would make sense only in connection with the failure to replace Saddam. Overall, intra-war deterrence would probably have been weak if Saddam had possessed the weapons the United States thought he did, because it is hard to see what he would have had to lose by doing as much damage to American interests as he could. The likely failure of deterrence in these circumstances, however, is consistent with standard deterrence ideas of when threats can and cannot be effective.

The rumors that Iraq threatened to destroy its own oil facilities in the face of an American attack also made some sense in deterrence terms. This action would have damaged something the United States valued greatly, in part because oil production was counted on to finance the occupation and reconstruction. Indeed, Iraq may have thought that the desire for oil motivated American policy and that destroying the fields would make an attack pointless.[37] But this was not what the United States cared most about. Furthermore, the United States wanted others to believe that oil was not its central concern, and to have been deterred by the threat of destroying oil fields would have confirmed an undesired image.

The United States also showed an appreciation for coercion in its treatment of allies. By making clear that it would move against Iraq with or without international support, it changed the situation that others faced from one in which they might be able to prevent a war to one in which they had to choose between a war without their sanction and a war with it. As Undersecretary of State John Bolton told the Russian government three weeks before the war started, "We're going ahead. … You are not going to decide whether there is war in Iraq or not. That decision is ours, and we have already made it. … The only question is whether the [U.N. Security] Council will go along with it or not."[38] Although their opposition did prevent a second vote, Russia's and France's endorsement of Resolution 1441 was largely a response to the position the United States put them in. For many others as well, once the option of avoiding war was no longer available, endorsing the war was the best choice in order to maintain the possibility of influencing the United States and keeping up the appearance that it was not acting unilaterally. As I will discuss further in the next chapter, there is something to the claim that what critics call arrogant unilateralism really is strong leadership that allows others to follow. Thus Saudi Arabia's Prince Bandar explained: "Once we join the club, then we can negotiate what Iraq will be like after the war. But without being part of the club, then we have no role the day after."[39] It was only the credible American threat to act unilaterally that produced this choice on the part of others, however. The United States made them an offer they couldn't refuse.

The contrasting American treatment of Iraq and North Korea also fits with deterrence theory. North Korea's chemical and nuclear capabilities make it too tough an adversary to tackle if there is any alternative. Furthermore, in the kind of irony that deterrence highlights, the presence of U.S. troops makes it harder for America to coerce North Korea, since they are hostages given to the latter. Even if they were withdrawn, the connection to Japan and South Korea would serve the same inhibiting function, since the United States values these countries and they would be badly damaged, if not destroyed, in a war. Iraq, on the other hand, was the "right size" enemy—troublesome enough to merit attention, but not so strong that it could deter a United States that was willing to run some risks. America's fear of North Korea both dovetails with and contradicts its belief that the United States could be deterred by a nuclear-armed Iraq. Just as the Bush administration affirmed a strong form of the stability-instability paradox in arguing that even a few Iraqi nuclear weapons would have made it difficult, if not impossible, for the United States to protect Iraq's neighbors, so it worries that North Korea's weapons could be used to coerce South Korea and Japan despite enormous U.S. military superiority. On the other hand, the relatively relaxed response to North Korea's open resumption of its nuclear program in late 2002, although in part imposed by the desire to concentrate on Iraq, may indicate a realization that the Korean weapons are much better for deterrence than for compellence, and therefore do little harm to American interests. But it is hard to see why the United States should have expected worse from Iraq, which has not behaved less predictably, brutally, or aggressively than North Korea.

INDIRECT DETERRENCE AND SELF-DETERRENCE

Cold War deterrence was bilateral; after the mid-1960s, the threat of assured destruction was mutual. Obviously this kind of deterrence did not restrain the United States in 2003 and would not do so in most confrontations in the future. But this does not mean that the United States is free to use all force available, including nuclear weapons.

While such use might cow others into submission, it also might set in train responses that could do great harm to American interests. In the war against Iraq, use of nuclear weapons would have engendered hatred in the Arab world that could have led to terrorism (perhaps with WMD) or to other Arab countries getting nuclear weapons. The reaction in western Europe and Japan would also have been severe, and might have led them to break the alliance and/or produce their own nuclear weapons. The expectation of these consequences presumably moderated the American use of force and gave others a bit more freedom of action.

Killing millions of Iraqis would also have deeply offended American values. A *New York Times* poll showed that if many Iraqi civilian casualties were expected, American support for the war dropped sharply, indeed more sharply than if many U.S. soldiers were expected to die.[40] Had the United States slaughtered innocent Iraqis, it would have destroyed people whom it valued. Although not a game of chicken in which war would have devastated the United States, by punishing Iraq, the United States would have punished itself. Indeed, during the Gulf War the United States stopped bombing Baghdad after hitting what it thought was a military headquarters but actually was a civilian air raid shelter, and in Kosovo the United States sought to spare not only civilians but also Serbian soldiers.[41] This is a new element; during the Cold War the United States was not inhibited by the thought that it would kill millions of Soviet civilians in a war—that was the main point of the deterrent. Deterrence will have to be constructed very differently if only the guilty can be killed.

Ironically, self-deterrence might have arisen had the Bush administration anticipated the course of postwar Iraq. From all appearances, its members actually believed their sunny predictions of American troops being greeted as liberators, economic reconstruction being financed from oil revenues, and political stability (indeed democracy) flowing with little American effort. Furthermore, many seem to have expected the consequences for the rest of the Middle East to be very salutary. Combined with the expectation of a quick military victory, this made the cost-benefit ratio of war appear to be quite favorable, irrespective of the questions of whether Saddam had WMD and whether the war was necessary. It now appears quite different, of course, and the fact that both political and psychological factors lead Bush and his colleagues to steadfastly affirm the wisdom of their decisions does not mean that they would have proceeded had they understood how difficult it would be to turn the military victory into a political one.

ALTERNATIVES TO DETERRENCE

In the academic world, the main alternative to deterrence is the spiral model in which threats, far from deterring, generate unnecessary conflict. During the Cold War, critics stressed that deterrence not only could fail under conditions when the theory said it should be effective, but also that it could produce political and psychological pressures that would increase rather than contain conflict.[42] Some of these arguments focused on the danger of using threats against states that were driven by insecurity rather than the impulse to expand; others concerned the multiple ways in which target states could misperceive or design around deterrent threats. The claim that deterrence is inherently fallible could lead one to conclude that a preventive war is necessary if the adversary is dangerous, while the claim that deterrence is counterproductive when the adversary is insecure leads to the call for more diplomacy and reassurances.[43] But few people believe that the spiral model applied to relations between the United States and Iraq, although it may to the confrontation with North Korea. As noted earlier, however, the United States could have tried returning to the pre–Gulf War policy of diplomatic engagement. This might not have worked, since Saddam might have rejected anything that precluded his dominating his neighbors and, according to the logic of deterrence, might have reacted to conciliation by concluding that the United States was weak and frightened, and thus pressed harder. Nevertheless, this policy was not beyond reason, and it is interesting that it received no attention. Countries and leaders do change their stripes, sometimes in ways that are hard to predict. Libya's Qaddafi was the chief rogue of the 1980s, yet first moderated his behavior and then traded his WMD for ties to the west.[44]

A second alternative to relying on threats, more applicable to relations with friends and potential enemies than with actual ones, is a concert or a quasi-constitutional order. The topic is central to discussions of the shape of future world politics among the developed states discussed in chapter 1, but here I merely want to note that in this relatively cooperative view of international relations, deterrence is relevant only in a very broad sense. States try to influence each other, but punishments consist mainly of exclusion from rewards and approval, with force playing little role. This could not have been the basis for policy toward Saddam, although the possibility that a transformed Iraq could be part of this order could be an inducement or even an inspiration to leaders of the liberated country.

Ironically, the Bush administration agrees with many of the old criticisms of deterrence, but seeing conciliation and reassurances as even more flawed, especially for dealing with states like Iraq, has been drawn to two other routes to security. The first is defense or, more generally, the threat and use of brute force rather than punishment. This not only applied to Iraq, but continues to underpin policies such as missile defense and providing Taiwan with the weapons that would permit it to beat back an attack from the PRC. The United States seeks to protect itself and its allies as much as possible, and it believes that the measures involved do not menace the legitimate interests of others. Of course the hope is that these capabilities will not have to be used because their existence will discourage challengers, but this goal is to be accomplished through the ability to defeat the adversary, not deter it by the threat of punishment.

Finally and more originally, the Bush administration has endorsed a policy of preventive war, based on the belief that defense, although not as fallible as deterrence, cannot be entirely relied upon. As I will discuss in more detail in the next chapter, the United States must be prepared to nip problems in the bud by attacking adversaries before they gain the ability to menace American interests, to refuse to "wait on events while dangers gather," as Bush put it in the State of the Union address less than five months after the 9/11 attacks. Since the United States is now the dominant state, any number of challengers could menace it, and although preventive war is to be employed only when other methods have failed, it has an important role to play.

The perceived need for the early use of force is part of the broader belief that American security, world stability, and the spread of the universal values of freedom and liberalism require the United States to assert its worldwide hegemony. This stance is not automatically inconsistent with affirming the efficacy of deterrence, but there are reasons for hegemony and preventive war to be linked. Bush's goals are extraordinarily ambitious, encompassing the defeat of all terrorists and tyrants and the remaking of not only international politics, but recalcitrant societies as well, both as ends in themselves and as means to U.S. security. As a result, the United States will be infringing on what adversaries (if not others) see as their vital interests. Coercion and, especially, deterrence are not likely to be sufficient for these tasks; these instruments share with traditional diplomacy the desire to minimize conflict by limiting one's own claims to interests that others can afford to respect. States that seek more may need brute force and preventive war (which gives some of us additional reasons to question the goals themselves). The belief that Saddam's regime would have been an unacceptable menace to American interests if it had developed nuclear weapons may then tell us not only about the models of deterrence that Bush and his colleagues reject but also about the expansive definition of U.S. interests that they hold.

4

UNDERSTANDING THE BUSH DOCTRINE

The invasion of Iraq, although important in itself, is even more note-worthy as a manifestation of the Bush Doctrine. In a sharp break from the President's pre-September 11 views that saw America's leadership, and especially its use of force, restricted to defending narrow and traditional vital interests, he enunciated a far-reaching program that calls for something very much like an empire.[1]

The Bush Doctrine has four components: a strong belief in the importance of a state's domestic regime in determining its foreign policy, and the related judgment that this is a time of great opportunity to transform international politics; the perception of great threats that can be defeated only by new and vigorous policies (most notably preventive war); a willingness to act unilaterally when necessary; and, as both a cause and a summary of these three elements, an overriding sense that peace and stability require the United States to assert its primacy in world politics. It is of course possible that what we are seeing is mostly an elaborate rationale for the overthrow of Saddam Hussein that will have little relevance beyond that. I think the Bush Doctrine is real, however. It is quite articulate, and American policy since the end of the war has been consistent with it. Furthermore, there is a tendency for people to act in accord with the explanations they have given for their own behavior, which means that the Doctrine could guide behavior even if it started as a rationalization.[2]

I will describe, explain, and evaluate the Bush Doctrine. These three tasks are hard to separate. Evaluation and explanation are particularly, and perhaps disturbingly, close, especially for realists who both see the Doctrine as unwise and believe that states usually behave quite rationally. In the end, I believe it to be the product of idiosyncratic and structural factors, both a normal reaction to an abnormal situation and a policy that is likely to bring grief to the world and to the United States. The United States may be only the latest in a long line of countries that are unable to place sensible limits on their fears and aspirations.[3]

DEMOCRACY AND LIBERALISM

This is not to say that the Bush Doctrine is entirely consistent, and one component may not fit well despite receiving pride of place in "The National Security Strategy of the United States," which starts thus: "The great struggles of the twentieth century between liberty and totalitarianism ended with a decisive victory for the forces of freedom—and a single sustainable model for national success: freedom, democracy, and free enterprise." The spread of these values opens the path to "make the world not just safer but better," a "path [that] is not America's alone. It is open to all."[4] This taps deep American beliefs and traditions enunciated by Woodrow Wilson and echoed by Jimmy Carter and Bill Clinton, and is linked to the conceit, common among powerful states, that America's values are universal and their spread will benefit the entire world. Just as Wilson sought to "teach [the countries of Latin America] to elect good men," so Bush will bring free markets and free elections to countries without them. Far from having to choose between ideals and self-interests, for the United States they are reinforcing. As Bush told the Air Force Academy graduating class in June 2004, "Some who call themselves 'realists' question whether the spread of democracy in the Middle Est should be any concern of ours. But the realists in this case have lost contact with a fundamental reality. America has always been less secure when freedom is in retreat. America always is more secure when freedom is on the march."[5] Furthermore, a world characterized by democracy, economic openness, and individualism is not only good for America, but is best for others. In furthering these goals, the United States is acting morally, and foreign policy, contrary to realist cynicism, is the realm of moral choice.[6] Indeed, only a foreign policy that seeks a wider good will be supported by Americans, Bush and his colleagues believe; the Nixon–Kissinger policy lost backing at home because of its cynical realpolitik.

This kind of view is disturbing, if familiar, to students of international politics in three ways. First, it exemplifies the propensity for people and states to believe that their values and beliefs are, and should be, widely shared. Of course people and states sometimes glory in their own uniqueness, which they see as a marker of their intellectual and moral superiority, but with the decline of racism and the growth of universalism as an ideal, actors want to think that all others will come to emulate them. Powerful actors in particular think that as they spread their influence, they are doing good in the world by converting others to their views. President Eisenhower, a more thoughtful and self-aware person than many of his critics realized, wrote to a friend: "We are [so] proud of our guarantees of freedom in thought and speech and worship, that, unconsciously, we are guilty of one of the greatest errors that ignorance can make—we assume that our standard of values is shared by all other humans in the world."[7] Second, there is an interesting parallel between Bush's view and most rational-choice theories. These theories see actors as homogeneous and downplay the importance of varied histories and cultures. It may be no accident that both Bush and these theories are American, since part of the American heritage is the view that people are highly malleable, that old bonds can be broken by new circumstances, and that people will seize opportunities for growth and improvement.

Bush's perspective is also familiar because it stresses the domestic sources of foreign policy, denies that all kinds of states will behave in the same way in the same situation, and flies in the face of much realism. It exemplifies Kenneth Waltz's "second image" thinking.[8] As I discussed in the previous chapter, because Saddam Hussein did evil at home, it was clear to Bush and to others who embrace this view that he would pursue evil abroad. The link between tyrants and terrorists that most realists find exaggerated, if not implausible, follows quite logically. Not only do both oppose the United States, but both will inevitably seek to disrupt the peaceful and just international order. They also reject civilized notions of morality and so have no compunctions about killing civilians.

Because the main source of a state's foreign policy is its domestic regime, the only route to lasting peace is through regime change, and once democratic regimes are established, they will live at peace and cooperate with one another. It is then not surprising that in his 2004 State of the Union Address, President Bush explicitly endorsed the theory of the democratic peace, albeit in very oversimplified form. This stance parallels Ronald Reagan's policy of not accepting a détente with the USSR that was limited to arms control, and instead insisting on a larger agenda that included human rights within the Soviet Union, thus implicitly calling for a new domestic regime. The Bush administration is heir to this tradition when it declares that any agreement with North Korea must address a range a problems in addition to nuclear weapons, including "the abominable way [the North] treats its people."[9] As in Iraq, regime change is necessary because tyrannical governments are prone to disregard agreements and to coerce their neighbors just as they mistreat their own citizens.

In this way, although Bush and his colleagues are realists in the large role for force that they see in international politics, they are classical liberals in their beliefs about what drives foreign policy. Just as the external relations of the United States stem from its fundamental values and conception of good government, so this is true for other countries as well. Thus democracy should be and can be spread around the globe. There is no incompatibility between Islam or any other culture and democracy; the example of political pluralism in one country will be emulated. The implicit belief is that democracy can take hold when the artificial obstacles to it are removed. Neo-conservatives were particularly vocal in arguing that it would be relatively easy to establish democracy in a post-Saddam Iraq and that doing so would further the cause of democratizing the Middle East.[10] Furthermore, more democracies will mean greater stability, peaceful relations with neighbors, and less terrorism: comforting claims that are questionable at best. Also questionable are the posited links between democracy and free markets, each of which can in fact undermine the other. But such doubts do not cloud official pronouncements or even the off-the-record comments of top officials. The United States now appears to have a faith-based foreign policy. (As I will discuss further in the final chapter, it is far from clear that this—or any other—administration will act on it, however. No American government has been willing to sacrifice stability in order to further democracy in countries such as Algeria, Egypt, Saudi Arabia, and Pakistan, and at some point Bush is likely to make the same choice in Iraq.)

Consistent with liberalism, this perspective is highly optimistic in seeing the possibility of progress. A week after September 11, Bush is reported to have told a close adviser: "We have an opportunity to restructure the world toward freedom, and we have to get it right." He expounded this theme in an address marking the six-month anniversary of the attack: "When the terrorists are disrupted and scattered and discredited, ... we will see then that the old and serious disputes can be settled within the bounds of reason, and goodwill, and mutual security. I see a peaceful world beyond the war on terror, and with courage and unity, we are building that world together."[11] In February 2002 the President responded to a reporter's question about the predictable French criticism of his policy by saying, "History has given us a unique opportunity to defend freedom. And we're going to seize the moment, and do it."[12] One month later he declared, "We understand history has called us into action, and we are not going to miss that opportunity to make the world more peaceful and more free."[13] The hope for transformation is also linked to Bush's belief that the American task is now nothing less than ridding the world of evil, a breathtaking ambition that stems in part from his religiosity, as I noted in chapter 2.

The absence of any competing model for organizing societies noted at the start of "The National Security Strategy of the United States" is part of the explanation for the optimism. Another is—or at least was—the expectation of a benign form of domino dynamics because the replacement of the Iraqi regime would embolden the forces of freedom and deter potential disturbers of the peace. Before the war Bush declared that when Saddam was overthrown, "other regimes will be given a clear warning that support for terror will not be tolerated. Without this outside support for terrorism, Palestinians who are working for reform and long for democracy will be in a better position to choose new leaders—true leaders who strive for peace."[14] After the war, Bush reaffirmed his belief that "a free Iraq can be an example of reform and progress to all the Middle East."[15] Even some analysts, including the *New York Times*'s Thomas Friedman, who are skeptical of much of the administration's policy believe that the demonstration effect of regime change in Iraq can be large and salutary.

The mechanisms by which these effects are expected to occur are not entirely clear. One involves establishing an American reputation for opposing tyranny. But the power of reputation is questioned by the Bush administration's skepticism toward deterrence documented in chapter 3, which works partly by this means. Another mechanism is the power of example: people will see that tyrants are not invulnerable and that democracy can provide a better life. But seeing one dictator overthrown (not an unusual occurrence) may not have much influence on others. The dynamics within the Soviet bloc in 1989–1991 were a product of special conditions, and while contagion, tipping, and positive feedback do occur, so does negative feedback. We may hope for the former, but it is unreasonable to expect it.

THREAT AND PREVENTIVE WAR

The second pillar of the Bush doctrine is that we live in a time not only of opportunity but also of great threat, the latter posed primarily by terrorists and rogue states. Optimism and pessimism are linked in the belief that if the United States does not make the world better, it will grow more dangerous. As Bush said in his radio address of March 8, 2003: "September 11th, 2001 showed what the enemies of America did with four airplanes. We will not wait to see what terrorists or terrorist states could do with weapons of mass destruction."[16] He elaborated in his West Point address of June 1, 2002:

> Today our enemies see weapons of mass destruction as weapons of choice. For rogue states these weapons are tools of intimidation and military aggression against their neighbors. These weapons may also allow these states to attempt to blackmail the U.S. and our allies to prevent us from deterring or repelling the aggressive behavior of rogue states. Such states also see these weapons as their best means of overcoming the conventional superiority of the U.S.[17]

These threats cannot be contained by deterrence. Terrorists are fanatics, and there is nothing they value that we can hold at risk; rogues like Iraq are risk-acceptant and accident-prone. Thus in the aftermath of the Iraq war, when it became clear that the United States had overestimated that country's WMD programs, Condoleezza Rice justified the decision to go to war by saying, "The most telling and eye-catching point in the judgment of five of the six intelligence agencies is that if left unchecked, Iraq would most likely have a nuclear weapon in this decade. The president of the United States could not afford to trust Saddam's motives or give him the benefit of the doubt."[18] The heightened sense of vulnerability increases the dissatisfaction with deterrence, but this stance also taps into the long-standing Republican critique of many American Cold War policies; one wing of the party always sought defense rather than deterrence (or, to be more precise, deterrence by denial instead of deterrence by punishment).[19]

Because even defense may not be possible against terrorists or rogues, the United States must be ready to wage preventive wars and to act "against ... emerging threats before they are fully formed," as Bush put it.[20] Prevention is not a new element in world politics.[21] As Paul Schroeder noted in the context of explaining World War I, "preventive wars, even risky preventive wars, are not extreme anomalies of politics, the sign of the bankruptcy of policy. They are a normal, even common, tool of statecraft. ... British history, for example, is full of them; the British empire was founded and sustained in great part by a series of preventive and preemptive war and conquests."[22] Britain was hardly alone. Israel launched a preventive strike against the Iraqi nuclear program in 1981; during the Cold War, U.S. officials contemplated attacking the USSR and the PRC before they could develop robust nuclear capabilities;[23] and the Monroe Doctrine and westward expansion in the nineteenth century stemmed in part from the American desire to prevent any European power from establishing a presence that could menace it.[24]

The United States was a weak country at that time; now the preventive war doctrine is based on strength, and on the associated desire to ensure the maintenance of American dominance. Critics argue that preventive wars are rarely necessary because deterrence can be effective and many threats are exaggerated or can be met with strong but less militarized policies. Bismarck called preventive wars "suicide for fear of death," and although the disparity of power between the United States and its adversaries means this is no longer the case, the argument for such wars still implies a high degree of confidence that the future will be bleak unless they are undertaken, or at least a belief that this world will be worse than the likely one produced by the war.

This policy faces three large obstacles. First, by definition, the relevant information is hard to obtain because it involves predictions about future threats. Thus, while in retrospect it is easy to say that the Western allies should have stopped Hitler long before 1939, at the time it was far from clear that he would turn out to be such a menace. No one who reads Neville Chamberlain's speeches can believe that he was a fool. In some cases, a well-placed spy might be able to provide solid evidence that the other had to be stopped, but in many others— perhaps including Nazi Germany—even this would not be sufficient because leaders do not themselves know how they will act in the future. Second and relatedly, even information on capabilities and past behavior may be difficult to come by and interpret, as the case of Iraq shows. Saddam's links to terrorists were murky and leaders in the United States and Britain not only publicly exaggerated but also privately overestimated the extent of his WMD programs. Third, unless all challengers are deterred by the exercise of the Bush Doctrine in Iraq, preventive war will have to be repeated as other threats reach a similar threshold. Doing so will require sustained domestic, if not international, support, which is held in check by the first two complications. While it is too early to say how American opinion will view Saddam's overthrow (and opinion is likely to change over time), a degree of skepticism that will inhibit the repetition of this policy seems probable.

National leaders are aware of these difficulties and generally hesitate to take strong actions in the face of such uncertainty. While one common motive for war has been the belief that the situation will deteriorate unless the state acts strongly, and indeed this kind of fear drives the security dilemma, leaders usually put off decisions if they can. They know that many potential threats will never eventuate or will be made worse by precipitous military action, and they are predisposed to postpone, to await further developments and information, to kick the can down the road. In rejecting this approach (in Iraq, if not in North Korea), Bush and his colleagues are behaving unusually, although this does not mean they are wrong.

Underpinning this stance is the feeling of vulnerability and the consequent belief that the risks and costs of inaction are unacceptably high. As noted in chapter 2, the shock of September 11 induced great fear and radically altered Bush's worldview. As the President has declared on many occasions, risks that were tolerable before 9/11 are now unacceptable and the new dangers are best met by taking the initiative. As Bush put it in his letter accompanying the submission of his "National Security Strategy," "In the new world we have entered, the only path to peace and security is the path of action," and the body of the document declared: "The greater the threat, the greater is the risk of inaction."[25] In the past, a state could let a potential threat grow because it might not turn into a major menace. Now, if one follows this cautious path and the worst case does arise, the price will be prohibitive. Thus Senator Orrin Hatch dismissed the argument that since the threat from Iraq was not imminent, the United States could have afforded to rely on diplomacy and deterrence by saying: "Imminence becomes murkier in the era of terrorism and weapons of mass destruction."[26] After the war, Bush similarly explained to Tim Russert that "it is essential that when we see a threat, we deal with those threats before they become imminent. It's too late if they become imminent. ... I'm dealing with a world in which we have gotten struck by terrorists with airplanes."[27] It then makes sense to strike much sooner than previously (which will mean striking more often), even though in some cases doing so will not have been necessary.

UNILATERALISM

The perceived need for preventive wars is linked to the fundamental unilateralism of the Bush Doctrine because it is hard to get a consensus for such strong action and other states have every reason to let the dominant power carry the full burden.[28] Unilateralism also has deep roots in segments of the Republican Party, was well represented in the Reagan administration, draws on long-standing American political traditions, and was part of Bush's outlook before September 11. Of course, assistance from others was needed in Afghanistan and solicited in Iraq. But these should not be mistaken for joint ventures; the United States did not bend its policy to meet others' preferences except for accommodating Britain's Tony Blair by seeking a second U.N. resolution on Iraq and announcing a road map for the Israeli–Palestinian dispute (which it never seriously pursued). In stressing that the United States is building coalitions in the plural rather than an alliance (the mission determines the coalition, in Rumsfeld's phrase), American leaders have made it clear that they will forgo the participation of any particular country rather than compromise.

The seeming exception of policy toward North Korea, in which the United States refused to negotiate bilaterally and insisted that the problem is one for the international community, is actually consistent with this approach. Others were not consulted on the policy, and in fact resisted it. The obvious purpose of the American stance was to get others (especially Japan and the PRC) to apply pressure on the adversary. While this is a legitimate aim and perhaps the best policy, it is one the United States selected on its own. Multilateralism here is narrowly instrumental, a way to avoid giving what the United States regards as a concession to North Korea and a means of weakening and isolating it, despite the fact that others believe this is unwise. Other very powerful states have adopted a similar stance. Paul Schroeder notes that the famous British late 19th century statesman William Gladstone, generally known as a liberal multinationalist, "had no intention of binding Britain to [the] collective decisions [of the Concert of Europe]. Britain had instead a right and duty to denounce sluggards and defectors among the powers and then to enforce the public law of Europe herself, with the aid of any powers willing to help her."[29]

Even before September 11, Bush displayed little willingness to cater to world public opinion or heed the cries of outrage from European countries as the United States interpreted its interests, and the interests of the world, in its own way. Thus the Bush administration walked away from the Kyoto Treaty, the International Criminal Court, and the protocol implementing the ban on biological weapons rather than trying to work within these frameworks and modify them. The United States also ignored European criticisms of its Middle Eastern policy.

On a smaller scale, it forced out the heads of the Organization for the Prohibition of Chemical Weapons and the Intergovernmental Panel on Climate Change. In response to this kind of behavior, European diplomats can only say: "Big partners should consult with smaller partners."[30] The operative word is "should." When, in the wake of the overthrow of Saddam, France's Chirac declared, "We are no longer in an era where one or two countries control the fate of another country," and Germany's Joschka Fischer said that common rules "must apply to the big, the medium-sized, and the small nations," they described the world as they would like it to be, not as it is.[31]

The Bush administration has defended each of its actions, but not its general stance. In part, the willingness and even the desire to move on its own may be a preferred style, perhaps rooted in general arrogance. Paul O'Neill claims that thorough and open discussion is foreign to Bush; many Republican congressmen have expressed dismay at the refusal of the administration to consult them; Elizabeth Drew quotes a prominent Republican as saying that "the lack of cooperation with the Hill is worse than noncooperation. It's 'We can act unilaterally—whether it's Congress or countries.'"[32] But a more principled, persuasive, and perhaps correct defense is built around the difficulty in procuring public goods. As long as leadership is shared, very little will happen because no one actor will be willing to shoulder the costs and responsibilities. "At this moment in history, if there is a problem, we're expected to deal with it," is how Bush explains it; "We are trying to lead the world," is what one administration official said when the United States blocked language in a UN declaration on child health that might be read as condoning abortion.[33] This is not entirely hypocritical: many of the countries that endorsed the Kyoto Protocol had grave reservations but were unwilling to stand up to strongly committed domestic groups.

Indeed, real consultation is likely to produce inaction, as was true in 1993 when Clinton called for "lift and strike" in Yugoslavia (i.e., lifting the arms embargo against Bosnia and striking Serbian forces). But because he believed in sharing power and was unwilling to move on his own, he sent Secretary of State Christopher to ascertain European views. This multilateral and democratic procedure did not work because the Europeans resisted being put on the spot, and in the face of apparent American indecision they refused to endorse such a strong policy. If the United States had informed the Europeans rather than consulted them, they probably would have complained, but would have gone along; what critics call unilateralism often is effective leadership. In 1991 a European spokesman said that the EU would take the lead in bringing peace to Yugoslavia: "This is the hour of Europe, not the hour of the Americans."[34] Unfortunately it wasn't, still isn't, and won't be for the foreseeable future. Could Arafat have been moved from his central position if the United States had sought consensus rather than staking out its own position? Could the six-party talks on Korea have taken place if the United States had asked whether others approved, instead of making it clear that the alternatives were even worse? Bush could also argue that just as Reagan's ignoring the sophisticated European counsels to moderate his rhetoric led to the delegitimation of the Soviet system, so his insistence on confronting tyrants has slowly brought others around to his general perspective, if not to his particular policies.

In this context, the strong opposition of allies to overthrowing Saddam was an advantage as well as a disadvantage to Bush. While it exacted domestic costs, complicated the effort to rebuild Iraq, and perhaps fed Saddam's illusion that he could avoid a war, it gave the United States the opportunity to demonstrate that it would override strenuous objections from allies if this was necessary to reach its goals. While this horrified multilateralists, it showed that Bush was serious about his doctrine. When Kofi Annan declared that an American attack without Security Council endorsement "would not be in conformity with the [UN] Charter," he may not have realized that for some members of the Bush administration, this made the move even more attractive.[35]

AMERICAN HEGEMONY

The final element of the Bush Doctrine, which draws together the others, is the establishment of American hegemony, primacy, or empire.[36] In the Bush Doctrine there are no universal norms or rules governing all states.[37] On the contrary, order can be maintained only if the dominant power behaves quite differently from the others. Thus the administration is not worried that its preventive war doctrine or attacking Iraq without Security Council endorsement will set a precedent for others because the dictates that apply to them do not bind the United States. Similarly, the United States sees no contradiction between its own expanding the ambit of a vigorous counter-proliferation policy and nuclear weapons to threatening their employment even if others have not used WMD first. American security, world stability, and the spread of liberalism require the United States to act in ways that others cannot and must not. This is not a double standard, but what world order requires.

Hegemony is implied when the Bush "Nuclear Posture Review" talks of dissuading future military competitors.[38] At first glance this seems to refer to Russia and China, but the point applies to the countries of western Europe as well, either individually or as a unit. This was clear in the draft defense guidance written by Paul Wolfowitz for Secretary of Defense Cheney at the end of the George H.W. Bush administration and also was implied by President George W. Bush when he declared to the West Point class of 2002: "America has, and intends to keep, military strengths beyond challenge—thereby making the destabilizing arms races of other eras pointless, and limiting rivalries to trade and other pursuits of peace."[39] This would mean not only sustaining such a high level of military spending that no other country or group of countries would be tempted to challenge it, but also using force on behalf of others so they will not need to develop potent military establishments of their own.[40] In an implicit endorsement of hegemonic stability theory that sees the international economy prospering only when one state dominates the driving belief is that the world cannot afford to return to traditional multipolar balance-of-power politics, which would inevitably turn dangerous and destructive.[41]

How Did We Get Here?

Although many observers—myself included—were taken by surprise by this turn in American policy, we probably should not have been. It is consistent with standard patterns of international politics and with much previous American behavior in the Cold War. As early as the start of World War II, American leaders understood that the United States would emerge as the prime architect of the new international politics; before the Soviet Union was perceived as a deadly menace, American leaders understood that theirs would be the major role in maintaining peace and prosperity.[42]

Even had the Soviet Union been more benign, instability, power vacuums, and the anticipation of future rivalries would have led the United States to use and increase the enormous power it had developed.[43] Of course the USSR did emerge as a threat, and American power was needed to contain it. The task could not be done by the United States alone, however. The world was not bipolar, especially because the United States sought to limit its defense spending and the prime target of the conflict was the allegiance of western Europe. The United States knew that allied, and especially European, support was necessary to resist Soviet encroachments, and allies, fearing a return to American isolationism, reciprocally made great efforts to draw the United States in.[44]

Although American power was central and consent often was forthcoming only because of veiled (or not so veiled) threats and rewards, on fundamental issues the United States had to take allied interests and views to heart. Thus Charles Maier exaggerates only slightly when he refers to "consensual American hegemony" within the West.[45]

As Europe stabilized and the American deterrent force became concentrated in intercontinental bombers and missiles, the need for allies, although still considerable, diminished. The United States could rebuff Britain and France at Suez in a way that it could not have done five years earlier; twenty-five years later, Reagan could pay even less heed to allied wishes. Of course, the United States could not do everything it wanted. Not only was it restrained by Soviet power, but to go it alone would have been to alienate domestic opinion, undermine the credibility of the commitment to Europe, and endanger an international economic system already under great pressure. Nevertheless, after the mid-1960s the degree to which the United States sought consensus and respected allies' desires varied from issue to issue and president to president. Above a significant but limited minimum level, cooperation with allies had become a matter of choice, not necessity.

The required minimum level of cooperation further decreased with the end of the Cold War and the emergence of unipolarity. The United States now has a greater share of world power than any state since the beginning of the state system, and it is not likely to lose this position in the foreseeable future.[46] Before George W. Bush's presidency, the United States used a mixture of carrots and sticks and pursued sometimes narrower, but often broader, conceptions of its interest. Bill Clinton, and George H.W. Bush before him, cultivated allies and worked to maintain large coalitions. Most scholars approve of this mode of behavior, seeing it as the best, if not the only, way for the United States to secure desired behavior from others, minimize the costs to itself, and smoothly manage a complex and contentious world.[47] These and most other scholars are sharply critical of Bush's unilateralism, but what is most telling here is that this prescription clashes with their earlier analyses that argued that the combination of the American domestic system, socialization into cooperative norms, and the development of strong international institutions meant that the United States was bound to continue working closely with others. It is now clear, however, that the previous choice of multilateralism was indeed a choice, revocable upon the appearance of changed circumstances and a different leader. The structure of world power meant that there was always a possibility that the United States would act on its own.

Until recently, however, it did not seem that the United States would in fact behave in a highly unilateral fashion and assert its primacy. The new American stance was precipitated, if not caused, by the interaction between the terrorist attacks and the election of George W. Bush, who brought to the presidency a more unilateral outlook than his predecessors and his domestic opponents. We can only speculate on what President Gore would have done. My estimate is that he would have invaded Afghanistan, but not proceeded against Iraq, or rejected treaties and other arrangements over a wide range of issues. To some extent, then, the current assertion of strong American hegemony may be an accident.

But it was an accident waiting to happen. To start with, there are structural reasons to have expected a large terrorist attack. Bin Laden had attacked American interests abroad and from early on sought to strike the U.S. homeland. His enmity stemmed primarily from the establishment of U.S. bases in Saudi Arabia, which was a product of America's worldwide responsibilities. (Ironically, the overthrow of Saddam may permit the United States to greatly reduce its presence in Saudi Arabia, although I doubt that bin Laden expected this result or that he will now be satisfied.) Furthermore, al-Qaeda was not the only group targeting the United States; as Richard Betts has argued, terrorism is the obvious weapon of weak actors against the leading state.[48]

Even without terrorism, both internal and structural factors predisposed the United States to assert its dominance. I think the latter are more important, but it is almost a truism of the history of American foreign relations that the United States rarely engages in deeply cooperative ventures with equals.[49] Unlike the European states that were surrounded by peers, once the United States had established its regional dominance, it could choose the terms on which it would work with others. Thus, when the United States intervened in World War I, it insisted that the coalition be called the "Allied and Associated Powers" (i.e., it was an associate, with freedom of action, not an ally). The structure of the American government, its weak party system, its domestic diversity, and its political traditions all make sustained cooperation difficult. It would be an exaggeration to say that unilateralism is the American way of foreign policy, but there certainly is a strong pull in this direction.

More important, the United States is acting like a normal state that has gained a position of dominance.[50] There are four facets to this argument. First and most general is the core of the realist outlook that power is checked most effectively, if not only, by counterbalancing power. Thucydides puts these words into the mouths of the Athenians in the famous Melian dialogue, and while he disapproves and knows the attitude will bring ruin, he probably agrees with the generalization:

> Our opinion of the gods and our knowledge of men lead us to conclude that it is a general and necessary law of nature to rule wherever one can. This is not a law that we made ourselves, nor were we the first to act upon it when it was made. We found it already in existence, and we shall leave it to exist for ever among those who come after us. We are merely acting in accordance with it, and we know that you or anybody else with the same power as ours would be acting in precisely the same way.[51]

It follows from the propensity of states to use the power at their disposal that those who are not subject to external restraints tend to feel few restraints at all. As Edmund Burke put it, in a position endorsed by Hans Morgenthau: "I dread our *own* power and our *own* ambition; I dread our being too much dreaded. It is ridiculous to say that we are not men, and that, as men, we shall never wish to aggrandize ourselves."[52] With this a driving idea, Waltz saw the likelihood of America's current behavior from the start of the post–Cold War era:

> The powerful state may, and the United States does, think of itself as acting for the sake of peace, justice, and well-being in the world. But these terms will be defined to the liking of the powerful, which may conflict with the preferences and the interests of others. In international politics, overwhelming power repels and leads others to try to balance against it. With benign intent, the United States has behaved, and until its power is brought into a semblance of balance, will continue to behave in ways that annoy and frighten others.[53]

Parts of the Bush Doctrine are unique to the circumstances, but it is the exception rather than the rule for states to stay on the path of moderation when others do not force them to do so.[54] Thus the existence of a security community among the world's most powerful and developed states discussed in chapter 1 ironically makes the Bush Doctrine possible. The lack of fear of war among these countries means that the United States is not restrained by the possibility that its peers will use force against it and allows the United States to focus on other dangers and to pursue other goals.

Second and relatedly, states' definitions of their interests tend to expand as their power does.[55] It then becomes worth pursuing a whole host of objectives that were out of reach when the state's security was in doubt and all efforts had to be directed to primary objectives. With increases in power and security, states seek what Arnold Wolfers called "milieu goals."[56] The hope of spreading democracy and liberalism throughout the world has always been an American goal, but the lack of a peer competitor now makes it more realistic—although perhaps not very realistic—to actively strive for it. Seen in this light, the Bush administration's perception that this is a time of great opportunity in the Middle East is the product not so much of the special circumstances in the region as of the enormous resources at America's disposal.

More specifically, the quick American victory in Afghanistan probably contributed to the expansion of American goals. Bush dropped the modifier "with a global reach" from his war on terrorists, and the United States sent first military trainers, and then a combat unit, to the Philippines to attack guerrillas who posed only a minimal threat to Americans and who have no significant links to al-Qaeda. Most dramatically, according to Bob Woodward, only ten days after the breakthrough on the battlefield in Afghanistan, Bush took Rumsfeld aside to ask him: "What kind of war plan do you have for Iraq?"[57] Similarly, the easy military victory in Iraq initially encouraged thought of a wider agenda, and perhaps threatening force against other tyrants ("moving down the list" was the phrase often employed).[58] Furthermore, at least up until a point, the exercise of power can increase power as well as interests. I do not think that the desire to control a large supply of oil was significant motivation for the Iraq war, but if the United States is able to consolidate its position in that country, it would gain an additional instrument of influence.

A third structural explanation for American behavior is that increased relative power brings with it new fears. The reasons are both objective and subjective. As Wolfers explained in his classic essay "National Security as Ambiguous Symbol," the latter can diverge from the former.[59] In one manifestation of this, as major threats disappear, people elevate ones that previously were seen as quite manageable.[60] I discussed the role of fear in chapter 2, and people now seem to be as worried as they were during the height of the Cold War, despite the fact that a terrorist or rogue attack, even with WMD, could cause only a small fraction of World War III's devastation. But there is more to it than psychology. A dominant state acquires an enormous stake in the world order and interests spread throughout the globe. Most countries are primarily concerned with what happens in their neighborhoods; the world is the hegemon's neighborhood, and it is not only hubris that leads it to be concerned with everything that happens anywhere. The result is a fusion of narrow and broad self-interest. At a point when most analysts were worried about the decline of American power, not its excesses, Waltz noted that for the United States, "like some earlier great powers …, the interest of the country in security came to be identified with the maintenance of a certain world order. For countries at the top, this is predictable behavior. … Once a state's interests reach a certain extent, they become self-reinforcing."[61]

The historian John S. Galbraith explored the related dynamic of the "turbulent frontier" that produced the unintended expansion of colonialism in the late 19th century. As a European power gained an enclave in Africa or Asia, usually along the coast or a river, it also gained an unpacified boundary that had to be policed. This led to further expansion of influence and often of settlement, and this in turn produced a new area that had to be protected and a new zone of threat.[62] There were few natural limits to this process. There are not likely to be many now. The wars in Afghanistan and Iraq have led to the establishment of U.S. bases and security commitments in Central Asia, an area previously beyond reach. It is not hard to imagine how the United States could be drawn further into politics in the region, and find itself using force to oppose terrorist or guerrilla movements that arise there, perhaps in part in reaction to the American presence. The same dynamic could play out in Colombia and, according to recent reports, in Africa.[63]

The fourth facet can be seen as a broader conception of the previous point. As realists stress, even states that find the status quo acceptable have to worry about the future.[64] Indeed, the more an actor sees the current situation as satisfactory, the more it will expect the future to be worse. Psychology is important here, too: prospect theory argues that actors are prone to accept great risks when they believe they will suffer losses unless they act boldly. The adoption of a preventive war doctrine may be a mistake, especially if taken too far, but is not foreign to normal state behavior, as I have discussed, and it appeals to states that have a valued position to maintain. However secure states are, only rarely can they be secure enough, and if they are currently very powerful, they will feel strong impulses to act now to prevent a deterioration that could allow others to harm them in the future.[65]

All this means that under the Bush Doctrine the United States is not a status quo power. Its motives may not be selfish, but the combination of power, fear, and perceived opportunity lead it to seek to reshape world politics and the societies of many nations. This tracks with and extends old ideas of the United States as a revolutionary country. As the first modern democracy, the United States was founded on principles of equality, progress, and a government subordinate to civil society that, while initially being uniquely American, had universal appeal and applicability. Indeed, not only Bush today but many Americans in previous eras believed that because a state's foreign policy is inseparable from its domestic regime, a safe and peaceful world requires the spread of these arrangements.[66] Under current conditions of terrorism and WMD, tyrannical governments pose too great a danger to be tolerated. The world cannot stand still: without strong American intervention, the international environment will become more menacing to America and its values, but with strong leadership the United States can increase its security and produce a better world. In a process akin to the deep security dilemma,[67] in order to protect itself, the United States is impelled to act in a way that will increase, or at least bring to the surface, conflicts with others. Even if the prevailing situation is satisfactory, it cannot be maintained by purely defensive measures. Making the world safe for American democracy is believed to require that dictatorial regimes be banished, or at least kept from obtaining weapons of mass destruction.

Hegemony, Iraq, and Europe

This perspective on the Bush Doctrine helps explain international disagreements about Iraq.[68] Most accounts of France's opposition stress its preoccupation with glory and its traditional jealousy of and disdain for the United States. More generally, Europe's resistance to the war is attributed to the peaceful worldview produced by its success in overcoming historical rivalries and creating a law-governed society (summarized by the phrase "Americans are from Mars, Europeans are from Venus").[69] Also frequently mentioned is the European distaste for the crude and bullying American style ("Bush is just a cowboy"). There is something to these positions, but are Europeans really so opposed to force and wedded to law? When faced with domestic terrorism, Germany and other European countries did not hesitate to employ unrestrained state power that John Ashcroft would envy, and their current treatment of minorities, especially Muslims, does not strike these populations as liberal. The French continue to intervene in Africa unilaterally, join other European states in playing as fast and loose with trade regulations as does the United States, and for some time disregarded legal rulings to drop their ban on British beef. Most European states favored the war in Kosovo despite the absence of UN sanction, supported the United States in Afghanistan, and, had they been attacked on September 11, might not have maintained their aversion to the use of force.

Even more glaringly, the claims for a deep cultural divide overlook the fundamental difference between how Europe and the United States are placed in the international system. The fact that the latter is hegemonic has three implications. First, only the United States has the power to do anything about problems like Iraq; the others have incentives to ride free. Second, the large European states have every reason to be concerned about American hegemony, and sufficient resources to seek to constrain it. This is not traditional power balancing, which is driven by security fears. The French are not afraid of an American attack, and the German worry is that the United States will withdraw too many of its troops. But they do fear that a world dominated by the United States would be one in which their values and interests would be served only at American sufferance. It is hardly surprising that an April 2002 poll showed that majorities within many European countries—often overwhelming majorities—felt that American policy toward Iraq and the Middle East was based "mainly on its own interests."[70] Condoleezza Rice had forgotten her knowledge of basic international politics when she expressed her shock that "there were times that it appeared that American power was seen [by France and Germany] to be more dangerous than, perhaps, Saddam Hussein."[71] The United States may be correct that American dominance serves Europe and the world, but we should not be startled when others beg to differ. The United States probably is as benign a hegemon as the world has ever seen. Its large domestic market, relatively tolerant values, domestic diversity, and geographic isolation all are helpful. But a hegemon it remains, and by that very fact it must make others uneasy.

Third, the Europeans' stress on the need to go through the Security Council shows less their attachment to law and world governance than their appreciation of power. France especially, but also Russia and China (two countries that are not from Venus), will gain enormously from the principle that large-scale force can be used only with the approval of the Council, of which they are permanent members. Indeed, Security Council membership is one of the few major resources at these countries' disposal. The statement of a Russian leader that "if someone tries to wage war on their own account, … without an international mandate, it means all the world is confusion and a wild jungle"[72] would carry more moral weight if Russia did not have a veto in the mandate-granting body. When the Europeans—including those not on the Council—argue that intervention is legitimate only if carried out with a consensus or widespread international support, what is meant is widespread European support, not Russian, Chinese, or Third World approval.

The United Kingdom does not readily fit this picture, of course. Structure always leaves room for choice, and Tony Blair told Parliament on September 24, 2002, that "it is an article of faith with me that the American relationship and our ability to partner [with] America in these difficult issues is of fundamental importance, not just to this country but to the wider world." Blair's personal views may be part of the explanation, but this has been the British stance ever since World War II, when it resisted becoming too much a part of Europe and sought to maintain a major role in the world through supporting rather than opposing the United States. But only one ally can have a "special relationship" with the hegemon, and Britain's having taken this role makes it harder for others to emulate it.

Structure also explains why many of the smaller European countries chose to support the United States in Iraq despite hostile public opinion. The dominance they fear most is not American, but Franco–German. The United States is more powerful, but France and Germany are closer and more likely to control them.[73] Seeking a distant protector is a standard practice in international politics. That France and Germany resented the resulting opposition is no more surprising than the American dismissal of "old Europe," with the resulting parallel that while France and Germany bitterly decried the American effort to hustle them into line, they disparaged and bullied the east European states that sided with the United States—quite un-Venusian behavior.

CONCLUSION

What will emerge depends in part on unpredictable events such as economic shocks, the course of events in Iraq, the targets and success of future terrorist attacks, and the characteristics of the leaders who arise through diverse domestic processes. The war against Saddam, however, already marks out the path on which the United States is embarked and illuminates the links between preventive war and hegemony, which was the reason for much of the opposition at home and abroad. Indeed, the war is hard to understand if the only object was to disarm Saddam or even to remove him from power. Even had the inflated estimates of his

WMD capability been accurate, the danger was too remote to justify the effort. But if changing the Iraqi regime was expected to bring democracy and stability to the Middle East, discourage tyrants and energize reformers throughout the world, and demonstrate the American willingness to provide a high degree of what it considers world order, whether others like it or not, then, as part of a larger project, the war makes sense.[74]

While the United States is indeed the strongest country in the world, its power is still subject to two familiar limitations, however: it is harder to build than to destroy, and success depends on others' decisions because their cooperation is necessary for the state to reach its goals. Of course American military capability is not to be ignored, and I doubt whether countries such as Iran, Syria, and North Korea will ignore it. They may reason as Bush expects, and limit their WMD programs and support for terrorism, if not reform domestically. But the prospects for long-run compliance are less bright. Although a frontal assault on American interests is perhaps unlikely, highly motivated adversaries will not give up the quest to advance their interests as they see them. The war in Iraq has increased the risks of their pursuing nuclear weapons, but it has also increased their incentives to do so. Amid the debate about what these weapons can and cannot accomplish, everyone agrees that they can deter invasion, which makes them very attractive to states that fear they might be in the American gun sights. Both Waltz's argument that proliferation will produce stability, and the contrary and more common claim that it would make the world more dangerous, imply that nuclear weapons will reduce American influence because others will have less need of U.S. security guarantees and will be able to fend off U.S. threats to their vital interests.[75] The American attempt to minimize the ability of others to resist U.S. pressures is the mark of a country bent not on maintaining the status quo but on fashioning a new and better world.

Military capabilities matter less in America's relations with allies and probably with Russia. From them the United States wants extensive cooperation on issues such as the sharing of highly sensitive information on terrorism, rebuilding failed states, preventing nuclear proliferation, and managing the international economy. There is little danger (or hope) that Europe will form a united counterweight to the United States and try to thwart it by active opposition, let alone the use of force. But political resistance is quite possible and, even more than with adversaries, the fate of the American design for world order lies in the hands of its allies.[76] Although the United States governs many of the incentives that allies and potential supporters face, what it needs from them cannot be coerced. It is possible that they will see themselves better off with the United States as an assertive hegemon, allowing them to gain the benefits of order while being spared the costs, and they may conclude that any challenge would fail or bring with it dangerous rivalry. Indeed, without the war in Iraq, I doubt that the spring of 2003 would have seen the degree of cooperation that the United States obtained from Europe in combating the Iranian nuclear program, and from Japan and the PRC in containing North Korea.

But I suspect that much will depend on allies' answers to several questions: Can the American domestic political system sustain the Bush Doctrine over the long run? Will the United States be open to allies' influence and values? Will it put pressure on Israel as well as on the Palestinians? More generally, will it seek to advance the broad interests of the diverse countries and peoples in the world, or will it exploit its power for its own narrower political, economic, and social interests? Bush's world gives little place for other states—even democracies—except as members of a supporting cast.

This is especially troublesome because much of Bush's vision depends on persuading others, not coercing them. He wants to spread democracy, the free market, and individualism. Although incentives and even force are not irrelevant here, at bottom this requires people to accept, if not embrace, a set of institutions and values. As noted at the start of this chapter, Bush believes that these are universal and represent the deepest aspirations of all peoples. But even if this is true, it is undeniable that people have not always adopted them, and building the world that Bush seeks is a political, social, and psychological task for which unilateral measures are likely to be unsuited and in which American military and economic strength can at best play a supporting role. Success requires that others share the American vision and believe that U.S. leadership is benign.

Conflating broader with narrower interests and believing that one has a monopoly on wisdom are obvious ways that a hegemon can come to be seen as tyrannical.[77] In 1919 Woodrow Wilson said that both nationalism and internationalism called for the United States to join the League of Nations: "The greatest nationalist is the man who wants his nation to be the greatest nation, and the greatest nation is the nation which penetrates to the heart of its duty and mission among the nations of the world. With every flash of insight into the great politics of mankind, the nation that has that vision is elevated to a place of influence and power which it cannot get by arms."[78] Wilson surely meant what he said, but his great certainty that he knew what was best for the world was troubling. In the 2000 presidential campaign, Bush said that the United States needed a "more humble foreign policy."[79] But its objectives and conceptions make the Bush Doctrine quite the opposite. The very boldness, if not the grandiosity, of the Doctrine must raise the question of whether it can succeed. World politics often changes dramatically, but largely in ways unintended by the participants, and whether it is amenable to such purposeful guidance is far from clear. As I will discuss in the final chapter, while the future of world politics will be influenced by the Bush Doctrine, it is more likely to prove an interlude than a blueprint.

5

WHERE DO WE GO FROM HERE?

Last chapters are supposed to be titled "Conclusions," or perhaps "Final Thoughts." Current international politics is in too much flux for that, however. Even more than usual, the future is unpredictable, and while I think it is very likely that the next few years will see another major terrorist attack against the American homeland, what is less foreseeable is how the United States will react to this shock. Even were this not my expectation, the thoughts in this chapter would be tentative, being susceptible to change not only by all sorts of events but also by arguments others will make or my own further thoughts. So all I can do is bring together some of the diverse strands of the previous chapters and address the likelihood that the Bush Doctrine can be sustained.

At the start, I want to stress the importance of the fact that the leading powers now form a Security Community, as I argued in chapter 1. Although we are now preoccupied with terrorism and the American response to it, the deeper and more lasting change in world politics is that the most powerful states in the international system no longer contemplate fighting each other. As frightening as many of the remaining threats are, they pale in comparison with those we would face were the Community not to exist. Furthermore, the existence of the Community allows the United States to focus on the threat from terrorism and WMD in the hands of rogues. Were there a chance of war with a peer state, meeting this danger would have to be the top priority; if other leading powers were worried about an attack either from the United

States or from each other, there would be no chance of gaining widespread cooperation against terrorists.

For some countries, of course, the freedom given the United States by the existence of the Community is itself a threat. I very much doubt whether the United States would have dared invade Iraq in an era of great-power rivalry. The other side of this coin is that the perceived opportunities for transforming world politics, although perhaps illusory, would never have been contemplated if the United States had peer rivals. Although the United States hoped to lead transformations after the two world wars, these projects rested on sustained great-power cooperation, and once it became clear that this would not be forthcoming, other ambitions necessarily fell by the wayside. Now there is room for them.

The structure of the international system is central to the main thrust of the American reaction to September 11 as well. As I argued in chapter 4, although many factors went into the development of American policy and a different president probably would have reacted differently, the fact that the system was unipolar meant that no other state was in a position to curb what many saw as a foolish and heavy-handed response, just as the others were not powerful enough to shoulder much of the burden of dealing with emerging threats. The tension between the United States and many of its allies is not surprising in light of how these countries are differently placed in the international system. Furthermore, the fact that these tensions are not great enough to endanger the Security Community means that the states need not moderate their scorn of each other in fear that harsh words and limited conflict might lead to a permanent break, let alone armed hostilities.

CAN THE BUSH DOCTRINE BE SUSTAINED?

But if the configuration of world politics encouraged such a highly assertive policy by the United States, it does not guarantee that this policy can endure. In fact, I think it will collapse of its own weight. The main reasons for this are the Bush Doctrine's internal contradictions and tensions, the nature of the American domestic political system, and the impossibly heavy burden placed on the American ability to understand the actors that are seen as potentially deadly menaces to it. Bush and his colleagues have said that the war on terror will be very long, which makes it difficult to sustain. Much depends on how events will unfold over the next few years. Support is more likely to be forthcoming if the threat continues to be seen as real, but people also believe that progress is being made. This is a difficult combination.

Internal Tensions

The Bush Doctrine combines a war on terrorism with the strong assertion of American hegemony. While these elements arguably reinforced each other in the overthrow of the Taliban, it is far from clear that this was true in Iraq or will be the case in the future. Rooting out terrorist cells throughout the world calls for excellent information, and this requires the cooperation of intelligence services in many countries. Of course America's power allows it to deploy major incentives to induce cooperation, but there may come a point at which opposition to U.S. dominance will hamper joint efforts. A minor example is the Europeans' refusal to extradite suspected terrorists to the United States unless it promises not to seek the death penalty, and the American resistance to making this concession. More important, I join many critics in believing that the basic unilateralism of the U.S. behavior that goes with such assertive hegemony erodes the willingness of allies to cooperate on a wide range of endeavors and that the war in Iraq has strained the alliance bonds in a way that will come back to haunt the United States.

Despite its realpolitik stress on the importance of force, the Bush Doctrine also rests on idealistic foundations: the claim for the centrality of universal values represented by America, the expected power of positive examples, and the belief in the possibility of progress. These have power through their acceptance by others, not through American might. They require that others change not only their behavior but also their outlooks, if not their values. For this to happen, the United States has to be seen as well-motivated and exemplifying shared ideals. As many commentators from across the political spectrum have argued, America's success in the Cold War derived in part from the openness of its domestic system to allied voices, its articulation of a common vision, and a sense of common interest. While we should not idealize this past or underestimate the degree to which allies, let alone neutrals, distrusted U.S. power and motives, neither should we neglect the ways in which influence was able to be exercised relatively cheaply and the West was able to gain a much greater degree of unity and cooperation than many contemporary observers had believed possible.

The Bush Doctrine calls for an even more cooperative world, in part because its goals are so ambitious. It is easy to dismiss Bush's frequent claims to be trying to rid the world of evil, but as I discussed in chapter 4, he is trying to transform international politics and many of the states and societies that generate it. Even more than the war in Vietnam, the struggle that Bush has embarked on requires winning the hearts and minds of the people. But in its articulation and implementation the

Doctrine is antithetical to the sort of changes in beliefs that it requires. Even had U.S. actions been carried out with skill and tact, the inherent unilateralism of the Doctrine would have reduced the extent to which others would not only have complied but also adopted the favored attitudes. As events turned out, of course, the lessons taught by Iraq were quite contrary to those desired. The lack of WMD, the inability to establish democracy, the failure of other countries in the Middle East to respond as predicted, the human rights violations exemplified by the abuses of Iraqi prisoners, and, perhaps above all, the unwillingness of the administration to admit its errors and listen to others means that future support, when forthcoming, will be grudging, conditional, and shallow. Unlike the Security Community, the Doctrine has within itself the seeds of its own destruction.[1]

Just as the means employed by the Bush Doctrine contradict its ends, so the latter, by being so ambitious, invite failure. Not only is it extremely unlikely that terror can ever be eradicated, let alone the world be rid of evil, but the war in Iraq is already lost. Of course, it was successful in overthrowing Saddam, but we need to remember that wars, like most human ventures, are rarely zero-sum. The fact that Saddam lost does not mean that the United States won. Ousting the old regime was less important in itself than as a means to other objectives: reducing terrorism, bringing democracy to Iraq, transforming the Middle East, and establishing the correctness and the legitimacy of the Bush Doctrine. See the war objectives presented to Bush by Undersecretary of Defense for Policy Douglas Feith in March 2003 in Bob Woodward *Plan of Attack* (New York: Simon & Schuster, 2004), p. 28; a sample of many officials' views 18 months later can be found in Tyler Marshall, "Heady U.S. Goals for Iraq Fall by Wayside," *Los Angeles Times*, September 27, 2004. Although the effects of the invasion have not yet played out, it is clearly a failure in these terms. The Doctrine is then off to a very bad start, and the reasons are not only overconfidence and incompetence, but also the basic mismatch between the Doctrine and the world it seeks to mold.

A related tension in the Bush Doctrine also is highlighted by Iraq. The administration argued that overthrowing Saddam was a part of the war on terrorism because of the danger that he would give WMD to terrorists; Bush calls Iraq the "the central front" in the counterterrorist effort; and he rhetorically asks, "If America were not fighting terrorists in Iraq, … what would these thousands of killers do, suddenly begin leading productive lives of service and charity?"[2] Most observers find this line implausible and believe that the war was at best a distraction from the struggle against al-Qaeda. American attention and forces were drawn off; world (and especially Arab) opinion has been alienated; and if the United States is fighting terrorists in Iraq, the main reason is not that they have flocked to that country to try to kill Americans, but that the occupation has recruited large numbers of people to the terrorist cause. Although evidence, let alone proof, for the last and crucial point is of course elusive, it is hard to avoid the inference that the war has created more terrorists than it has killed and has weakened the resolve of others to combat them. This view is held by a wider range of observers, including France's leading anti-terrorism investigator and Pakistan's president Pervez Musharraf as well as (more predictably) France's Chirac:[3] If correct, it means that the centerpiece of the war on terror has made the problem worse and has increased the danger of attacks against the United States and its allies. Whether correct or not, if widely believed it will make others even less willing to trust American judgment.

Indeed, the policies required to build support for overthrowing Saddam may have undermined key aspects of the Bush Doctrine. Diplomatic, military, and intelligence resources that could have been used to seek out terrorists, especially in Afghanistan, were redeployed against Iraq. In perhaps an extreme case, in June 2002 the White House vetoed a plan to attack Abu Mussab al-Zarqawi and his poison laboratory in northern Iraq because it might have disturbed the efforts to build a domestic and international coalition to change the regime.[4] Zarqawi later emerged as the leading terrorist in Iraq and second only to Osama bin Laden in the overall most wanted list. Most obviously, the attempt to develop support for the war led national leaders to degrade and distort intelligence on Iraqi WMD. While effective in the short run, this not only demoralized the intelligence community but also diminished the future American ability to use intelligence to persuade audiences at home and abroad. The application of the Bush Doctrine then probably increased the obstacles to applying it again.

The war has also led public approval of the United States around the world to plummet. The United States is generally seen as a major threat to peace, and in many countries George Bush is more disliked than Osama bin Laden.[5] Foreign policy is not a popularity contest, but in many ways, often hard to specify, these views eventually will be reflected in reduced support for and cooperation with the United States. There is a related tension within American policy in that while the Bush Doctrine rests in part on a great faith in democracy abroad, if other countries' policies become more responsive to public opinion, they will become more anti-American. In the key Arab states of Jordan, Egypt, and Saudi Arabia, cooperation with the United States could not be sustained if the public had greater influence; the elections in Pakistan in September 2002 reduced the regime's stability and complicated the efforts to combat al-Qaeda, results that would have been magnified had the elections been truly free; in Europe the public is even more critical of the United States than are the leaders; and in the unlikely event that Iraq becomes a democracy, it is likely to embody illiberal values and oppose the United States.

Even without the stimulus of the American occupation of Iraq, the highly assertive American policy around the world may increase the probability that the United States will be the target of terrorist attacks as others attribute most of the world's ills to America. Whether terrorists seek vengeance, publicity, or specific changes in policy, the dominant state is likely to be the one they seek to attack. American power then produces American vulnerability.[6] If the United States placed priority on reducing its attractiveness as a target for terrorism, it could seek a reduced role in world politics. The real limits to what could be done here should not disguise the tension between protection from terror and hegemony.

The Bush Doctrine argues that combating terrorism and limiting nuclear proliferation go hand in hand. They obviously do in some cases. The danger that a rogue state could provide terrorists with WMD, although exaggerated and incorrect in the case of Iraq, is not fictitious, and controlling the spread of nuclear weapons and nuclear material contributes to American security. But this does not mean that there are no tradeoffs between nonproliferation and rooting out terrorism. Most obviously, Iraq's drain on American military resources, its time and energy, and the support of the international community means that the ability to deal with Iran and North Korea has been sharply limited. These two countries figured prominently in administration fears before 9/11 and arguably are more dangerous and perhaps more likely to provide weapons to terrorists than was Iraq. But the way the Bush administration interpreted the war on terror has hindered its ability to deal with these threats and, in an added irony, if Iran gets nuclear weapons, the U.S. may be forced to provide a security guarantee for Iraq or permit that country to develop its own arsenal. Furthermore, even if better conceived, combatting terrorism can call for alliances with regimes that seek or spread nuclear weapons. The obvious example is Pakistan, a vital American ally that has been the greatest facilitator of proliferation. The United States eventually uncovered A.Q. Kahn's network and forced Musharraf to cooperate in rolling it up, but it might have moved more quickly and strongly had it not needed Pakistan's support against al-Qaeda. This compromise is not likely to be the last, and the need to choose between these goals will continue to erode the Bush Doctrine's coherence.

In wartime, other goals are sacrificed to the war effort. As Winston Churchill famously said when he explained why he was sending aid to the Soviet Union after that country was attacked by Nazi Germany: "I have only one purpose, the destruction of Hitler, and my life is much simplified thereby. If Hitler invaded Hell, I would make at least a favorable reference to the Devil in the House of Commons."[7] Consistent with this maxim, one of the sharpest changes in U.S. foreign policy since September 11 has been the softening of the strongly anti-PRC position. China is no longer referred to as a "strategic competitor," and U.S. defense policy is no longer justified in terms of the need to meet the menace from China (although many of the weapons being purchased would be more useful in a war against China than in the fight against terrorism). This stance can be continued as long as the PRC behaves in ways that are acceptable to the United States and the Taiwan issue remains muted. But over the long run more difficult times have to be expected, and how the Bush Doctrine will cope with them and simultaneously keep the focus on terrorism is not clear. The broader question is whether the war on terrorism really is the overriding objective for American foreign policy and whether it can or should dominate all other concerns. As some of the latter (e.g., supporting American economic interests, furthering human rights, traditional security considerations) come to command renewed attention, it may be hard to continue acting as though this is a real war.

Other tensions, if not contradictions, are implicit in the Bush Doctrine's call for preventive military action. By definition, this means moving before there is incontrovertible evidence that the adversary will do great damage if it is not stopped. While such actions may be brave, they will always be subject to criticism for being reckless. An American preventive or even preemptive attack before Iraq invaded Kuwait would not have been supported by world and domestic opinion, and probably would have been judged a mistake in retrospect, for example.

Finally, the Bush Doctrine is vulnerable because while it rests on the ability to deploy massive force, the U.S. Army, despite being capable of great military feats, is not large enough to simultaneously garrison a major country and attack another adversary, and may not even be sufficient for the former task over a prolonged period. Troops must be withdrawn from one theater relatively quickly if the United States is to be able to cope with other threats. This dilemma is brought out most sharply in Iraq. It is far from clear that the occupation can be sustained without destroying the system of a volunteer army, reserves, and national guard that has proven so successful since the draft was abolished more than a quarter-century ago.

Imperial Overstretch?

Of course all policies embody tensions, and the ones I have discussed may be no more fatal than those that characterized containment during the Cold War. They are sometimes resolved by trying to do everything in order to avoid hard choices. Limits on resources can make this impossible, however, and the Bush Doctrine's very ambitious objectives bring to the fore the question of whether it can be supported by the American economic and political system. Before turning to the latter, I want to discuss the more familiar claim that the United States, like so many great powers before it, is falling victim to "imperial overstretch."[8] The basic point is that expansion inevitably leads to decline as the country takes on ever more extensive and expensive commitments. The process is like that of the turbulent frontier described in chapter 4, only on a scale so large that the state itself is entrapped. Each territory conquered or, in the current day, brought under influence must be protected against its neighbors and subversive forces. Although these countries contribute something to the upkeep of the empire (be it formal or informal), the costs mount as the dominant state becomes the enemy of all of those who oppose it in any part of the world, and is forced to expend resources at a pace that saps its economic strength.

This is a common trajectory. Money is necessary in order to wage wars; states with larger economies are likely to prevail; expensive wars can destroy a victor's economy and sow the seeds for future defeats. In early modern Europe, rulers often lost battles and even wars because they literally ran out of funds to pay their armies, which melted away or went over to the other side.[9]

The wars fought by France in the mid-18th century not only were limited by its ability to raise money, but left a crushing debt that helped set the stage for the French Revolution.[10] In the twentieth century, Germany lost two world wars in part because its financial and industrial resources were not adequate to defeat the enemies that opposed its reckless expansion, and the Soviet Union disintegrated in part because its inefficient economy could not withstand the burden of competing with the West.

This past, fascinating as it is, does not tell us much about the likely fate of the United States and the Bush Doctrine, however. The U.S. defense budget is small as a portion of gross domestic product (about 3.6 percent); the proportion devoted to the war on terrorism, although impossible to determine with any precision, obviously is even smaller. The U.S. economy can afford this war, even for the indefinite future. Granted, there are economic impediments to continuing on the current path. Deficits in the federal budget and in the balance of payments are enormous, and make the United States vulnerable to external pressures because they cannot be sustained without heavy inflows from abroad.[11] But, as many commentators have noted, increased defense spending is not the major cause of the problem. The United States could easily balance its budget if it were willing to increase taxes. Bush has done the opposite, making this the first war in American history in which taxes have gone down, not up. A discussion of the politics and beliefs that lie behind this policy would be a digression here, but the essential point is that, unlike the cases sketched in the previous paragraph, the American policy is not doomed to fail because of lack of resources. The problem of an army too small for multiple commitments is probably a better case of "imperial overstretch," but even here it is willpower rather than manpower that is in short supply. Higher pay or the reinstitution of a modest draft could provide what is needed.

A more political argument is that these resources cannot be tapped because of resistance from Bush supporters. Those in the highest income brackets who have benefited so much from the tax cuts would not support the expansive foreign policy if they were not being rewarded in this way, and their backing is necessary to sustain this policy. This argument is not without its appeal, but I do not think it is correct. The rich are very happy with Bush's tax cuts, but there is no evidence that they would not have favored him and his foreign policy without them. Some targeted favors and spending programs, especially increases in agricultural subsidies, may have been necessary to maintain domestic support for the administration, but the tax cuts were not required.

Domestic Regime and Politics

This general line of argument points in the right direction, however. Public opinion, the structure of the U.S. government, and domestic politics make it difficult to sustain the Bush Doctrine or any other clear policy. "It seemed that the United States was a very difficult country to govern," Charles de Gaulle said to Prime Minister Harold Mac Millan when explaining his disdain for the unsteady course of American policy.[12] The general was correct.

Contrary to the common impression, democracies, and especially the United States, do not find it easy to sustain a consistent line of policy when the external environment is not compelling. Domestic priorities ordinarily loom large, and few Americans think of their country as having an imperial mission. Wilsonianism may provide a temporary substitute for the older European ideologies of a *mission civilisatrice* and the white man's burden, but since it rests on the assumption that its role will be not only noble but also popular, I am skeptical that it will endure if it meets much opposition from those it is supposed to benefit. Significant casualties will be corrosive, and when the going gets tough, I think the United States will draw back.

Under most circumstances, neither any one interest nor the American state itself is strong enough to impose coherent guidance, which means that courses of action are shaped less by a grand design than by the pulling and hauling of varied interests, ideas, and political calculations. This is the model of pluralism that is believed by most scholars to capture a great deal of American politics.[13] During the Cold War, realists argued that the national interest abroad, unlike the public interest at home, was palpable because the external environment was sufficiently compelling to override domestic differences and enable even a relatively weak state to follow a policy of some consistency.[14] But the prevalence of realist calls for countries and their leaders to pursue the national interest in the face of conflicting domestic claims indicates that the latter are so powerful that they are likely to prevail under ordinary circumstances.

No American policy can be sustained without domestic support. One might think that this could be arranged with adequate public education: if the experts agree, the public can be brought around. In the late 1940s the architects of containment were able to work with opinion leaders to develop strong foundations for the policy, but by the end of the century, trust in government and other organizations was low and the sort of civic leaders who were powerful earlier had disappeared. Only conspiracy theorists see the Council on Foreign Relations as much more than a social and status group. "Captains of industry" are absent, with the possible exception of a handful of leaders in the communications and information sectors who lack the breadth of experience of earlier elites. Union leaders have disappeared even faster than unions. University presidents, who were national figures at midcentury, have become money-raisers. Those newspapers that have survived are much less relied upon than was true in the past, and television anchors do not have the expertise and reputation that would allow them to be influential, even if the large corporations that own the networks would permit them to try. Known to the public now are celebrities, largely from sports and the entertainment industry, who lack the interest and knowledge necessary to undertake the public educational campaigns we saw in the past.

Under pluralism, different groups, interests, and values predominate in different areas and at different times. Although temporarily submerged by the attacks of September 11, domestic politics and conflicting interests are likely to reassert themselves. Even in the first three years of the war, problems have appeared. Fear of offending vehemently pro-Israel groups in the country at large and within his own party have complicated Bush's search for an effective policy in the Middle East, although few of the options these groups foreclosed were attractive to him. Pressures for trade protection have increased frictions with countries whose support is needed in the war. To bolster his chances for reelection, Bush felt he had to grant tariff relief to the steel industry, with the resultant outcry from allies and others. He similarly backed an agricultural support bill that contradicted his calls for other countries to reduce protection, nullified much of the increase in American foreign aid, and provided further evidence that the United States would not respect the rules that it called upon others to follow.

Separation of powers means that the President cannot control Congress, which can undermine the President's policies. In a minor but telling example, the need to garner crucial votes for a broad package of trade legislation made Bush promise representatives from textile-producing districts that he would maintain strict limits on clothing made in Pakistan, creating resentment in that country.[15] Furthermore, the judiciary also is independent, giving citizens the ability to brings suits that run contrary to the policies of the executive branch, as shown by several human rights cases brought under the Alien Tort Claims Act, a 1789 law resurrected and put to new purposes, and by the families of 9/11 victims who are suing leading figures in Saudi Arabia for having financed Islamic extremism.

The contentious nature of the American system has come into play as the war in Iraq, having not turned out as expected, has divided the country and sharply revealed the vulnerabilities of the Bush Doctrine. The pacification effort has proved difficult, leading to a steady stream of American casualties. While it is not true that American opinion is as casualty-averse as conventional wisdom has it,[16] the public is intolerant of wars that drag on for little apparent purpose. Casualties by them-selves do not undermine support, but they can do so when combined with other factors. Thus it matters that the United States was not greeted as the liberator, that no weapons of mass destruction (WMD) were found,[17] and that the entire Middle East has not been transformed. Underlining all of these concerns, of course, is the central question of whether overthrowing Saddam weakened al-Qaeda and reduced the terrorist threat to the United States. The answer cannot be known with certainty, and the Bush administration vigorously defends the invasion in these terms. But since it also announces that the terrorist threat has not diminished,[18] it seems likely that the claim that the Bush Doctrine is effectively coping with the terrorist threat will continue to be met with significant public skepticism.

Even if the situation in Iraq were to improve, sustaining support for the war on terror will be difficult because it is a very long-term strug-gle, and one that lacks clear markers of progress. Even during World War II sustained public support was in doubt.[19] Without territory to be gained, it is now much harder to tell whether the United States is on the right track. So it is not surprising that even though the Republican Party is still seen by the electorate as better able to provide for Ameri-can security than are the Democrats, the latter felt it sensible to make the Bush Doctrine a major campaign issue.

At first glance, it would seem that much as the experts criticize the Bush Doctrine for its unilateralism, on this score at least it rests on secure domestic foundations. The line that drew the most applause in the President's 2004 State of the Union Address was "America will never seek a permission slip to defend the security of our country." In fact, the public is sensibly ambivalent. Although few would argue that lack of international support should stop the United States from acting when a failure to do so would endanger the country, polls taken in the run-up to the war in Iraq indicated that international endorse-ment would have added as much as twenty percentage points to sup-port for attacking.[20] Even in a country with a strong tradition of unilateralism, people realize that international support translates into a reduced burden on the United States and increased legitimacy that can both aid the specific endeavor at hand and strengthen the patterns of cooperation that serve American interests. Furthermore, many people take endorsement by allies as an indication that the American policy is sensible, both is a great deal of the reason why Blair's support for Bush was so important domestically and means that the Bush Doctrine is particularly vulnerable to British defection.[21]

In summary, although the combination of Bush's predisposition and the attack of September 11 have produced a coherent doctrine, the required domestic support is likely to erode. Congress will become increasingly assertive as the war continues, especially if it does not go well; the Democrats, while lacking a consistent policy of their own, have not accepted the validity of Bush's strategy; although the public is united in its desire to oppose terrorism, the way to do so is disputed. The United States remains a very difficult country to govern.

Requirements for Intelligence

It is particularly difficult for the Bush Doctrine to maintain public support because its ambitious policy goals make failure likely on a number of occasions and require more accurate assessment of the international environment than intelligence can provide.[22] The problem here centers on the perceived need for preventive wars. Although members of the Bush administration have stressed that this tool is to be used only as a last resort, the basic idea of nipping threats in the bud, of acting when there is still time, implies a willingness to accept false positives in order to avoid more costly false negatives. That is, the United States must act on the basis of far from complete information because if it hesitates until the threat is entirely clear, it will be too late: it cannot afford to wait until the smoking gun is a mushroom cloud, to use the phrase the administration favored before the Iraq war. In principle, this is quite reasonable. The costs of a WMD attack could be so high as to make it rational to launch a preventive war even though this might not actually be necessary.

Even if this approach is intellectually defensible, however, it is not likely to succeed politically. The reason is twofold. First, the very nature of a preventive war means that the evidence is ambiguous and the supporting arguments are subject to rebuttal. If Britain and France had gone to war with Germany before 1939, large segments of the public would have believed that the war was not necessary. If it had gone badly, the public would have been inclined to sue for peace; if it had gone well, public opinion would have questioned its wisdom. The cost of a war that is believed to be unnecessary will be high in terms of both international and domestic opinion and will sap the support for the policy. (Indeed, in the case of Iraq, the administration chose to continue to assert that the war was forced on it despite the clear evidence that the central claims used to justify it were incorrect.) Even if the public does not judge that the administration should be turned out of power for its mistake, it is not likely to want the adventure to be repeated.

The second problem is that preventive war asks a great deal of intelligence. It does not bode well for the Bush Doctrine that the war in Iraq involved a massive intelligence failure concerning WMD (which is different from saying that it was caused by this failure), and that the United States started the war two days ahead of schedule because agents claimed to know the whereabouts of Saddam and his sons, with the amazing accuracy of the munitions that destroyed the location only underlining the falsity of the information. Because the idea of intelligence failure is so central, I want to take some time to unpack the numerous issues involved, after which I will return to the question of what went wrong.

First, intelligence can be wrong in the sense of diverging from what later and more complete information tells us. It is clear that the Iraq estimates were badly in error, and for many purposes this obvious point is the most important one because if accurate estimates are necessary for a policy of preventive war, then the viability of the policy is called into question.

We cannot use hindsight to judge the second kind of intelligence failure, in which intelligence analysis fails to reflect the information that was available at the time. Because most of the latter remains classified, we do not know if this was the case in Iraq. The Senate Select Committee on Intelligence (SSCI) argues that it was, but its analysis is marred by hindsight bias and the application of unrealistic standards.[23] Hindsight is displayed by the fact that it generally sees judgments that were later borne out as being reasonable and those that were incorrect as being unreasonable. This is an implausibly tidy view of the world. It also implies that to be well founded, a judgment that Iraq had vigorous WMD programs had to be supported by unambiguous firsthand reports. Obviously, these are to be desired, but to argue that conclusions require them is to condemn intelligence to silence on most important issues. My guess is that when the relevant underlying documents are eventually declassified, most of the analysts' judgments will appear reasonable, although we are sure also to find grounds for alternatives that were not explored at the time.

A third meaning or kind of intelligence failure is a gap between the evidence that was gathered and the information that should have been obtained. This obviously requires difficult judgments about what it was reasonable to expect intelligence to have learned. For example, while it is a truism that the United States is short on information from spies, it would have taken especially great skill, effort, and luck to have secured the services of a highly placed agent who could have been of great assistance. Saying that the United States was misled because it did not have an agent or listening device in Saddam's office is a bit like my favorite counterfactual, "If my grandmother had wheels, she'd be a bus": not particularly useful. On occasion a country will have information of this importance, but one cannot count on it.[24]

In the case of Iraq the question is often posed as whether the intelligence was faulty or whether the Bush administration distorted it. I think the answer is "both." The possibility of intelligence being "politicized" (i.e., being a product of policy more than an input to it), like the concept of intelligence failure, comes in multiple forms, of which two are the most obvious.[25] One is decision makers' giving inaccurate accounts of intelligence reports, and the other is their putting pressure on intelligence so that they get back the message they want to hear. I believe that both forms were present. Top administration officials, especially the Vice President and the Secretary of Defense, made claims that went significantly beyond what was in intelligence estimates, and indeed contradicted them. When they did not say that their statements were grounded in agreed-upon intelligence, this was implied. Most famously, the President said that the British reported that Saddam had sought uranium from Africa (true, but a reasonable listener would infer that American intelligence agreed, which was not true); the Vice President said that Iraq had reconstituted its nuclear program; he and the Secretary of Defense said that there was solid evidence for connections between Iraq and al-Qaeda; and many policy makers insisted that the WMD threat was "imminent." The U.S. intelligence community thought that the second statement went too far and that the third and fourth were wrong. Indeed, CIA director Tenet testified that he privately corrected officials for claims like these.[26]

Officials also engaged in "cherry-picking" and "stove-piping." The former is highlighting reports of questionable validity that support the policy to the exclusion of more numerous and better-established ones to the contrary; the latter is the delivery of selected raw intelligence to policy makers, bypassing intelligence analysts who could critically evaluate it. These practices can be defended as within the prerogatives and even the duties of top officials to reach their own conclusions, but when used to justify policies to the public, they incorrectly imply the backing of the intelligence community.

Politicization in the form of pressure on intelligence to bolster the conclusions policy makers have already reached is harder to demonstrate, and SCCI finds no evidence for it. But its report is quite partisan, its conclusions on this point are rejected by many of its Democratic members,[27] and I believe that it is clearly correct only regarding the most blatant forms of politicization. That is, analysts were not ordered to reach specified conclusions. But this is not to say that they were not influenced by the knowledge of what the political leaders had made very clear they wanted and expected intelligence to say.[28] It became obvious that the intelligence community had stretched to support policy when it released declassified reports that painted a more vivid and certain picture of WMD capabilities than it had presented in the classified counterparts, dropping fifteen "probablies" and several dissenting opinions.[29]

Although the extent to which analysis was influenced by political pressures will remain subject to debate even when the documents are open and the officials are free to tell their stories, it is clear that analysts and intelligence managers knew that any suggestion that Saddam might not have a robust WMD program would immediately draw hostile fire from their superiors. Faced with really strong evidence that these programs did not exist, a working-level analyst probably would have gone to her superior, but short of this (and it is hard to imagine decisive evidence for the negative case), no one had any incentives to raise the question. Indeed, in this political climate no one could even ask if the conventional wisdom about Saddam's WMD programs should be reexamined.

Nevertheless, I think there is little reason to doubt that most intelligence officers truly believed that Saddam was actively pursuing WMD programs. Complaints that they acted on duress in this area are relatively few and, as I will discuss below, their judgments were highly plausible. Furthermore, in other areas the CIA came to conclusions that were unpalatable to the administration. Three months before the war the National Intelligence Council warned that the aftermath of the invasion was not likely to be easy and that attacking might increase support for terrorists in the Islamic world.[30] Even more strikingly, intelligence consistently denied that there was significant evidence for Saddam's role in 9/11 or that he might turn over WND to al-Qaeda. Individual analysts and the intelligence community as a whole held to this position in the face of administration statements to the contrary, endlessly repeated inquiries and challenges that I think can only be interpreted as pressure, and the formation of a unit in the Defense Department dedicated to finding evidence for such connections. The efforts of the administration to gain the answers it desired showed a corruption of the policy-making process, but the lack of success not only speaks to the integrity of the intelligence officials, but also casts doubt on the claim that the reports on WMD were badly biased by the desire to please.

The intense political atmosphere probably created what might be called a "hostile climate" that was not conducive to critical analysis and that led intelligence to produce judgments of excessive certainty, however. The desire to avoid the painful value trade-off between pleasing policy makers and following professional standards created what psychologists call "motivated bias" in favor of producing estimates that would support, or at least not undermine, policy. This is not unusual; in the 1930s there was a close correlation between British policy toward Germany and intelligence on the military balance. Rather than the latter influencing the former, however, the estimates changed in the wake of policy shifts.[31]

It is worth noting that politicization represents the tribute that vice pays to virtue and may be a modern phenomenon. That is, leaders, at least in the United States and United Kingdom, now need to justify their foreign policies by saying that they are based on the findings of intelligence professionals, as is illustrated by the fact that Secretary of State Powell demanded that Director of Central Intelligence Tenet sit right behind him when he gave his speech to the UN outlining the evidence on Iraq. This is a touching faith in the concept of professionalism and how much can be known about other states. It is not the only way things could be. A leader could say, "I think Saddam is a terrible menace. This is a political judgment, and I have been elected to make difficult calls like this. Information rarely can be definitive, and while I have consulted widely and listened to our intelligence services and other experts, this is my decision, not theirs." This is politically very difficult to do, however, and a policy maker who wants to proceed in the face of ambiguous or discrepant information will be hard pressed to avoid at least some politicization of intelligence. This is true despite the fact that intelligence is often wrong and political judgments right. In the most important case, when Winston Churchill prevailed on his colleagues to continue fighting Nazi Germany in June 1940, he utilized estimates of German strength that were even more faulty than U.S. intelligence on Iraq. Many of the best decisions are based more on intuition than on defensible calculations.[32]

Two rough measures of politicization are comparisons of the intelligence prepared under Bush with that of German and French views and with the baseline analysis inherited from the Clinton administration.

The allied intelligence services apparently agreed that Iraq had significant stockpiles of chemical weapons and sought nuclear ones, although the nuances may have been different. This was true for the Clinton-era estimates as well. As it became clear that the Bush administration was committed to overthrowing Saddam, however, the estimates hardened, dropping adjectives and qualifiers that indicated uncertainty and adding ones of emphasis and urgency. Although little of the information that came in after September 11 proved to be accurate, intelligence reported a more robust program, including the claim that Iraq had restarted its nuclear program and had a stockpile of biological agents.[33] Nevertheless, the gap between the Bush and Clinton estimates was less than that which separated the latter from what we now believe was true.

The errors in the Clinton baseline bring us back to the fundamental question of why the intelligence was so wrong even when it was not under great pressures.[34] I doubt if we will have a full understanding even after all the current investigations are complete,[35] but putting aside the degradation caused by politicization, I think eight factors were at work.[36]

First and most fundamentally, here, as in many other cases, intelligence is hard and there is no a priori reason to expect success. Intelligence services are engaged in a competitive game, with hiders and deceivers usually having the advantage. Failure may not call for any special explanation, but perhaps is what we should expect in the absence of particularly favorable circumstances. This is not a new insight: the only fault with what Clausewitz has to say is that he implies that the difficulties are less in peacetime: "Many intelligence reports in war are contradictory; even more are false, and most are uncertain."[37] As I will discuss further at the end of this section, understanding the other side and seeing the world through the regime's eyes is particularly difficult when these views and behavior are odd or even irrational. Second and relatedly, the United States lacked well-placed agents who could provide the best information. In their absence, the United States did receive many reports, but most were unreliable or deceptive and the signal-to-noise ratio was quite unfavorable. Some of these reports may have been inadvertently misleading if they accurately reported things that Saddam's officials believed or were told because it turns out that Saddam was misleading them.[38] Ironically, the problem was magnified by the fact that Iraqi WMD program became a top priority for American intelligence. Since everyone in the intelligence chain, from sources to top analysts, knew that the government was extraordinarily interested in what Iraq was doing in this area, all sorts of reports were generated and passed on, thereby producing the incorrect impression that with this much smoke, there had to be fire. Third, aerial photography and signals intelligence, which can be very valuable, could not yield a great deal here. Most Iraqi communications went by land lines rather than radio, and so could not be intercepted; aerial reconnaissance could reveal that buildings that previously housed WMD programs were being rebuilt, but could not tell what they contained. Indeed, it seems that even photographs of one site that appeared to be incriminating because they showed decontamination trucks were inadvertently misleading because they were of a drill that was staged to prepare the Iraqis for the possible resumption of production.[39] Fourth, intelligence agencies learned—and overlearned—from the past.[40] After the 1991 Gulf War intelligence was shocked to learn how much it had underestimated Iraq's WMD programs, especially in the nuclear area, and it was not going to make this error again. Relatedly, intelligence had learned how effective Saddam's programs of deception and denial were, and this meant that any failure to find specific evidence could be attributed to Iraq's success at hiding it. All this was compounded by the lessons taught by the Rumsfeld Commission of 1998 that berated the CIA for basing its missile estimates on the assumption that adversaries would follow the same methodical path to these weapons as the United States had followed.

These four obstacles are unique in their details, but apply quite generally. The next is particularly important in the United States, although it can be present in other countries as well: the CIA is forbidden to comment on American policy. Although it is understandable for decision makers not to want their intelligence services looking over their shoulders, there is a serious problem in the frequent instances when the other side's behavior is in part a reaction to what the United States is doing or what it thinks the United States may do. In this case, if some of Saddam's intransigence was due to his belief that Bush would seek to overthrow him no matter what he did, intelligence was not in a good position to elucidate his calculations.

The final three reasons for the failure in Iraq stem from general cognitive biases. Most obviously, once a view of the other side becomes established, it will remain unquestioned in the absence of powerful information to the contrary. Intelligence analysts, like everyone else, assimilate incoming information to their preexisting beliefs. In the early 1990s almost everyone came to believe that Saddam had active WMD programs. Without complete and thorough inspections to show that this was not the case, it was natural that people would interpret ambiguous information not only as consistent with, but also as confirming, this "fact."[41] Relatedly, analysts engaged in "bootstrapping": evidence that was accepted in part because it fit with the established views was then used to buttress the validity of them.

The driving role of preexisting beliefs and images is shown by the fact that people who were predisposed to believe that Saddam might ally with Osama bin Laden gave great credit to the scattered and ambiguous reports to such ties, while those whose general views of the Iraqi regime made them skeptical that it would do this found the evidence quite unconvincing. Similarly, the different evaluations of the reports that Iraq was trying to acquire uranium from Niger and that his unmanned aircraft might be intended to strike the United States are explained not by the evidence, which was held in common by all involved, or by better or worse reasoning power, but rather by the analysts' general beliefs that such policies would or would not make sense. The influence of beliefs was magnified by a common failing, this one representing a standard but unfortunate neglect of appropriate social science reasoning. Intelligence professionals try to detect the pattern from scattered, incomplete, and ambiguous bits of evidence. But, like most people, they rarely take the next step of treating what they think they see as a hypothesis, which would entail asking what else they would expect to see if their belief was correct.[42] Even more rarely do they examine competing explanations in this way. Taking these steps would not have guaranteed the right answer, but it might have helped. Posing the question "If Iraq is building stockpiles of chemical and biological weapons and actively pursuing an atomic bomb, what traces should we be able to detect?" might have led intelligence officials to come up with a number of propositions that they could have sought to verify. At least some of the results presumably would have been negative, and while this would not have proven that the underlying belief was incorrect, it could have provided a sensible platform for doubt.

The final explanation for the failure is closely related to the first one and is perhaps the most important: given Saddam's behavior, his protestations to have disarmed were implausible.[43] That is why most opponents of the war did not dispute the basic claim that Saddam had an active WMD program. If he did not, then why did he not welcome the inspectors and show that he had complied? Doing so under Clinton could have led to the sanctions being lifted; doing so in 2002–2003 was the only way he could have saved his regime. Iraq could have provided a complete and honest accounting of its weapons programs, as called for by the UN resolution, and while the Bush administration would not have been convinced, other countries might have been and domestic opposition might have been emboldened. Similarly, Iraq could have mounted an effective rebuttal to Powell's UN speech. The regime's failure to do things like this left even opponents of the war with little doubt that Saddam had active and serious WMD programs. It made great sense that he would be trying to keep his program secret; it did not make any sense that he was exaggerating it to impress the United States, his fellow Arabs, and perhaps domestic opinion.

The postwar Iraq Survey Group led first by David Kay and then by Charles Duelfer has revealed not only the quiescent if not moribund state of Saddam's WMD programs but also some of the reasoning behind his actions. While the Duelfer report is speculative and based on only scattered information because Saddam and his top lieutenants did not speak freely, it tells us that the best available evidence indicates that Saddam was particularly concerned about maintaining the appearance of WMD in order to deter Iran, that he feared that unlimited inspections would allow the United States to pinpoint his location and assassinate him, that private meetings between the inspectors and scientists were resisted on the general grounds that "any such meeting with foreigners was seen as a threat to the security of the Regime," and that "Iraq did not want to declare anything that documented use of chemical weapons for fear the documentation could be used against Iraq in law suits.[44]

Saddam's central motivation apparently was to first end sanctions and inspections and then to reconstitute his programs, all the while keeping his real and perceived adversaries at bay. "This led to a difficult balancing act between the need to disarm to achieve sanctions relief while at the same time retaining a strategic deterrent. The Regime never resolved the contradiction inherent in this approach."[45] This is putting it mildly. Full compliance with the inspectors was the only way that sanctions were going to be lifted, especially after 9/11. It is true that revealing that he had no WMD would have reduced his deterrence, but the fear of such weapons could not and did not prevent an American attack, and Iran was hardly spoiling for a fight and could not have assumed that the West would stand aside while it greatly increased its influence by moving against Iraq even if it so desired. Saddam's policy was then foolish and self-defeating, and this goes a long way to explaining the Western intelligence failure. When the truth is as bizarre as this, it is not likely to be believed. I will return to the implications of this puzzle later, but here I just want to stress that when the truth is implausible, it is not likely to be believed.

Although this last factor made the Iraq case particularly difficult, future cases are not likely to be easy, and intelligence will continue to be faulty. Of course the CIA will get some important cases right, but I suspect that success will be more the exception than the rule. A policy that can work only if the underlying assessments of other actors are quite accurate is likely to fail. Thus not only did the administration put a great pressure on intelligence to provide reports that would justify the invasion, thereby making short-run gains at the cost of reducing everyone else's confidence in the system, but, more generally, the Bush Doctrine places a heavier burden on intelligence than it can bear. The National Security Strategy document says that in order to support preventive options the United States "will build better, more integrated intelligence capabilities to provide timely, accurate information on threats, wherever they emerge," but this is not likely to be possible.[46]

Rebuttal

Proponents of the Bush Doctrine can argue that this line of argument is irrelevant. As noted earlier, the dominant view in the administration corresponds to Kenneth Waltz's second image of international politics: a state's foreign policy follows from its domestic political system.[47] This is a very American approach, extending back to Woodrow Wilson, if not earlier, and has significant appeal to liberal elites and the public. It also fits with a cursory look at the twentieth century's history, with Stalin and Hitler being two leaders who tyrannized over their own subjects before turning their venom on the wider world. In this view, evil regimes follow evil foreign policies. It follows that consequential assessment errors will be quite rare. Even when intelligence has difficulty estimating the other's capabilities, as proved to be the case in Iraq, it is very easy to tell when its regime is repressive. Thus, knowing that North Korea, Iran, and Syria are brutal autocracies tells us that they will seek to dominate their neighbors, sponsor terrorism, and threaten the United States.

In the wake of the failure to find WMD after the war, this became the main line of the Bush administration's defense of its actions. The fact that Iraq had only "WMD program-related activities" rather than WMD did not matter much, it argued, because this would affect only the timeline of the danger. Perhaps the United States had a few more years to respond than was believed, but since removing Saddam was the only way to remove the danger, this error was minor. The regime was evil, and it followed that at some point it would menace its neighbors and the United States. As Bush told Tim Russert, "Saddam was dangerous with the ability to make weapons."[48] This approach turns on its head the normal mantra of conservative intelligence analysis: that one should concentrate on capabilities, not intentions. For a regime like this, Bush and his colleagues claim, what is crucial is that it was evil and had the intention to get WMD as soon as possible.

This approach has two difficulties, however. First, taken to its logical conclusion it implies a very much reduced need for intelligence. It does not take spies or expensive satellites to determine that a country is repressive, and if that is all we need to know, we can save a great deal of money. Second, even if it is true that the countries that abuse their neighbors are those that have abused their own people, many of the latter follow a quiescent foreign policy. Mao's China, for example, was second to none in internal oppression but followed a cautious, if not benign, foreign policy. Thus, while knowing that only repressive regimes are threats to the United States would indeed be useful, it does not tell us which of these regimes are menaces and which are not. This knowledge, then, does not solve the basic conundrum facing the doctrine of preventive war of deciding which countries are threats and when the danger is sufficiently grave to merit taking the offensive.

Understanding Adversaries

My previous discussion, like most treatments of the subject, has concentrated on specific intelligence problems highlighted by the misestimates of Iraq's WMD programs. But the war also revealed a broader kind of failure, one that is quite common and that also makes it difficult to sustain the Bush Doctrine: the inability to understand the way Saddam viewed the United States and the rest of the world and the strategy that he was following. The two kinds of failures are linked. As I noted, the main, if rarely articulated, reason why almost all observers believed that Saddam had a thriving WMD program was that his behavior did not make sense if this was not the case. Why did he not show that he did not have WMD when this was the only way he might save himself? I will offer some tentative explanations for Saddam's behavior below, but the puzzle is more important than the answer. It shows that things that common sense indicates must be true sometimes are not; that our understanding of the details of the adversary's capabilities and specific behaviors is often influenced by our general image of them rather than the latter being derived from the former; and that policies may be based on undisputed but disturbingly incorrect beliefs about what others are like.

Linked to the failure to understand what Saddam was up to was the failure of the United States to adequately convey its intentions and capabilities to him. As subsequent events demonstrated, the United States had the ability to rapidly overthrow Saddam, if not to rapidly pacify the country, and to capture him. It also seemed clear—at least to most of the world—that the United States would carry out its threat if need be. Saddam then seemed willfully blind, and as a result the United States could not coerce him despite the fact that it had the capability to defeat him and had made highly credible threats to do so. This is puzzling. During the Cold War we became accustomed to the disturbing fact that while the United States could not protect itself, it could deter the Soviet Union from attacking or undertaking major adventures. Elaborate, controversial, and I believe basically correct theories were developed to explain how deterrence was possible in the absence of defense. But we now have the reverse situation, and this represents the failure of both policy and theory. Because the United States had the ability to defeat Saddam and the incentives to do so if necessary, Saddam should have backed down and invasion should not have been necessary.

Four possible explanations are compatible with general theories of coercion but cast doubt on the effectiveness of many American strategies. First, despite the fact that observers around the world believed the American threats, Saddam may not have. Dictatorships are notoriously impervious to unpleasant information; dictators are usually closed-minded, and often kill those who bring bad news. Saddam could have believed that even if his troops could not defeat the invading army, they could delay it long enough to force mediation by France and Russia.[49] Perhaps he also thought that the United States would be deterred by the recognition that it could not consolidate its military victory in the face of insurgency, nationalism, and political divisions among the anti-Baathist groups. While this chain of reasoning now has some appeal, it is far from clear that it was Saddam's and, on balance, it remains hard to see how Saddam could have expected to keep the United States at bay.[50]

Second, Saddam could have preferred martyrdom to compliance. Political and perhaps physical death could have given him personal honor and great stature in the Arab world; both could have been gratifying and furthered Saddam's political dreams. While we cannot rule this out, these values and preferences do not seem to accord with his previous behavior. Third, Saddam may have underestimated the incentives that Bush felt to overthrow him. As hard as this is to believe,

Duelfer reports that high-level interrogations indicate that "by late 2002 Saddam had persuaded himself that the United States would not attack Iraq because it already had achieved its objectives of establishing a military presence in the region."[51]

Fourth, as I noted in chapter 3, Saddam may have believed that he did not have an alternative that would leave him in power. As Thomas Schelling stressed long ago, making threats credible will do no good unless the actor simultaneously conveys a credible promise not to carry out the undesired action if the other side complies.[52] During most of the run-up to the invasion, the Bush administration made clear that its goal was regime change, which, it reminded us, was the objective of the Clinton administration as well. Only for a few months in late 2002, when the administration sought support from Congress and the United Nations, did it argue that it would be satisfied by Saddam's compliance with previous UN resolutions. It would have been easy, and indeed rational, for Saddam to have believed that this American position was insincere; that submitting would have given him at best a brief lease on life; and that the only possible route to survival was to bluff and exaggerate his WMD capability in the hope that the United States would back down rather than risk the high casualties that WMD could inflict.[53]

This argument is certainly plausible and probably is part of the answer to the puzzle. But doubts are raised about the adequacy of this or the previous particularistic accounts by the fact that the phenomenon is quite general.[54] The United States failed to understand the beliefs and calculations that led Stalin to authorize the North Korean invasion of South Korea in June 1950 and Mao to intervene several months later, for example. Other countries can be similarly blind; despite its intensive study of its adversary, Israel was unable to grasp the strategy that led Anwar Sadat to launch his attack across the Suez Canal in October 1973—or to go to Jerusalem four years later, for that matter.

What is most striking and relevant to the Bush Doctrine is that since the end of the Cold War, there have been five instances in which the United States had to use force because the threat to do so was not perceived as credible, despite being supported by adequate capability and willpower. The first case was Panama in 1989. Here it can be argued that Noriega had little reason to believe the threat because the United States had not carried out operations like this before, public support was unclear, and memories of Vietnam lingered. Furthermore, as in Iraq, the adversary's leader might not have been able to change his behavior in a way that would have allowed him to remain in power.

The second case is the Gulf War. Because the United States made no attempt to deter Saddam, the puzzle here is not why Saddam invaded Kuwait, although the explanation remains in some dispute,[55] but his unwillingness to withdraw despite the presence of 500,000 coalition troops poised against him. In fact, he may have been convinced at the last minute, with the war attributable to the difficulties in making arrangements with so little time remaining and the American preference to destroy the Iraqi forces rather than allowing them to withdraw and be available for future adventures. Other factors may also have been at work, such as Saddam's residual belief that he could deter the United States by inflicting a large number of casualties, or his calculation that a bloodless withdrawal would cost him more in the eyes of his own people and his Arab neighbors than a limited military defeat. Nevertheless, this incident is a puzzling failure of coercion despite massive military superiority and a display that convinced most observers that the United States would use it.

The third case is Haiti in 1996. Although Clinton did not have to fight to oust the junta, he did have to put the invasion force into the air before Cedras and his colleagues believed that they had no choice but to abdicate.[56] This was, then, a close-run thing, and while the previous American hesitations may have given Haitian leaders reason to doubt that the United States would use force, as the American position hardened most observers understood that Clinton would act if he needed to, and so we cannot attribute Cedras's refusal to yield to Clinton's failure to make his intention clear. Of course here, as in Panama, the resistance was greatly heightened by the fact that the American demand entailed removing the adversary from power. It remains striking, however, that this coercion proved so difficult.

The next case of failed coercion was the operation in Kosovo. Clinton and his colleagues believed that if Milošević did not back down in the face of the American/NATO threat to use force, he would do so after a day or two of bombing. In the event, it took much more than that; although an actual invasion was not needed, the amount of force required was quite large. Again the reason is in part that the United States demanded a great deal from Milošević. He viewed Kosovo as part of Serbia, had gained power through arousing public opinion on this issue, and had reason to fear that he would be overthrown if he withdrew (as in fact proved to be the case). Indeed, the puzzle of why he did not back down initially is complemented by the unanswered questions surrounding his eventual concessions. What happened during the campaign to lead him to change his mind? Many individual authors are sure of the answer, but each gives a different one and we cannot yet determine the relative importance of the bombing of Serbian army units, the damage to Belgrade, the targeting of assets that belonged to Milošević's circle of supporters, the lack of backing and eventual pressure from Russia, and the fear of a ground invasion. What is clear and crucial is that the United States did not understand Milošević's perceptions and strategy, just as he almost surely did not understand the American preferences and options.

These thumbnail sketches lead to four conclusions. First, intelligence failures are often bilateral if not multilateral.[57] That is, the American surprise at finding that its adversaries could not be coerced was mirrored by the adversaries' misreading of what the United States would do. Intelligence requires empathy, seeing the world as the other sees it, and this is particularly difficult when the other sees you in a way very different from the way you see yourself.

Second, whatever policy the United States adopts, it is important for it to try to do a better job of understanding its adversaries and conveying its promises and threats to them.[58] Although the task is difficult, it is striking how little the U.S. government has sought to learn from these troublesome cases, despite the fact that it now has access to many of the decision makers on the other side. The American propensity to treat past events as mere history is nowhere more evident and costly than here. The trickle of information that has reached the public about Saddam's reasoning is intriguing, and perhaps indicates that this case is receiving more attention, if for no reason other than its political importance. There is some evidence that Saddam doubted both that the United States would leave him in power even if he showed that he had no WMD and that Bush would carry out his threat to invade. Other reports are that he was more concerned with the danger of domestic and Arab opposition and that he felt that inspections of his palaces would be humiliating. He may also have thought that he could play for time and that the U.S. drive for war would lose momentum.[59] Obviously this is only a start, and it is far from clear that the United States will try and be able to do the job as thoroughly as it should.

Third, it is unlikely that even excellent studies will provide a sufficient base of knowledge to prevent all such errors in the future. The ways in which adversaries can perceive and calculate are too numerous and surprising to permit confident projections. The meetings of Cold War veterans since the mid-1990s reveal mutual amazement that the other side could have believed what it did, and the current task is more difficult than the one the United States faced during the Cold War. Then it dealt with one fairly stable adversary over a prolonged period; now it has to assess a wide variety of very different kinds of actors with different goals, beliefs, and worldviews, many of which the United States has taken seriously for only a few years.

Finally, the Bush Doctrine places heavy demands on judging adversaries. If the United States is to block proliferation and engage in preventive wars when rogues get close to gaining WMD, it will need far better understanding of others than it has been able to muster so far. Conversely, if the United States is not able to gain more discriminating intelligence about the capabilities and intentions of potential rogues, the Bush Doctrine will require it to use force to change any number of regimes. But it is unlikely that American domestic politics would support such a policy.

Democracy as the Answer?

Here, as in the earlier problem of intelligence failure, the Bush administration's faith in democracy provides a rebuttal: threats like these will disappear as more and more countries become democratic. I am doubtful, however, that the United States will in fact vigorously support the establishment of democracies abroad, that such efforts will succeed, and that democratic regimes will always further American interests.

The first question is whether the United States will run risks to establish democracies abroad. This question of course arose during the Cold War, and the basic problem was summarized in Kennedy's oft-quoted reaction to the assassination of the dictator of the Dominican Republic, Rafael Trujillo, in May 1961: "There are three possibilities, in descending order of preference: a decent democratic regime, a continuation of the Trujillo regime, or a Castro regime. We ought to aim at the first, but we really can't renounce the second until we are sure that we can avoid the third."[60] Despite the fact that the United States has more room to maneuver now that it does not have to worry about a new regime allying with a major enemy state, there appears to be a great deal of continuity between the U.S. policy during the Cold War, what it did in the first decade after it, and Bush's actions. While the United States hopes to replace hostile dictatorships with democracies, only rarely does it push for democracy when doing so could destabilize friendly regimes. It would be tiresome to recount the sorry but perhaps sensible history of U.S. policies toward Egypt, Pakistan, and Saudi Arabia, and I will just note that when the latter arrested reformers who had called for a constitutional monarchy and independent human rights monitoring, all Colin Powell could say was, "Each nation has to find its own path and follow that path at its own speed."[61]

Ironically, the war on terrorism, although accompanied by greater stress on the value of democracy, has made the United States less willing to act accordingly because it has increased the American need for allies throughout the globe. Without the war, the United States might have put more pressure on the nondemocratic states of the former Soviet Union or at least not supported them. But the perceived need for bases in Central Asia has led the United States to embrace a particularly unsavory set of regimes. The pressure to democratize Pakistan is similarly minimal, in part because of the fear that greater responsiveness to public opinion would lead to an unacceptable Islamic regime. This danger, and that of any kind of instability, are magnified because of Pakistan's nuclear arsenal. Although Egypt lacks nuclear weapons, instability in such a powerful and centrally placed country is also greatly to be feared, and so despite an occasional sentence in a speech,[62] Bush, like his predecessors, feels he cannot afford to do anything that might lead to the worst possible outcome. In other parts of the Middle East and areas such as the Caspian basin, it is the need for a secure flow of oil that leads the United States to support nondemocratic regimes. In fact, it seems that there are few places on the globe that are unimportant enough to run the experiment of vigorously supporting democracies where they do not now exist.

For the Bush administration, furthermore, strategic considerations do not tell the whole story. It appears to be driven more by the politics of the regimes it is dealing than by an abstract commitment to democracy, as is shown by its stance toward, if not its role in, the unconstitutional as well as the constitutional opposition to Chávez in Venezuela and Aristide in Haiti.[63] In a continuation of the Cold War pattern, leftist governments are seen as dangerous, and authoritarian regimes of the right are acceptable. On other occasions it is the specific policies of a leader that make him unacceptable despite his popular approval. The American refusal to treat Arafat as the Palestinians' leader was rooted in the belief that he was unwilling to stop terrorism or even had sponsored it, not his inability to win an election, and the United States withdrew its recognition of President Rauf Denktash of Turkish Cyprus when he opposed proposals for reunifying the island.[64]

But even vigorous support for democracy might not produce that outcome. The fate of Iraq may not yet be determined, and at this writing anything appears to be possible, from a partially democratic regime to a civil war to the return of a national strongman to the loss of national unity. But it is hard to believe that the near future will see a full-fledged democracy in that country, with extensive rule of law, open competition, a free press, and checks and balances.[65] The best that could be hoped for would be a sort of semi-democracy, such as we see in Russia or Nigeria, to take two quite different countries. The prospects of a reconstruction that resembled that of Italy, Germany, or Japan after World War II always were slim, and would have required an American occupation much larger and perhaps longer than the Bush administration (or most Americans) were willing to tolerate.[66] This is not to say that American efforts will be entirely wasted. Indeed, contrary to conventional wisdom, when the United States made serious efforts to spread liberalism and democracy in its twentieth-century interventions, it often did move countries in that direction.[67] Today as well, we are likely to see a range of results, some quite beneficial.

The Bush administration's position is much more optimistic, however, arguing that for democracy to flourish, all that is needed is for repression to be struck down. The implicit belief is that democracy can take hold when the artificial obstacles to it are removed. Far from being the product of unusually propitious circumstances, a free and pluralist system is the "natural order" that will prevail unless something special intervenes;[68] with a bit of support, all countries can become democratic. President Bush devoted a full speech to this subject, saying: "Time after time, observers have questioned whether this country, or that people, or this group, are 'ready' for democracy—as if freedom were a prize you win for meeting our own Western standards of progress. In fact, the daily work of democracy is itself the path of progress."[69] This means that for him, one obvious criticism of the war in Iraq is misguided. While it is true that you cannot force people to be democratic, this is not necessary. All that is needed is to allow people to be democratic.

We would all like this vision to be true, but it probably is not. Even if there are no conditions that are literally necessary for the establishment of democracy, this form of government is not equally likely to flourish under all conditions. Poverty, deep divisions, the fusion of secular and religious authority, militaristic institutions, lack of a democratic tradition and commitment to individualism, and a paucity of attractive careers for defeated politicians all inhibit democracy.[70] Although Bush is at least partly right in arguing that some of these conditions arise out of authoritarian regimes, they are causes as well, and there is no reason to expect the United States to be able to make most countries democratic even if it were to bend all its efforts to this end.

Indeed, movements for reform and democracy may suffer if they are seen as excessively beholden to the United States. As Colin Powell noted after one American attempt of this type had to be abandoned in the face of cries of U.S. bullying, "I think we are now getting a better understanding with the Arab nations that it has to be something that comes from them. If you don't want us to help, you don't want us to help."[71]

Is it even true that the world would be safer and the United States better off if many more countries were democratic? Would the extension of democracy lead to an expansion of the Security Community? Although a full examination of the behavior of democracies is beyond the scope of this book, I doubt that democracy is a panacea. The best-established claim that democracies rarely if ever fight each other is not entirely secure, and the more sophisticated versions of this theory stress that joint democracy will not necessarily produce peace unless other factors, especially economic interdependence and a commitment to human rights, are present as well.[72] This makes sense because democracy is compatible with irreconcilable conflicts of interest. Furthermore, even if well-established democracies do not fight each other, states that are undergoing transitions to democracy do not appear to be similarly pacifistic.[73] Putting these problems aside, there is no reason to expect democracies to be able to get along well with nondemocracies, which means that establishing democracy in Iraq or in any other country would not make the world more peaceful unless its neighbors were similarly transformed.

The Bush administration has also argued that other countries are much more likely to support American foreign policy objectives if they are democratic. The basic point that democracies limit the power of rulers has much to be said for it, but it is far from clear how far this will translate into shared foreign policy goals. After all, at bottom, democracy means that a state's policy will at least roughly reflect the objectives and values of the population, and there is no reason to believe that these should be compatible between one country and another. Why would a democratic Iraq share American views on the Arab–Israeli dispute, for example? Would a democratic Iran be a closer ally than the Shah's regime was? If Pakistan were truly democratic, would it oppose Islamic terrorism? In the spring of 2004 Paul Bremer declared, "Basically Iraq is on track to realize the kind of Iraq that Iraqis want and that Americans want, which is a democratic Iraq."[74] Leaving aside the unwarranted optimism, the assumption that Iraqis and Americans want the same thing is a touching but misplaced faith in universal values and harmony of interests among peoples, and therefore among democratic regimes. Indeed, it now appears that the only possible way for Iraq to be pro-American would be for it to be nondemocratic (although it is likely to end up being both authoritarian and anti-American).[75]

THE SHAPE OF THINGS TO COME?

I regret that in closing I have few firm predictions and confident pre-scriptions. At least one point is clear, however. There is every reason to believe that the Security Community among the leading powers will be maintained. This may be stating the obvious. I doubt if many more readers expect a war among the developed countries than to find the law of gravity repealed. But the fact that we now take the Community for granted, like gravity, does not make it any less important or easier to understand (again like gravity). I discussed the competing explanations and my synthesis in chapter 1, and here want to argue that even the great frictions that have developed because of the divergent American and European reactions to 9/11 will not lead to a return to normal power politics among these countries. Most of the European states badly want to restrain the United States, or gain more influence over it. The United States, especially under Bush, strongly resists these attempts. But no one thinks that the Europeans can or will try to reach these ends through military threats.

It is indeed arguable, as many Europeans and not a few American believe, that the Bush Doctrine represents a bid for hegemony if not empire. In the past, such (over)reaching would have led to the forma-tion of a grand blocking coalition that would have been ready to resort to force. This is inconceivable now. The high costs of war, the gains from staying at peace, and the common values within the Community work together so powerfully that while the Europeans may refuse to cooperate with the United States and use diplomacy to try to thwart it, there are sharp limits to how far the relationship can deteriorate.

This will not change even in the unlikely event that Europe unites. The expansion of the EU and the smaller states' fears of the larger ones, especially France and Germany, inhibit real unity. Greater coordination is of course possible, as is the development of a small, independent Euro-pean expeditionary force. The United States has opposed these moves in the past,[76] and the Bush administration and its friends have argued that a united Europe would hinder American foreign policy and lead to destabilizing rivalry, and therefore should be thwarted.[77] There may then well be increased conflict within the Community, but there is no danger of bloodshed.

Further steps toward European unity could lead to an American military withdrawal from much of Europe, and indeed in any event the United States is likely to move most of its troops out of Germany. Will this make war among the Europeans thinkable again? The American military presence was a necessary condition for the establishment of the Community, guaranteeing as it did that Germany could not turn on its neighbors. As late as 1989–1990, French and British leaders hoped to see Germany remain divided in order to ensure that this peril would not arise. Many Europeans—including Germans—would be made uneasy by the withdrawal of American forces for this reason, but the unease is more likely to produce vigorous attempts by the European countries, and especially Germany, to reassure each other than to set off a spiral of insecurity and fears that would undermine the Community.[78]

IRREVERSIBLE CHANGES

If the Bush Doctrine and the war in Iraq have not broken the Community, they have weakened Western unity and called into question the potency of deterrence, which was a cornerstone of stability during the Cold War. As I argued in chapter 3, there were good reasons to believe that Saddam Hussein could have been deterred even had he developed nuclear weapons. But the leaders of the Bush administration thought otherwise, and their beliefs and willingness to launch a war based on them are now facts. This matters because deterrence rests in part on potential challengers' understanding that the defender has great confidence in its deterrent threats. Now that the United States has shown that it—or at least the Bush administration—lacks faith in the efficacy of deterrence not only against terrorists but also against small states, the use of force against Iraq may not be sufficient to inhibit further challenges. Even if future administrations adopt a different stance and affirm the role of deterrence, some damage may be permanent.

The largely unilateral overthrow of Saddam has set in motion even more important irreversible changes in relations with allies. Before Bush came to power, the emerging consensus was that the United States was committed to multilateralism. This is not to say that it would never act without the consent of its leading allies, but that on major issues it would consult fully, listen carefully, and give significant weight to allies' views.[79] International institutions, deeply ingrained habits, the sense of shared values and interests, close connections at the bureaucratic levels, public support for this way of proceeding, and the understanding that long-run cooperation was necessary and possible only if the allies had faith that the United States would not exploit its superior power position all led to a structure that inhibited American unilateralism. This partial world order, it was argued, served American interests as well as those of its partners because it induced the latter to cooperate with each other and with the United States, reduced needless frictions, and it laid the foundations for prosperity and joint measures to solve common problems. This way of doing business had such deep roots that it could absorb exogenous shocks and the election of new leaders.

Recent events have shown that while the argument may have been correct normatively, it was not correct empirically. Perhaps it would have been wise for the United States to have continued on the multilateral path, to have maintained a broad coalition, and to have given its allies more influence over the way it fought terrorism. But we can now see that it was wrong to conclude that the international system and U.S. policy had evolved to a point that compelled this approach. Even if the many unilateralist measures the United States took before September 11 were not sufficient evidence, the Bush Doctrine and the war in Iraq show that the United States would and could act against the liberal internationalist norms.

This does not mean that the United States is now firmly set on a new course. Indeed, this chapter has argued that the Bush Doctrine cannot be sustained. Despite his reelection, Bush's domestic support rests on the belief that he is making the United States safer, not an endorsement of a wider transformationist agenda. Especially in the absence of a clear political victory in Iraq, support for assertive hegemony is limited at best. But if Bush is forced to retract, it is extremely unlikely that he will revert to the sort of coalition building that Clinton favored. Of course there will be a new president elected in 2008, but even if he or she wanted to pick up where Clinton left off this will not be possible. Although allies would meet the United States more than halfway in their relief that policy had changed, they would realize that the permanence of the new American policy could not be guaranteed. A new 9/11 or a new George Bush could arise in the future; lasting American cooperation simply cannot be assumed. The familiar role of anarchy in limiting the ability of states to bind themselves has been highlighted by Bush's behavior, and will not be forgotten. The basic structural fact of enormous American power and the concomitant possibility for the United States to go off on its own that made Bush's assertive unilateralism an accident waiting to happen will cast a deep shadow over future world politics.

The United States and others, then, face a difficult task. The collapse of the Bush foreign policy will not leave clear ground on which to build. Although the Security Community will remain, new policies and forms of cooperation will have to be jury-rigged above the rubble of the recent past. Having asserted the right (and the duty) to maintain order and provide what it believes to be collective goods, any retraction by America not only will be greeted with initial relief by many, but also is likely to produce disorder, unpredictability, and opportunities for others.

Over 80 years ago, Walter Lippmann famously argued that the public could not act responsibly in politics, and especially in foreign policy, because it was driven by stereotypes and images of the external world that were crude and rigid.[80] There is much to this, but ironically it now applies to large segments of the Republican foreign policy elite more than to the general public. Lippmann's description of how stereotypes do more than conserve our intellectual effort is particularly appropriate and disturbing: "The systems of stereotypes may be the core of our personal tradition, the defenses of our position in society …. They may not be a complete picture of the world, but they are a picture of a possible world to which were we are adapted. In that world people and things have their well-known places, and do certain expected things."[81] Ideologies can provide a comforting way of understanding a complex world and a guide to swift action. But even under the best of circumstances, they are likely to disort, to miss a great deal, and to inhibit adjustment to changing circumstances. When the world is new and confusing, the temptation to rely on stereotypes and ideologies is greatest. But these are just the circumstances under which this pattern in most dangerous.

Machiavelli famously asked whether it is better to be feared or to be loved. The problem for the United States is that it is likely to be neither. Bush's unilateralism and perceived bellicosity weakened the ties to allies, dissipated much of the sympathy that the United States had garnered after 9/11, and convinced many people that America was seeking an empire with little room for their interests or values. It will be hard for any future administration to regain the territory that has been lost. Perhaps if the occupation of Iraq had gone well and if the United States had been able to use this as leverage to pressure and persuade other countries in the region to reform, it might have been productively feared. If the war had been used to broker a settlement between Israel and the Palestinians, the United States might have gained much more support and approval, if not love. But with the failure to establish order and an alternative (and friendly) government in Iraq, these possibilities appear dim.

Bush's policy has left the United States looking neither strong nor benign, and we may find that the only thing worse than a successful hegemon is a failed one. We are headed for a difficult world, one that is not likely to fit any of our ideologies or simple theories.

Notes

Notes to Introduction

1. Frederick Dunn et al., *The Absolute Weapon: Atomic Power and World Order*, edited by Bernard Brodie (New York: Harcourt Brace, 1946; Freeport, N.Y.: Books for Libraries, 1972), p. 52.

2. Psychologists have established what most of us already suspect from examining others (especially those who disagree with us): people systematically are more confident of the validity of their views than they should be, in the sense that they say they have 90 percent confidence in things that are true much less than 90 percent of the time. For a review, see Hillel Einhorn and Robin Hogarth, "Confidence in Judgment: Persistence of the Illusion of Validity," *Psychological Review* 85 (October 1978): 395–416; for a broader analysis, see Philip Tetlock, *Clashing Conceptions of Good Judgment: Cognitive Styles, Biases, and Correctives* (Princeton, N.J.: Princeton University Press, forthcoming, 2005). For a discussion of overconfidence and foreign policy decisions, see Dominic Johnson, *Overconfidence and War: The Havoc and Glory of Positive Illusions* (Cambridge, Mass.: Harvard University Press, 2004).

3. Quoted in Max Rodenbeck, "Islam Confronts Its Demons," *New York Review of Books*, April 29, 2004, p. 16; also see Paul Schroeder, " The War Bin Laden Wanted," *American Conservative*, October 25, 2004, 14–19.

4. See the list presented to the president in Bob Woodward, *Plan of Attack* (New York: Simon & Schuster, 2004), p. 328.

5. Melvyn Leffler analyzes American policy at the start of the Cold War in these terms in his magisterial *A Preponderance of Power: National Security, the Truman Administration, and the Cold War* (Stanford, Calif.: Stanford University Press, 1992).

6. For my own views, see Robert Jervis, "Legacies of the Cold War," *Brown Journal of World Affairs* 2 (Summer 1995): 21–27.

7. John Mearsheimer, *The Tragedy of Great Power Politics* (New York: Norton, 2001); Dale Copeland, *The Origins of Major War* (Ithaca, N.Y.: Cornell University Press, 2000); Eric Labs, "Beyond Victory: Offensive Realism and the Expansion of War Aims," *Security Studies* 6 (Summer 1997): 1–49.

8. For an important discussion of the analytic difficulties created by the fact that we are trying to explain the behavior of actors who are acting according to similar theories, see Erik Gartzke, "War Is in the Error Team," *International Organization*, 53 (Summer 1999): 567–587.

9. See Kenneth Waltz's exchange with Colin Elman in *Security Studies* 6 (Autumn 1996): 7–61.

10. Robert Jervis, *Perception and Misperception in International Politics* (Princeton, N.J.: Princeton University Press, 1976), pp. 128–142; and Irving Janis and Leon Mann, *Decision Making: A Psychological Analysis of Conflict, Choice, and Commitment* (New York: Free Press, 1977).

11. The impact of the scandal was greatly magnified by the existence of photographs that not only provided incontrovertible evidence but, even more important, also were vivid and suitable for television as well as the print media. Similarly, one reason why 9/11 is primarily associated with the attack on the World Trade Center rather than the Pentagon is that we have stunning photographs of the second plane flying into the tower and the subsequent collapses of both towers, whereas the Pentagon did not collapse and there are no pictures of the plane hitting it.

12. For the first two years after the attacks, Bush and his colleagues made no attempt to hide the fact that their attention was focused elsewhere. It was only the politically charged 9/11 hearings that led them to belatedly and unconvincingly deny this. Although the desire to avoid a partisan split led the 9/11 Commission to avoid explicitly assigning responsibility, the text in fact makes clear that the Bush administration did not see terrorism as a high priority and was not perceptually sensitive to evidence of an impending attack: the 9/11 Commission Report, *Final Report of the National Commission on Terrorist Attacks upon the United States* (New York: Norton, 2004), ch. 8. For a good discussion of how this case fits with surprise attacks in general, see Daniel Byman, "Strategic Surprise and the September 11 Attacks: A Review Essay," *Annual Review of Political Science*, vol. 8 (Palo Alto: Annual Reviews, forthcoming 2005); also see chapter 2, note 39.

13. For the relevant literature, see ch. 5, note 35. In the case of the September 11 warnings, it is worth noting that the famous PDB of August 6, like many intelligence documents, was written in a style that minimized its impact; available at www.npr.org/911hearings/pdb.pdf. Although its heading was appropriate—"Bin Laden Determined to Strike in U.S."—its message was blurred in the presentation. The first sentence was "Clandestine, foreign government, and media reports indicate Bin Laden since 1997 has wanted to conduct terrorist attacks in the US." I do not think it is only hindsight that leads me to believe that it should have been "Bin Laden has long sought to stage a major terrorist attack within the U.S. homeland and he is now acquiring the ability to do so." Whether anything could have been done on the basis of such a warning is another question, of course.

Notes to Chapter 1

1. Quoted in Andreas Osiander, *The States System of Europe, 1640–1990* (Oxford: Clarendon Press, 1994), p. 265.

2. Winston Churchill, Cabinet memo, "Cruisers and Parity," July 20, 1927, in Martin Gilbert ed., *Winston S. Churchill*, vol. 5, companion pt. 1, *Documents: The Exchequer Years, 1922–1929* (Boston: Houghton Mifflin, 1981), p. 1033. In 1929 the United States developed a plan for a war with Great Britain growing out of commercial rivalry: "1929 File Reveals War Plan on Britain," *Los Angeles Times*, December 19, 1975.

3. Alexis de Tocqueville, *Democracy in America*, vol. 1 (New York: Vintage Books, [1835] 1945), p. 7.

4. John Mueller, *Retreat from Doomsday: The Obsolescence of Major War* (New York: Basic Books, 1989). Also see Emanuel Adler, "Europe's New Security Order," in Beverly Crawford ed., *The Future of European Security* (Berkeley: Center for German and European Studies, Institute for International and Area Studies, University of California, 1992), pp. 287–326; John S. Duffield, "Transatlantic Relations after the Cold War: Theory, Evidence, and the Future," *International Studies Perspectives* 2 (February

2001): 93–115; James Goldgeier and Michael McFaul, "A Tale of Two Worlds: Core and Periphery in the Post–Cold War Era," *International Organization* 46 (Spring 1992): 467–491; Robert Jervis, "The Future of World Politics: Will It Resemble the Past?" *International Security* 16 (Winter 1991/1992): 39–73; Michael Mandelbaum, "Is Major War Obsolete?" *Survival* 40 (Winter 1998/1999): 20–38; Martin Shaw, *Global Society and International Relations* (Cambridge: Polity Press, 1994); Max Singer and Aaron Wildavsky, *The Real World Order: Zones of Peace/Zones of Turmoil* (Chatham, N.J.: Chatham House, 1993); Richard Ullman, *Securing Europe* (Princeton, N.J.: Princeton University Press, 1991); Stephen Van Evera, "Primed for Peace: Europe after the Cold War," *International Security* 15 (Winter 1990/1991): 7–57; also see the essays by Eliot Cohen, Charles Doran, and Donald Kagan, in "Is Major War Obsolete? An Exchange," *Survival*, 41 (Summer 1999): 139–152. For broader claims about the declining role of violence in the world, see James Payne, *A History of Force* (Sandpoint, Idaho: Lytton, 2004); Paul Schroeder, "Does the History of International Politics Go Anywhere?", in Schroeder, *Systems, Stability, and Statecraft: Essays on the International History of Modern Europe* David Wetzel, Robert Jervis, and Jack Levy, eds. (New York: Palgrave Macmillan, 2004, pp. 267–284); Alexander Wendt, "Why a Worldwide State Is Inevitable," *European Journal of International Relations* 9 (December 2003): 491–542; John Mueller, *The Remnants of War* (Ithaca, N.Y.: Cornell University Press, 2004); K.J. Holsti, *Taming the Sovereigns: Institutional Change in International Politics* (New York: Cambridge University Press, 2004). For a general discussion of the role of great power war in the past, see Jack Levy, *War in the Modern Great Power System* (Lexington: University Press of Kentucky, 1983).

5. Karl W. Deutsch et al., *Political Community and the North Atlantic Area: International Organization in the Light of Historical Experience* (Princeton, N.J.: Princeton University Press, 1957). Also see Emanuel Adler and Michael Barnett, eds., *Security Communities* (New York: Cambridge University Press, 1998); and Matthew Melko, *52 Peaceful Societies* (Oakville, Ont.: Canadian Peace Research Institute Press, 1973).

6. James Eayrs, *In Defence of Canada*, vol. 1, *From the Great War to the Great Depression* (Toronto: University of Toronto Press, 1965), pp. 70–78.

7. Quoted in Martin Gilbert, *Winston S. Churchill*, vol. 6, *Finest Hour 1939–1941* (London: Heinemann, 1983), pp. 860–861. But wars in fact may not settle the disputes, especially in the post–World War II era: see Page Fortna, "Where Have All the Victories Gone? War Outcomes in Historical Perspective," paper presented to the American Political Science Association meeting, Chicago, September 3, 2004.

8. Evan Luard, *War in International Society: A Study in International Sociology* (London: I.B. Tauris, 1986), p. 77.

9. One reason for the difference between my analysis and Mearsheimer's is that he focuses more on the danger of a war with Russia or China. See John Mearsheimer, *The Tragedy of Great Power Politics* (New York: Norton, 2001).

10. Arnold Wolfers, *Discord and Collaboration: Essays on International Politics* (Baltimore: Johns Hopkins University Press, 1962) pp. 73–76.

11. Samuel Huntington, "Why International Primacy Matters," *International Security* 17 (Spring 1993): 68–83; Charles Kupchan, *The End of the American Era* (New York: Knopf, 2002); Kenneth Waltz, "The Emerging Structure of International Politics," *International Security* 18 (Fall 1993): 44–79, and "Structural Realism after the Cold War," *International Security* 25 (Summer 2000): 5–41. There is more ambiguity on this point in David Calleo, *Rethinking Europe's Future* (Princeton, N.J.: Princeton University Press, 2001); Christopher Layne, "US Hegemony and the Perpetuation of NATO," *Journal of Strategic Studies* 23 (September 2000): 59–91; John Mearsheimer, "Back to the Future: Instability in Europe after the Cold War," *International Security* 15 (Summer 1990): 5–56, and *The Tragedy of Great Power Politics*.

12. Layne, "US Hegemony and the Perpetuation of NATO"; "Excerpts from Pentagon's Plan: Prevent the Re-emergence of a New Rival," *New York Times*, March 8, 1992, and Patrick Tyler, "Pentagon Drops Goal of Blocking New Superpowers," *New York Times*, May 24, 1992.

13. For a good discussion of the reasons for and implications of an independent European military force, see Barry Posen, "ESDP and the Structure of World Power," *International Spectator* 39 (January 2004): 5–17; for a broader discussion of ESDP, see Jolyon Howorth, *Saint-Malo Plus Five: An Interim Assessment of EDSP*, Groupment d'Études et de Recherches, Notre Europe, Policy Paper no. 7 (November 2003), available at www.notre-europe.asso.fr/IMG/pdf/policypaper7.pdf. Independent Task Force on European Defence, "European Defence: A Proposal for a White Paper" (Paris: Institute for Security Studies, May 2004).

14. Robert Art, "Why Western Europe Needs the United States and NATO," *Political Science Quarterly* 111 (Spring 1996): 1–39; Mearsheimer, *Tragedy of Great Power Politics*, pp. 385–396.

15. Richard Betts, "Systems of Peace or Causes of War? Collective Security, Arms Control and the New Europe," *International Security* 17 (Summer 1992): 5–43.

16. Less popular in the United States is a neo-Marxist account of the need and possibilities for capitalists in the advanced industrial countries to work together to maintain their positions of dominance—what Karl Kautsky called ultra-imperialism at a time when most Marxists thought that classical imperialism would bring the European countries to fight each other. For discussions, see Stephen Gill, *American Hegemony and the Trilateral Commission* (New York: Cambridge University Press, 1990); Fred Halliday, *Rethinking International Relations* (Vancouver: University of British Columbia Press, 1994), ch. 3; Martin Shaw, *Theory of the Global State: Globality as Unfinished Revolution* (New York: Cambridge University Press, 2000), chs. 6–9; Kees Van der Pijl, *Transnational Classes and International Relations* (New York: Routledge, 1998). Also see Tarak Barkawi and Mark Laffey, "The Imperial Peace: Democracy, Force, and Globalization," *European Journal of International Relations* 5 (December 1999): 403–434.

17. Alexander Wendt, *Social Theory of International Politics* (Cambridge: Cambridge University Press, 1999), here draws on the social-psychological work of Morton Deutsch (*The Resolution of Conflict: Constructive and Destructive Processes* [New Haven, Conn.: Yale University Press, 1973]), which is not as well known to political scientists as it should be. For a discussion of the central role of interactions in politics, see Robert Jervis, *System Effects: Complexity in Political and Social Life* (Princeton, N.J.: Princeton University Press, 1997). The starting place for constructivism in international politics is Hedley Bull, *The Anarchical Society: A Study of Order in World Politics* (New York: Columbia University Press, 1977).

18. Quoted in Stephen Van Evera, "The Cult of the Offensive and the Origins of the First World War," *International Security* 9 (Summer 1984): 27; this article provides a thorough discussion of the relationship between nationalism and war. For a more pessimistic view, see Mearsheimer, "Back to the Future," pp. 20–21, 25.

19. Quoted in Amitava Kumar, "Bristling on the Subcontinent," *The Nation*, April 23, 2001, p. 29; for a counterpart in India, see Amy Waldman, "Among India's Tribes, a Campaign for Hearts and Minds," *New York Times*, April 19, 2004; for a brief general survey, see Kathleen Kennedy Manzo, "Muslim Textbooks Seen as Intolerant," *Education Week*, April 21, 2004, pp. 1, 15.

20. Mary Hampton, "NATO, Germany, and the United States: Creating Positive Identity in Trans-Atlantia," *Security Studies* 8 (Winter 1998/1999): 240–244; Colin Kahl, "Constructing a Separate Peace: Constructivism, Collective Liberal Identity, and Democratic Peace," *Security Studies* 8 (Winter/Spring 1998/1999): 94–144; Thomas Risse-Kappen, "Democratic Peace—Warlike Democracies? A Social Constructivist Interpretation of

the Liberal Argument," *European Journal of International Relations* 1 (1995): 491–517; Margaret Hermann and Charles Kegley, "Rethinking Democracy and International Peace: Perspectives from Political Psychology," *International Studies Quarterly* 39 (December 1995): 511–533; Wendt, *Social Theory of International Politics*, pp. 353–357. Also see Henry Nau, *At Home Abroad: Identity and Power in American Foreign Policy* (Ithaca, N.Y.: Cornell University Press, 2002).

21. Bruce Cronin, *Community under Anarchy: Transnational Identity and the Evolution of Cooperation* (New York: Columbia University Press, 1999); and Karl Deutsch, *Nationalism and Social Communication* (New York: Wiley, 1953).

22. Lars-Erik Cederman ed., *Constructing Europe's Identity: The External Dimension* (Boulder, Colo.: Lynne Rienner, 2001).

23. Badredine Arfi, "Ethnic Fear: The Social Construction of Insecurity," *Security Studies* 8 (Autumn 1998): 151–203.

24. For the growing illegitimacy of conquest, see Tanisha Fazal, "State Death in the International System," *International Organization* 58 (Spring 2004): 311–344; Mark Zacher, "The Territorial Integrity Norm: International Boundaries and the Use of Force," *International Organization* 55 (Spring 2001): 215–250; Anna Simons, "The Death of Conquest," *National Interest*, no. 71 (Spring 2003): 41–49.

25. The best discussion of this kind of learning is Paul Schroeder, *The Transformation of European Politics, 1763–1848* (New York: Oxford University Press, 1994). Note, however, that this refers to the learning that occurred at the end of the Napoleonic Wars, and the fact that this did not lead to a permanent security community can be read as a cautionary tale. Also see Schroeder, "Does the History of International Politics Go Anywhere?"

26. In fact Wendt's analysis relies heavily on changed material circumstances, in contradiction to his theoretical formulation: *Social Theory of International Politics*, pp. 343–366.

27. Dennis Wrong, *Skeptical Sociology* (New York: Columbia University Press, 1976).

28. Bruce Russett and John Oneal, *Triangulating Peace: Democracy, Interdependence, and International Organizations* (New York: Norton, 2001).

29. The literature is voluminous: for good discussions see James Lee Ray, *Democracy and International Conflict: An Evaluation of the Democratic Peace Proposition* (Columbia: University of South Carolina Press, 1995), and "Does Democracy Cause Peace?" in *Annual Review of Political Science*, vol. 1 (Palo Alto, Calif.: Annual Reviews, 1998); Bruce Russett, *Grasping the Democratic Peace: Principles for a Post–Cold War World* (Princeton, N.J.: Princeton University Press, 1993); Russett and Oneal, *Triangulating Peace*, chs. 2–3; Dan Reiter and Allan Stam, *Democracies at War* (Princeton, N.J.: Princeton University Press, 2002). David Rousseau, *Democracy and War: Institutions, Norms, and the Evolution of International Conflict* (Stanford: Stanford University Press, 2005); Paul Huth and Todd Allee, *The Democratic Peace and Territorial Conflict in the Twentieth Century* (New York: Cambridge University Press, 2003). For critiques see Joanne Gowa, *Ballots and Bullets: The Elusive Democratic Peace* (Princeton, N.J.: Princeton University Press, 1999); David Mares, *Violent Peace: Militarized Interstate Bargaining in Latin America* (New York: Columbia University Press, 2001), ch. 4; Sebastian Rosato, "The Flawed Logic of Democratic Peace Theory," *American Political Science Review* 97 (November 2003): 585–602; Erik Gartzke, "The Futility of War: Capitalism and Common Interests as Determinants of the Democratic Peace," unpublished MS, Columbia University. Other scholars argue that the benign behavior is a product not of the broad category of democracy, but of the subset of behaviors that are liberal and/or mature: John Owen, *Liberal Peace, Liberal War: American Politics and International Security* (Ithaca, N.Y.: Cornell University Press, 1997); Edward Mansfield and Jack Snyder, "Democratization and the Danger of War," *International Security* 20 (Summer 1995): 5–38, and *Electing to Fight: Why Emerging Democracies Go*

To War (Cambridge, Mass.: MIT Press, 2005); Michael Ward and Kristian Gleditsch, "Democratizing for Peace," *American Political Science Review* 92 (March 1998): 51–62.

30. For the latest exchange see Donald Green, Soo Yeon Kim, and David Yoon, "Dirty Pool," *International Organization* 55 (Spring 2001): 441–468; Russett and Oneal, *Triangulating Peace*; Nathaniel Beck and Jonathan N. Katz, "Throwing the Baby Out with the Bath Water: A Comment on Green, Kim, and Yoon," *International Organization* 55 (Spring 2001): 487–496; and Gary King, "Proper Nouns and Methodological Propriety: Pooling Dyads in International Relations Data," *International Organization* 55 (Spring 2001): 497–507.

31. Jack Levy, "Domestic Politics and War," in Robert Rotberg and Theodore Rabb, eds., *The Origin and Prevention of Major Wars* (Cambridge: Cambridge University Press, 1989), p. 88.

32. Ralph White, "Why Aggressors Lose," *Political Psychology* 11 (June 1990): 227–242; but see the discussion of the intelligence failure in Iraq in chapter 5 of this volume and Chaim Kaufmann, "Threat Inflation Failure of the Marketplace of Ideas: The Selling of the Iraq War," *International Security* 29 (Summer 2004): 5–48.

33. James Fearon, "Domestic Political Audiences and the Escalation of International Disputes," *American Political Science Review* 88 (September 1994): 577–592; Kenneth Schultz, *Democracy and Coercive Diplomacy* (New York: Cambridge University Press, 2001); Kristopher Ramsay, "Politics at the Water's Edge: Crisis Bargaining and Electoral Competition," *Journal of Conflict Resolution*, 48 (August 2004): 459–486. For qualifications and doubts, see Bernard Finel and Kristin Lord, eds., *Power and Conflict in the Age of Transparency* (New York: Palgrave, 2000).

34. Bruce Bueno de Mesquita, James Morrow, Randolph Siverson, and Alastair Smith, "An Institutional Explanation of the Democratic Peace," *American Political Science Review* 93 (December 1999): 791–807; Bueno de Mesquita, Smith, Siverson, and Morrow, *The Logic of Political Survival* (Cambridge, Mass.: MIT Press, 2003); Hein Goemans, *War and Punishment: The Causes of War Termination and the First World War* (Princeton, N.J.: Princeton University Press, 2000). A related argument is Jack Snyder, *Myths of Empire: Domestic Politics and International Ambition* (Ithaca, N.Y.: Cornell University Press, 1991).

35. David Lake, "Powerful Pacifists: Democratic States and War," *American Political Science Review* 86 (March 1992): 24–37; Reiter and Stam, *Democracies at War*; Stephen Biddle and Stephen Long, "Democracy and Military Effectiveness: A Deeper Look," *Journal of Conflict Resolution*, 48 (August 2004): 525–546.

36. But not all: Rudolph Rummel, "Democracies ARE Less Warlike Than Other Regimes," *European Journal of International Relations* 1 (March 1995): 457–479.

37. For Russett's discussion of what he deems an "important anomaly," see his *Grasping the Democratic Peace*, pp. 120–124; for a rebuttal see Mares, *Violent Peace*, pp. 102–104.

38. Gabriel Almond, *The American People and Foreign Policy* (New York: Harcourt Brace, 1950); Walter Lippmann, *Essays in the Public Philosophy* (Boston: Little, Brown, 1955).

39. William Thompson, "Democracy and Peace: Putting the Cart before the Horse?" *International Organization* 50 (Winter 1996): 141–174.

40. Henry Farber and Joanne Gowa, "Polities and Peace," *International Security* 20 (Fall 1995): 123–146, and "Common Interests or Common Polities?" *Journal of Politics* 59 (May 1997): 123–146. Also see Miriam Elman, ed., *Paths to Peace: Is Democracy the Answer?* (Cambridge, Mass.: MIT Press, 1997); and Christopher Layne, "Kant or Cant: The Myth of the Democratic Peace," *International Security* 19 (Fall 1994): 5–49.

41. For this and related issues, see Erik Gartzke, "Kant We All Get Along? Motive, Opportunity, and the Origins of the Democratic Peace," *American Journal of Political Science* 42, no. 1 (1998): 1–27, and "Preferences and Democratic Peace," *International Studies Quarterly* 44 (June 2000): 191–212; Zeev Maoz, "The Controversy over the Democratic

Peace: Rearguard Action or Cracks in the Wall?" *International Security* 22 (Summer 1997): 162–198; Russett and Oneal, *Triangulating Peace*; Randall Schweller, "Democracy and the Post–Cold War Era," in Birthe Hansen and Bertel Heurlin, eds., *The New World Order* (New York: St. Martin's Press, 2000).

42. Most scholars take the latter view, but that does not mean this is what most versions of the theory actually imply.

43. Alexander Wendt, "Collective Identity Formation and the International State," *American Political Science Review* 88 (June 1994): 384–396; Wendt, *Social Theory of International Politics*, pp. 344–349. Earlier functional theorists of integration argued similarly: Jennifer Sterling-Folker, "Competing Paradigms or Birds of a Feather? Constructivism and Neoliberal Institutionalism Compared," *International Studies Quarterly* 44 (March 2000): 106–107.

44. Quoted in Kenneth Bourne, *The Foreign Policy of Victorian England, 1830–1902* (Oxford: Clarendon Press, 1970), p. 85. For a general treatment of Cobden's views, see Peter Cain, "Capitalism, War, and Internationalism in the Thought of Richard Cobden," *British Journal of International Studies* 5 (October 1979): 229–247. The best-known statement is of course Norman Angell, *The Great Illusion*, 3rd rev. and enl. ed. (New York: G.P. Putnam's Sons, 1911), although it is important to note that he believed that interdependence made war self-defeating, not impossible. See J.D.B. Miller, *Norman Angell and the Futility of War: Peace and the Public Mind* (Houndmills, U.K.: Macmillan, 1986). Also interesting is Frank Russell, *Theories of International Relations* (New York: Appleton-Century, 1936), ch. 23. For the recent correlating evidence, see Susan McMillan, "Interdependence and Conflict," *Mershon International Studies Review* 41, supp. 1 (May 1997): 33–58; Edward Mansfield and Brian Pollins, eds., *Economic Interdependence and International Conflict* (Ann Arbor: University of Michigan Press, 2003); Katherine Barbieri, *The Liberal Illusion: Does Trade Promote Peace?* (Ann Arbor: University of Michigan Press, 2002); Patrick McDonald, "Peace through Trade or Free Trade?" *Journal of Conflict Resolution* 48 (August 2004): 547–572; Russett and Oneal, *Triangulating Peace*, ch. 4; and Erik Gartzke, "Interdependence Really Is Complex," unpublished MS, Columbia University. For arguments that interdependence has been exaggerated and misunderstood, see Kenneth Waltz, "The Myth of National Interdependence," in Charles Kindleberger, ed., *The International Corporation* (Cambridge, Mass.: MIT Press, 1970), pp. 205–223, *Theory of International Politics* (Reading, Mass.: Addison-Wesley, 1979), ch. 7, and "Globalization and Governance," *PS: Political Science and Politics* 32 (December 1999): 693–700. For a discussion of the effect of war on the economies of neutrals, see Eugene Gholz and Daryl Press, "The Effects of Wars on Neutral Countries: Why It Doesn't Pay to Preserve the Peace," *Security Studies* 10 (Summer 2001): 1–57. Most traditional liberal thinking and the rest of my brief discussion assume symmetry; as Albert Hirschman, *National Power and the Structure of Foreign Trade* (Berkeley and Los Angeles: University of California Press, 1945), showed, asymmetric dependence can provide the basis for exploitative bargaining.

45. Hull's views, although not the phrase, can be found in Cordell Hull, *The Memoirs of Cordell Hull*, vol. 1 (New York: Macmillan, 1948), pp. 355, 363–365.

46. "The Foreign Economic Policy of the State Department," *Department of State Bulletin* 12 (May 27, 1945): 979.

47. Klaus Knorr, *On the Uses of Military Power in the Nuclear Age* (Princeton, N.J.: Princeton University Press, 1966); Richard Rosecrance, *The Rise of the Trading State: Commerce and Conquest in the Modern World* (New York: Basic Books, 1986), and *The Rise of the Virtual State: Wealth and Power in the Coming Century* (New York: Basic Books, 1999).

48. But for evidence that bad relations do not necessarily impede trade, see Katherine Barbieri and Jack Levy, "Sleeping with the Enemy: The Impact of War on Trade," *Journal of Peace Research* 36 (July 1999): 463–479.

49. Helen Milner, *Resisting Protectionism: Global Industries and the Politics of International Trade* (Princeton, N.J.: Princeton University Press, 1988); and Rosecrance, *The Rise of the Trading State*, ch. 7.

50. See, e.g., Scott James and David Lake, "The Second Face of Hegemony: Britain's Repeal of the Corn Laws and the American Walker Tariff of 1846," *International Organization* 43 (Winter 1989): 1–30; and Milner, *Resisting Protectionism*.

51. Quoted in Volker Berghahn, *Germany and the Approach of War in 1914* (New York: St. Martin's Press, 1973), p. 97. For the importance of honor as a cause of war throughout history, see Donald Kagan, *On the Origins of War and the Preservation of Peace* (New York: Doubleday, 1995).

52. Albert Hirschman, *The Passions and the Interests: Political Arguments for Capitalism before Its Triumph* (Princeton, N.J.: Princeton University Press, 1977), and *Rival Views of Market Society and Other Recent Essays* (New York: Viking, 1986), chs. 3 and 5; and Joseph Schumpeter, *The Theory of Economic Development* (Cambridge, Mass.: Harvard University Press, 1934).

53. Peter Liberman, *Does Conquest Pay? The Exploitation of Occupied Industrial Societies* (Princeton, N.J.: Princeton University Press, 1996); also see Mearsheimer, *Tragedy of Great Power Politics*, pp. 148–152. For a partial rebuttal see Stephen Brooks, "The Globalization of Production and the Changing Benefits of Conquest," *Journal of Conflict Resolution* 43 (October 1999): 646–670.

54. Dale Copeland, "Economic Interdependence and War: A Theory of Trade Expectations," *International Security* 20 (Spring 1996): 5–42, and "Trade Expectations and the Outbreak of Peace: Détente 1970–74 and the End of the Cold War 1985–91," *Security Studies* 9 (Autumn 1999/Winter 2000): 15–58.

55. Norrin Ripsman and Jean-Marc Blanchard, "Commercial Liberalism under Fire: Evidence from 1914 and 1936," *Security Studies* 6 (Winter 1996/1997): 4–51.

56. Barbieri and Levy, "Sleeping with the Enemy"; Robert Keohane, "Governance in a Partially Globalized World," *American Political Science Review* 95 (March 2001): 1; Waltz, "The Myth of National Interdependence" and *Theory of International Politics*.

57. Russett and Oneal, *Triangulating Peace*, p. 136.

58. Joanne Gowa, *Allies, Adversaries, and International Trade* (Princeton, N.J.: Princeton University Press, 1994).

59. Quoted in Paul Kennedy, *The Rise of Anglo-German Antagonism, 1860–1914* (Boston: George Allen & Unwin, 1980), p. 315; but also see Liberman, "Trading with the Enemy."

60. We tend to lose sight of the linked role of American pressure and the European belief that uniting was the only way to resist the United States: see Mark Sheetz, "Continental Drift: Franco-German Relations and the Shifting Premises of European Security," unpublished dissertation, Department of Political Science, Columbia University, 2002; Marc Trachtenberg, ed., *Between Empire and Alliance: America and Europe during the Cold War* (Lanham, MD: Rowman & Littlefield, 2003).

61. Russett and Oneal, *Triangulating Peace*, ch. 5.

62. Robert Keohane, *After Hegemony: Cooperation and Discord in the World Political Economy* (Princeton, N.J.: Princeton University Press, 1984). Much of the literature is summarized in Lisa Martin and Beth Simmons, "Theories and Empirical Studies of International Institutions," *International Organization* 52 (Autumn 1998): 729–757.

63. Robert Jervis, "Neorealism, Neoliberalism, and Cooperation: Understanding the Debate," *International Security* 24 (Summer 1999): 42–63, and "Correspondence: Institutionalized Disagreement," *International Security* 27 (Summer 2002): 174–177; James March and Johan Olsen, "The Institutional Dynamics of International Political Orders," *International Organization* 52 (Autumn 1998): 943–969.

64. Although we identify this factor as new, in 1947 the British scholar Harold Laski declared that "America bestrides the world like a colossus; neither Rome at the height

of its power nor Great Britain in the period of its economic supremacy enjoyed an influence so direct, so profound, or so pervasive." "America—1947," *The Nation*, December 13, 1947, p. 641. For discussions of current and future American hegemony, see William Odom and Robert Dujarric, *America's Inadvertent Empire* (New Haven, Conn.: Yale University Press, 2004); Mark Sheetz, "Debating the Unipolar Moment," *International Security* 22 (Winter 1997/1998): 168–172; William Wohlforth, "The Stability of the Unipolar World," *International Security* 24 (Summer 1999): 5–41; and Kenneth Waltz, "The Emerging Structure of World Politics," *International Security* 18 (Fall 1993): 44–79, and "Structural Realism after the Cold War." In an exception to the propensity for liberals to ignore the possible pacifying effects of hegemony, Russett and Oneal (*Triangulating Peace*, pp. 184–191) propose a rebuttal by looking at earlier eras, but these are not comparable to the current situation.

65. Jacek Kugler and Douglas Lemke, eds., *Parity and War: Evaluations and Extensions of The War Ledger* (Ann Arbor: University of Michigan Press, 1996); George Modelski, *Long Cycles in World Politics* (Seattle: University of Washington Press, 1987); A.F.K. Organski and Jacek Kugler, *The War Ledger* (Chicago: University of Chicago Press, 1980); William Thompson, *On Global War: Historical-Structural Approaches to World Politics* (Columbia: University of South Carolina Press, 1988). In his epilogue Robert Gilpin (*War and Change in World Politics* [Cambridge: Cambridge University Press, 1981]) discusses the reasons why future hegemonic transitions might be carried out peacefully.

66. The literature on this subject is very large. My analysis on the stabilizing effects of nuclear weapons is Robert Jervis, *The Meaning of the Nuclear Revolution* (Ithaca, N.Y.: Cornell University Press, 1989). Interestingly enough, John Herz, one of the leading exponents of the security dilemma and of postwar American realism, argued that nuclear weapons could buy time until the superpowers established something akin to a world government; see his *International Politics in the Atomic Age* (New York: Columbia University Press, 1959), especially chs. 11 and 12. For a discussion of how nuclear weapons influenced the thought of major Realist thinkers, see Campbell Craig, *Glimmer of a New Leviathan* (New York: Columbia University Press, 2003).

67. Glenn Snyder, "The Balance of Power and the Balance of Terror," in Paul Seabury, ed., *The Balance of Power* (San Francisco: Chandler, 1965), pp. 184–201; also see Jervis, *Meaning of the Nuclear Revolution*, pp. 19–23, 74–106.

68. The same logic applies to the indeterminate effect of the high costs of damaging relations that is a consequence of economic interdependence, but only in attenuated form. Relations are bad when two states confront one another with nuclear weapons, but they are likely to be good under conditions of interdependence, which means that the threat to sever ties will harm relations and decrease economic activity. Thus, even if the state prevails by using coercive tactics, it will pay a price for doing so. For related arguments, see Erik Gartzke, Quan Li, and Charles Boehmer, "Investing in the Peace: Economic Interdependence and International Conflict," *International Organization* 55 (Spring 2001): 391–438; and James Morrow, "How Could Trade Affect Conflict?" *Journal of Peace Research* 36, no. 4 (1999): 481–489.

69. Robert Jervis, "Cooperation under the Security Dilemma," *World Politics* 30 (January 1978): 167–214; Stephen Van Evera, *Causes of War: Power and the Roots of Conflict* (Ithaca, N.Y.: Cornell University Press, 1999); but also see Kier Lieber, *Offense–Defense Theory and the Prospects for Peace* (Ithaca, N.Y.: Cornell University Press, forthcoming).

70. Arie M. Kacowicz, *Zones of Peace in the Third World: South America and West Africa in Comparative Perspective* (Albany: State University of New York Press, 1998), ch. 2, finds satisfaction with the status quo responsible for peace in several areas outside the Security Community.

71. Joseph Grieco, *Cooperation among Nations: Europe, America, and Non-Tariff Barriers to Trade* (Ithaca, N.Y.: Cornell University Press, 1990); Michael Mastanduno, "Do Relative Gains Matter? America's Response to Japanese Industrial Policy," *International Security* 16 (Summer 1991): 73–113.

72. Mueller, *Retreat from Doomsday.*

73. Quoted in William Henry Harbaugh, *The Life and Times of Theodore Roosevelt* (New York: Collier Books, 1961), p. 99.

74. For a discussion of homogeneous and heterogeneous systems, see Raymond Aron, *Peace and War: A Theory of International Relations*, translated by Richard Howard and Annette Fox (Garden City, N.Y.: Doubleday, 1966), pp. 99–124, 373–403; and Stanley Hoffmann, "International Systems and International Law," in Klaus Knorr and Sidney Verba, eds., *The International System: Theoretical Essays* (Princeton, N.J.: Princeton University Press, 1961), pp. 207–209. For evidence of the central role of common values in relations between individuals and groups, see Milton Rokeach and Louis Mezei, "Race and Shared Belief as Factors in Social Choice," *Science* 151 (January 14, 1966): 167–172.

75. Paul Diehl, ed., *A Road Map to War: Territorial Dimensions of International Conflict* (Nashville, Tenn.: Vanderbilt University Press, 1999); Paul Hensel, "Territory: Theory and Evidence on Geography and Conflict," in John Vasquez, ed., *What Do We Know about War?* (Lanham, Md.: Rowman & Littlefield, 2000), pp. 57–84; Paul Huth, *Standing Your Ground: Territorial Disputes and International Conflict* (Ann Arbor: University of Michigan Press, 1996), and "Territory: Why Are Territorial Disputes between States a Central Cause of International Conflict?" in Vasquez, *What Do We Know about War?* pp. 85–110; Kacowicz, *Zones of Peace in the Third World*; John Vasquez, *The War Puzzle* (New York: Cambridge University Press, 1993); Mark Zacher, "The Territorial Integrity Norm: International Boundaries and the Use of Force," *International Organization* 55 (Spring 2001): 215–250.

76. Ronald Inglehart, *The Silent Revolution: Changing Values and Political Styles among Western Publics* (Princeton, N.J.: Princeton University Press, 1977), and *Modernization and Postmodernization: Cultural, Economic, and Political Change in 43 Societies* (Princeton, N.J.: Princeton University Press, 1997).

77. Jervis, "The Future of World Politics," p. 55; Mueller, *Retreat from Doomsday*, chs. 10–11; Wendt, *Social Theory of International Politics*, pp. 310–312. The movement toward women's rights and the tolerance of diversity has waned as well as waxed in many parts of the world, however, especially within Muslim countries.

78. For a general discussion of interaction and feedbacks, see Jervis, *System Effects.*

79. Andrew Hurrell, "An Emerging Security Community in South America?" in Emanuel Adler and Michael Barnett, eds., *Security Communities* (New York: Cambridge University Press, 1998); Kacowicz, *Zones of Peace in the Third World*; Mares, *Violent Peace*; Felix Martin-Gonzalez, "The Longer Peace in South America, 1935–1995," Ph.D. dissertation, Department of Political Science, Columbia University. For general discussions of the changing incidence and nature of war, see K.J. Holsti, *The State, War, and the State of War* (New York: Cambridge University Press, 1996); Stuart Kaufman, "The End of Anarchy: The Society of Nations, Institutions, and the Decline of War," paper presented at the 2001 Annual Meeting of the International Studies Association, Chicago; and John Mueller, *Remnants of War.*

80. Charles Tilly, *Coercion, Capital, and European States, AD 990–1990* (Cambridge, Mass.: Blackwell, 1990), p. 74.

81. See the statements of European and American leaders in Patrick Tyler, "As Cold War Link Itself Grows Cold, Europe Seems to Lose Value for Bush," *New York Times*, February 12, 2003; for an account of European-American disputes over Iraq, see Philip Gordon and

Jeremy Shapiro, *Allies at War: America, Europe, and the Crisis over Iraq* (New York: McGraw-Hill, 2004).

82. Paul Schroeder, "Historical Reality vs. Neo-Realist Theory," *International Security* 19 (Summer 1994): 108–148.

83. The phrase was coined by Samuel Huntington, but his policy prescriptions are aimed at having the United States avoid this outcome by refraining from imposing its values and culture on others.

84. See Robert Pape, "Soft Balancing against the United States," unpublished paper, University of Chicago; Jeremy Pressman, "If Not Balancing, What? Forms of Resistence to American Hegemony," Belfer Center for Science and International Affairs Discussion Paper 2004-02, Kennedy School of Government, Harvard University, March 2004. Also see Ethan Kapstein and Michael Mastanduno, eds., *Unipolar Politics: Realism and State Strategies after the Cold War* (New York: Columbia University Press, 1999); G. John Ikenberry, ed., *America Unrivaled: The Future of the Balance of Power* (Ithaca, N.Y.: Cornell University Press, 2002); Ikenberry, "Strategic Reactions to American Preeminence: Great Power Politics in the Age of Unipolarity," unpublished paper, Georgetown University, July 2003; Peter Lieberman, "Ties That Blind: Will Germany and Japan Rely Too Much on the United States?" *Security Studies* 10 (Winter 2000/2001): 98–138; and Joseph Joffe, "How America Does It," *Foreign Affairs* 76 (September/October 1996). Jack Levy argues that in the past, balancing was automatic only against land powers, not sea powers, and this may have obvious relevance today: "Balances and Balancing: Concepts, Propositions, and Research Design," in John Vasquez and Colin Elman, eds., *Realism and the Balancing of Power: A New Debate* (Upper Saddle River, N.J.: Prentice Hall, 2003), pp. 128–153.

Of course much may depend on America's behavior, particularly whether it follows a policy of selective engagement and maintains the role of an offshore balancer or intervenes more frequently and directly. See, for example, Robert Art, *A Grand Strategy for America* (Ithaca, N.Y.: Cornell University Press, 2003); Mearsheimer, *Tragedy of Great Power Politics*; and Christopher Layne, "The 'Poster Child for Offensive Realism': America as a Global Hegemon," *Security Studies* 12 (Winter 2002/2003): 120–164.

85. Robert Keohane and Joseph Nye, eds., *Power and Interdependence: World Politics in Transition* (Boston: Little, Brown, 1977).

86. See, for example, Marc Busch, *Trade Warriors: States, Firms, and Strategic Policy in High Technology* (New York: Cambridge University Press, 1999); Paul Krugman, *Rethinking International Trade* (Cambridge, Mass.: MIT Press, 1990).

87. For a related debate about the fungibility of military power, see Robert Art, "American Foreign Policy and the Fungibility of Force," *Security Studies* 5 (Summer 1996): 7–42, and "Force and Fungibility Reconsidered," *Security Studies* 8 (Summer 1999): 183–189; and David Baldwin, "Force, Fungibility, and Influence," *Security Studies* 8 (Summer 1999): 173–182.

88. Philip Cerny, "Plurilateralism: Structural Differentiation and Functional Conflict in the Post–Cold War World Order," *Millennium* 22 (Spring 1992): 27–51; Ronnie Lipschutz, *After Authority: War, Peace, and Global Politics in the 21st Century* (Albany: State University of New York Press, 2000); Osiander, *The States System of Europe*; James Rosenau, *Turbulence in World Politics: A Theory of Change and Continuity* (Princeton, N.J.: Princeton University Press, 1990); Martin van Creveld, *The Rise and Decline of the State* (New York: Cambridge University Press, 1999). For a discussion of how the changed environment will affect state structures and strength, see Michael Desch, "War and Strong States, Peace and Weak States?" *International Organization* 50 (Spring 1996): 237–268; for the pre–Civil War United States, see Daniel Deudney, "The Philadelphian

System: Sovereignty, Arms Control, and Balance of Power in the American States-Union, circa 1787–1861," Ibid. 49 (Spring 1995): 191–228.

89. Keohane, "Governance in a Partially Globalized World."
90. See, for example, G. John Ikenberry, *After Victory: Institutions, Strategic Restraint, and the Rebuilding of Order after Major Wars* (Princeton, N.J.: Princeton University Press, 2001); John G. Ruggie, *Winning the Peace: America and World Order in the New Era* (New York: Columbia University Press, 1996); and John Steinbruner, *Principles of Global Security* (Washington, D.C.: Brookings Institution Press, 2000).
91. Art, "Why Western Europe Needs the United States and NATO."
92. Waltz, "Globalization and Governance" and "Structural Realism after the Cold War"; Layne, "US Hegemony and the Perpetuation of NATO."
93. Mueller, *Retreat from Doomsday*; Payne, *History of Force*.
94. Gilpin, *War and Change in World Politics*; Paul Kennedy, *Rise and Fall of the Great Powers: Economic Change and Military Conflict from 1500 to 2000* (New York: Vintage, 1989).
95. Kugler and Lemke, *Parity and War*; Organski and Kugler, *The War Ledger*. Also see Modelski, *Long Cycles in World Politics*.

Notes to Chapter 2

1. The most plausible argument that September 11 has strengthened the case for missile defense has not been widely made: it would increase the credibility of the threat to attack states that both possess weapons of mass destruction and harbor terrorists.
2. See, for example, Robert Kagan and William Kristol, eds., *Present Dangers: Crisis and Opportunity in American Foreign and Defense Policy* (San Francisco: Encounter Books, 2000); also see the Defense Guidance drafted by Paul Wolfowitz for Secretary of Defense Cheney at the end of the George H.W. Bush administration and discussed in chapter 4.
3. See, for example, Mary Dudziak, ed., *September 11 in History: A Watershed Moment?* (Durham, N.C.: Duke University Press, 2003); Eric Hershberg and Kevin Moore, eds., *Critical Views of September 11: Analyses from around the World* (New York: New Press, 2002). For a good review of some of this literature see Lisa Anderson, "Shock and Awe: Interpretations of the Events of September 11," *World Politics*, 56 (January 2004): 305–325. It might be fair to ask whether my own views have changed in the wake of September 11. In one way they clearly have—as I will note, I did not expect it to lead to such a drastic change in U.S. policy, and so it has challenged my understanding of U.S., if not of international, politics. My policy preferences have altered much less. The attacks did convince me that I had not taken terrorism seriously enough and that stronger measures were needed to deal with it, but they did not change my general support for working with allies and selective engagement rather than the assertive hegemony that Bush has pursued and that subsequent chapters will explore.
4. I have discussed several dynamics like this in Robert Jervis, *System Effects: Complexity in Political and Social Life* (Princeton, N.J.: Princeton University Press, 1997), ch. 6.
5. Quoted in Joseph Kahn, "The World's Economies Slide Together into Recession," *New York Times*, November 25, 2001.
6. The Bush administration's rejection of deterrence goes beyond terrorism, however. Even before September 11, the president advocated the deployment of missile defense because "rogue" states could not be deterred, and as I will discuss in the next chapter, the overthrow of Saddam Hussein rested on the premise that threats could not be sufficient to keep his behavior within acceptable bounds. The doctrine of preventive war, analyzed in chapter 4, also rejects deterrence. A recent academic critique of deterrence that shares the administration's perspective is Keith Payne, *The Fallacies of*

Cold War Deterrence and a New Direction (Lexington: University Press of Kentucky, 2001). Partly because of these views, Payne served in the Bush administration Department of Defense.

7. Gregory Mitrovich, *Undermining the Kremlin: America's Strategy to Subvert the Soviet Bloc, 1947–1956* (Ithaca, N.Y.: Cornell University Press, 2000).

8. David Rhoad, "On Paper Scraps, Talk of Judgment Day and Words to Friends at Home," *New York Times*, November 24, 2001.

9. Once established, however, al-Qaeda cells can operate without central facilities, although they have to operate differently. See Paul Pillar, "Counterterrorism after Al-Qaeda," *Washington Quarterly* 27 (Summer 2004): 101–113.

10. It can be argued that this stance, and the attack against Afghanistan, will weaken states by ignoring their sovereignty and perhaps opening the door to other modifications of this cornerstone of the state system. But sovereignty always has been complex, flexible, and pragmatic. See Stephen Krasner, *Sovereignty: Organized Hypocrisy* (Princeton, N.J.: Princeton University Press, 1999). For arguments that September 11 and the reactions to it show the continuing validity of established conceptual frameworks, see Colin Gray, "World Politics as Usual after September 11: Realism Vindicated," in Ken Booth and Tim Dubbe, eds., *Worlds in Collision: Terror and the Future of Global Order* (New York: Palgrave Macmillan, 2002), pp. 226–234; and Kenneth Waltz, "The Continuity of International Politics," in Booth and Dubbe, eds., *Worlds in Collision*, pp. 348–353.

11. This is why Samuel Huntington's *The Clash of Civilizations and the Remaking of World Order* (New York: Simon & Schuster, 1996), far from proclaiming the superiority of the West and calling for the Westernization of the world, calls for toleration of different cultures and decries the West's attempts to force its values and way of life on others. Interfering in other cultures is a recipe for greatly increasing conflict to no good end.

12. Quoted in Douglas Jehl, "Democracy's Uneasy Steps in Islamic World," *New York Times*, November 23, 2001. Also see Serge Schmemann, "U.N. Gets a Litany of Antiterror Plans," *New York Times*, January 12, 2002; and Neil MacFarquhar, "Syria Repackages Its Repression of Muslim Militants as Antiterror Lesson," *New York Times*, January 14, 2002.

13. "President Bush Discusses Progress in the War on Terror," "White House Press Release, July 12, 2004, p. 2; Douglas Jehl, "U.S. Sees no Basis to Prosecute Iranian Opposition 'Terror' Group being held in Iraq," *New York Times*, July 27, 2004. A brief but good discussion arguing that democracy would not end Islamic terrorism is Marina Ottaway and Thomas Carothers, "Middle East Democracy," *Foreign Policy* no.145 (November/December 2004): 28.

14. Rowan Scarborough, "'This Is War,' Rumsfeld Told Bush," *Washington Times*, February 23, 2004.

15. See Michael Howard, "What's in a Name? How to Fight Terrorism," *Foreign Affairs* 81 (January/February 2002): 8–13; Ronald Spiers, "How Do You Know When You Win?" *Rutland Herald*, March 23, 2004; Philip Heymann, *Terrorism, Freedom and Security: Winning without War* (Cambridge, Mass.: MIT Press, 2003). For a contrary view, see John Lynn, *Battle: A History of Combat and Culture* (Boulder, Colo.: Westview, 2003), which argues that "a prime reason to define terrorism as war is to impose some restraints on the campaigns against terrorism."

16. Quoted in James Bennet, "Israeli Soldier Killed in Gaza; Nablus Mourns a Hamas Leader," *New York Times*, November 25, 2001.

17. Quoted in William Safire, "Israel or Arafat," *New York Times*, December 3, 2001. Also see the remarks quoted in James Bennet, "Israelis Storm Village in the West Bank," *New York Times*, October 25, 2001, and "15 Israelis Die in Bus Attack," *New York Times*, December 3, 2001.

18. Quoted in James Bennet, "New Clashes in Gaza; Hamas to Limit Suicide Attacks," *New York Times*, December 22, 2001.

19. Rachel Swarms, "West's Envoys Unhappy, Find Zimbabwe Unhelpful," *New York Times*, November 24, 2001. Also see Tony Hawkins, "Harare to Hold Talks Today on Sanctions Threat," *Financial Times*, December 17, 2001.

20. Quoted in "President's Words: 'Lift This Dark Threat,'" *New York Times*, November 7, 2001. A possible middle ground is that while the war is not against only al-Qaeda, neither is it against all terror. Instead, it is against "militant" or "extremist" Islam. See, for example, Eliot Cohen, "World War IV," *Wall Street Journal*, November 20, 2001; Anonymous (Michael Scheuer), *Imperial Hubris: Why the West Is Losing the War on Terror* (Dulles, Va: Brassey's, 2004). This makes some sense, in terms of the identification of the enemy, but still does not tell us whether it is useful to consider this a war. Vice President Cheney said that "our strategy in the war on terror is based on a clear understanding of the enemy," but did not go on to explain who the enemy was; "Vice President's Remarks on War on Terror at AEI," White House Press Release, Office of the Vice President, July 24, 2003.

21. See David Sanger, "As the Battlefield Changes, So Does the War Itself," *New York Times*, December 23, 2001, sec. 4, p. 3; Serge Schmemann, "Caution: This Weapon May Backfire," *New York Times*, December 30, 2001, sec. 4, p. 1. In response to a particularly bloody attack on Indian soldiers and their families in Kashmir, the assistant secretary of state for South Asia, who was visiting the region, declared: "It's just the kind of barbarism that the war on terrorism is determined to stop." Quoted in Sudanand Dhume, "Violence in Kashmir Hinders U.S. Efforts to Allay Tensions," *Wall Street Journal*, May 15, 2002. The reasons for the administration's shift to unstinting support for the Sharon government are not entirely clear. Domestic politics may have played a part, in the form of the desire to court conservative Christian groups that now take this position. Bush may also have come to see the struggle against Palestinian suicide bombers as identical to the fight against al-Qaeda, perhaps in part because the latter calls for the destruction of Israel.

22. Douglas Feith (undersecretary of defense for policy), speech to American–Israel Public Affairs Committee, April 21, 2002, available at www.defense.gov/speeches/2002/s20020421-feith.html. Also see Robert Keohane, "The Public Delegitimation of Terrorism and Coalition Politics," in Booth and Dubbe, eds., *Worlds in Collision* (New York: Palgrave Macmillan, 2002), pp. 141–151.

23. John Mueller, *Retreat from Doomsday: The Obsolescence of Major War* (New York: Basic Books, 1989); also see James Payne, *A History of Force* (Sandpoint, Idaho: Lytton, 2004).

24. For a good statement of the sacrifices that Bush might ask of Americans, see Thomas Friedman, "Ask Not What …," *New York Times*, December 9, 2001, sec. 4, p. 14.

25. Quoted in Elisabeth Bumiller and Katharine Seelye, "Bush Defends Wartime Call for Tribunals," *New York Times*, December 15, 2001. In defending the claim to refuse any sort of judicial review of the detention of American citizens as enemy combatants, the government's lawyer told the Supreme Court that "where the government is on a war footing, you have to trust the executive to make" these judgments. Quoted in Linda Greenhouse, "Court Hears Case on U.S. Detainees," *New York Times*, April 29, 2004. Four months after the terrorist attacks, "President Bush … issued an executive order barring union representation at United States attorneys' offices and at four other agencies in the Justice Department … out of concern that union contracts could restrict the ability of workers in the Justice Department to protect Americans and national security." Steven Greenhouse, "Bush, Citing Security, Bans Some Unions at Justice Dept.," *New York Times*, January 16, 2002.

26. In June 2004 the Supreme Court ruled that the executive branch could not indefinitely hold people labeled as enemy combatants without some form of judicial review.

David Stout, "Supreme Court Affirms Detainees' Right to Use Courts," *New York Times*, June 28, 2004.

27. Quoted in R.W. Seton-Watson, *Disraeli, Gladstone, and the Eastern Question* (New York: Norton, 1972), p. 222.

28. Robert Pape, "The Strategic Logic of Suicide Terrorism," *American Political Science Review* 97 (August 2003): 343–362; Mia Bloom, "Palestinian Suicide Bombing: Public Support, Market Share, and Outbidding," *Political Science Quarterly*, 119 (Spring 2004): 61–88.

29. E.E. Schattschneider, *The Semi-Sovereign People* (New York: Holt, Rinehart, & Winston, 1960).

30. See the initial version of this chapter, which was written in the fall of 2001 and appeared as "An Interim Assessment of September 11: What Has Changed and What Has Not," *Political Science Quarterly* 117 (Spring 2002): 37–54.

31. Joshna Moravchik, "Terrorism's Silent Partner at the U.N.," *Los Angeles Times*, October 19, 2004.

32. It also took many American leaders by surprise. See, for example, Condoleezza Rice, "Promoting the National Interest," *Foreign Affairs* 79 (January/February 2000): 45–62. "This is a different Putin," Rice said at the signing of the agreement making Russia a partial member of NATO (quoted in David Sanger, "NATO Formally Welcomes Russia as a Partner," *New York Times*, May 29, 2002). For changes in Russian policy since 9/11, see William Jackson, "Encircled Again: Russia's Military Assesses Threats in a Post-Soviet World," *Political Science Quarterly* 117 (Fall 2002): 373–400; Robert Legvold, "All the Way: Crafting a U.S.–Russian Alliance," *National Interest* no. 70 (Winter 2002/2003): 21–32; Stephen Sestanovich, "Dual Frustration: America, Russia and the Persian Gulf," *National Interest*, no. 70 (Winter 2002/2003): 153–162; Bobo Lo, *Vladimir Putin and the Evolution of Russian Foreign Policy* (Oxford: Blackwell, 2003); Dmitri Trenin has a series of relevant briefing papers issued by the Carnegie Moscow Centre, available at http://www.carnegie.ru/en/staff/56232.htm.

33. The reaction to the stationing of a few NATO aircraft in Lithuania was particularly harsh: Steven Myers, "As NATO Finally Arrives on Its Border, Russia Grumbles," *New York Times*, April 3, 2004.

34. See, for example, David Lampton, "The Stealth Normalization of U.S.–China Relations," *National Interest*, no. 73 (Fall 2003): 37–48; Harold Brown, Joseph Prueher, and Adam Segal, *Chinese Military Power: Report of an Independent Task Force* (New York: Council on Foreign Relations, 2003), available at http://www.cfr.org/pdf/China_TF.pdf; Evan S. Medeiros and M. Taylor Fravel, "China's New Diplomacy," *Foreign Affairs* 82 (November/December 2003): 22–35; and Robert Sutter, "Why Does China Matter?" *Washington Quarterly* 27 (Winter 2003): 75–89. Wu Xinbo, "The Promise and Limitations of a Sino–U.S. Partnership," *Washington Quarterly* 27 (Autumn 2004): 115–26.

35. For a brief but good summary of Bush's "hands-off" attitude toward many issues that had deeply engaged his predecessor, see Ivo Daalder and James Lindsay, *America Unbound: The Bush Revolution in Foreign Policy* (Washington, D.C.: Brookings Institution Press, 2003), pp. 66–67.

36. "President Thanks World Coalition for Anti-terrorism Efforts," White House press release, March 11, 2002; David Sanger, "In Reichstag, Bush Condemns Terror as New Despotism," *New York Times*, May 24, 2002. Perhaps the fullest official statement of this view is "Remarks by the President at the United States Air Force Academy Graduation," White House press release, June 2, 2004.

37. "Remarks by the President in Photo Opportunity with the National Security Team," White House press release, September 12, 2001; "President's Remarks at National Day of Prayer and Remembrance," White House press release, September 14, 2001. Bush

later described his personal responsibility to Bob Woodward in similar terms: *Bush at War* (New York: Simon & Schuster, 2002), p. 67.

38. See, for example, George Kennan, *American Diplomacy, 1900–1950* (Chicago: University of Chicago Press, 1951); Robert Divine, *Perpetual War for Perpetual Peace* (College Station: Texas A&M University Press, 2000). For a related argument, see Frank Ninkovich, *Modernity and Power: A History of the Domino Theory in the 20th Century* (Chicago: University of Chicago Press, 1994).

39. Quoted in James Harding, "Conflicting Views from Two Bush Camps," *Financial Times*, March 20, 2003. Also see Woodward's reports in *Bush at War*, pp. 102, 205, 281, and his *Plan of Attack* (New York: Simon & Schuster, 2004) pp. 91, 421; and Peter Schweizer and Rochelle Schweizer, *The Bushes: Portrait of a Dynasty* (New York: Doubleday, 2004). For perceptive analyses, see Frank Bruni, "For President, a Mission and a Role in History," *New York Times*, September 22, 2001; Steve Erickson, "George Bush and the Treacherous Country," *LA Weekly*, February 13, 2004, pp. 28–33; and Ron Suskind, "Without a Doubt," *New York Times Magazine*, October 17, 2004, p. 44. Another ruler who believed that God was guiding him and would save his empire from overextension was Spain's Philip II: see Geoffrey Parker, *The Grand Strategy of Philip II* (New Haven, Conn.: Yale University Press, 1998), and *Empire, War, and Faith in Early Modern Europe* (London: Allen Lane, 2002).

40. Bush's language is unusually filled with references to fear although whether this is sincere or designed to garner support is not clear: for analyses, see Olivia Ward, "Stunning Victory in a Propaganda War," *Toronto Star*, September 8, 2003; Renana Brooks, "Nation of Victims," *The Nation*, June 30, 2003, pp. 20–22. A minor illustration of the power of fear was the closing of a New York subway station when a first-year art student taped to the girders and walls 37 black boxes with the word "fear" on them, an unlikely thing for a bomber to do: Michael Kimmelman, "In New York Art Is Crime and Crime Becomes Art," *New York Times*, December 18, 2002. For a study of how people's willingness to sacrifice civil liberties is affected by their fear of a future attack, see Darren Davis and Brian Silver, "Civil Liberties vs. Security: Public Opinion in the Context of the Terrorist Attacks on America," unpublished MS; Leonie Huddy, Stanley Feldman, Charles Taber, and Gallya Lahav, "The Politics of Threat: Cognitive and Affective Reactions to 9/11," paper presented at the Annual Meeting of the American Political Science Association, Boston, August 29–September 1, 2002; Leonie Huddy, Stanley Feldman, Theresa Capelos, and Colin Provost, "The Consequences of Terrorism: Disentangling the Effects of Personal and National Threat," *Political Psychology* 23 (September 2002): 485–510. For a general theory of the impact of feelings of vulnerability on policy, see Charles Kupchan, *The Vulnerability of Empire* (Ithaca, N.Y.: Cornell University Press, 1994); Zbigniew Brzezinski correctly poses the question of "whether a world power can really provide global leadership on the basis of fear and anxiety" in his "Remarks from the 'New American Strategies for Security and Peace' Conference, October 28, 2003," available at The American Prospect Online, http://www.prospect.org/webfeatures/2003/10/brzezinski-z-10-31.html.

41. According to Woodward, George Tenet believed that "Bush had been the least prepared of all of [the administration leaders] for the terrorist attacks": *Bush at War*, p. 318. As Bush himself said, before September 11 "I was not on point" (ibid., p. 39), and so it is not surprising that when they learned that a plane had crashed into the World Trade Center, both he and Condoleezza Rice thought "What a strange accident" (BBC interview with Condoleezza Rice, August 1, 2002, available at www.bbc.co.uk/radion4/news/withus.shtml. Also see Woodward, *Bush at War*, p. 15, and James Bamford, *A Pretext for War: 9/11, Iraq, and the Abuse of America's Intelligence Agencies* (New York: Doubleday, 2004), p. 36. Only when having to defend themselves before the 9/11 Commission did members of the Bush administration take the implausible

position that they had put counterterrorism at the top of their agenda. Were this the case, they were remarkably incompetent. In fact, they saw the more important threats as emanating from states. This mind-set, in addition to the normal problems of presidential transition and the new administration's scorn for anything its predecessor did, largely explains why al-Qaeda received relatively little attention from the Bush administration until the attacks.

42. Transcript of press conference, *New York Times*, February 1, 2003. In the aftermath of the war in Iraq, several well-placed observers, including NSC official Richard Clarke and former secretary of the treasury Paul O'Neill, have argued that not only several members of the Bush administration but also the president himself were preoccupied by Iraq even before 9/11 and immediately saw Saddam's hand in the attack despite the lack of evidence and the implausibility of the connection. I see no reason to doubt these reports, but do not believe that the overthrow of the regime or the drastic reorientation of the Bush foreign policy would have taken place without the terrorist attack.

43. Quoted in James Risen, David Sanger, and Thom Shanker, "In Sketchy Data, Trying to Gauge Iraq Threat," *New York Times*, July 20, 2003; also see Woodward, *Bush at War*, p. 27.

44. See the survey by the Program on International Policy Attitudes, University of Maryland, "The Separate Realities of Bush and Kerry Supporters," October 21, 2004 (http://www.pipa.org/OnlineReports/Pres_Election_04/Report10_21_04.pdf).

45. Bernard Brodie, "The Development of Nuclear Strategy," *International Security* 2 (Spring 1978): 83. John Lewis Gaddis stresses that the attacks of September 11 greatly heightened Americans' sense of vulnerability and notes historical parallels in 1812 and 1914: *Surprise, Security, and the American Experience* (Cambridge, Mass.: Harvard University Press, 2004).

46. John Dinges, *The Condor Years: How Pinochet and His Allies Brought Terrorism to Three Continents* (New York: New Press, 2004), pp. 217–218.

47. Quoted in Bamford, *A Pretext for War* (New York: Doubleday, 2004), p. 324.

48. Tim Russert, interview with George Bush, *Meet the Press*, February 8, 2004, available at www.msnbc.msn.com/id/4179618/; Colin Powell made the same argument in "Remarks on the Occasion of George Kennan's Centenary Birthday," February 20, 2004, available at www.state.gov/secretary/rm/29683.htm. Bush's explanation of why he did not respond to the intelligence warnings in August 2001 is interesting in this connection: "Of course we knew that America was hated by Osama bin Laden. ... The question was, who was going to attack us, when and where, and with what" (quoted in Adam Nagourney and Philip Shenon, "Bush Says Brief on Qaeda Threat Was Not Specific," *New York Times*, April 12, 2004). The statement is correct, but the lack of such information did not inhibit Bush from attacking Iraq. Tony Blair expressed similar sentiments: Lizette Alvarez, "Blair Defends War in Iraq in Debate in Parliament," *New York Times*, July 21, 2004.

49. "Transcript of the candidates' first debate in the presidential campaign," *New York Times*, October 1, 2004.

50. Bush made this especially clear in his interview with Russert; the lack of WMD might have made a difference to Colin Powell: see the report in the *New York Times* editorial, "The Failure to Find Iraqi Weapons," September 26, 2003.

51. "'Ultimate Penalty': Excerpts from Interview with President Bush," December 16, 2003, available at http://abcnews.go.com/sections/primetime/US/bush_sawyer_excerpts_1_031216.html.

52. Daniel Kahneman and Amos Tversky, eds., *Choices, Values, and Frames* (New York: Russell Sage Foundation, 2000). Stephen Brooks argues that the central difference between Offensive and Defensive Realism is that the former believes that states must, and do, act against threats they see as possible without carefully seeking to measure

the probability involved: "Dueling Realisms," *International Organization* 51 (Summer 1997): 445–477.

53. "Transcript of President Bush's Remarks on the End of Major Combat in Iraq," *New York Times*, March 2, 2003; emphasis added. He used a similar formulation three months later: "President Meets with Small Business Owners in New Jersey," June 16, 2003, White House press release. Britain's Tony Blair expressed similar sentiments: Lizette Alvarez, "Blair Defends War in Iraq in Debate in Parliament," *New York Times*, July 21, 2004.

54. There is an interesting parallel here to the United States after World War II. See Melvyn Leffler, *A Preponderance of Power: National Security, the Truman Administration, and the Cold War* (Stanford, Calif.: Stanford University Press, 1992), especially pp. 50–52. Mueller also points out that the United States is much less vulnerable to terrorism than is often assumed: "Devils and Duct Tape: Assessing Threats during and after the Cold War," Paper presented at the International Studies Association Meeting at Montreal, March 17–20, 2004.

Notes to Chapter 3

1. The best discussion and critique of American reliance on deterrence during the Cold War is Alexander George and Richard Smoke, *Deterrence in American Foreign Policy: Theory and Practice* (New York: Columbia University Press, 1974). The irony is that while the Bush administration rejects much of deterrence, which many critics would applaud, it adopts a policy more heavily reliant on the use of force. For an interesting theoretical discussion of American policy toward Iraq in terms of deterrence, see Galia Press-Barnathan, "A War against Iraq and International Order: From Bull to Bush," *International Studies Review* 6 (June 2004): 195–212.

   It can be argued that it was not deterrence that the Bush administration worried about, but rather the danger that Saddam would give WMD to terrorists. For three reasons I find this far-fetched and think that it was enunciated largely to capitalize on the public's fear of terrorism rather than being the driving motivation behind the policy. First, the United States believed that Saddam had possessed WMD for a decade without passing them on and had no reason to expect that he would change his behavior. As I discussed in the previous chapter, September 11 induced a sea change in Bush's views; no one argued that it changed Saddam's. Second and relatedly, like most dictators, Saddam was dedicated to keeping power and control in his own hands. He would not have been predisposed to share his most powerful weapons, especially not with a group like al-Qaeda, which had denounced him. Third, the basic argument not only of Bush but also of informed opponents of Saddam was that he wanted to dominate the Middle East, and it is not clear how terrorist attacks on the United States would have furthered this goal. September 11 certainly did not. If it were known that Saddam was behind an attack, he might have grown more respected in some eyes and more feared in others, but he would also have signed his death warrant, because the United States would surely have destroyed him. As the CIA argued, it was very unlikely that Saddam would seek to attack the United States absent an American attack on him, and it is similarly hard to believe that he would have put his fate in the hands of others. Indeed, given the American suspicions of him, he would have had every incentive to see that no terrorists got, let alone used, WMD. For a compendium of statements by high administration officials of the links between Iraq and al Qaeda, see what the Bush administration said, *New York Times*, section 4, June 20, 2004.

2. Not all WMD are created equal; nuclear weapons remain much more potent than chemical weapons, with biological agents being a great and frightening unknown.

3. Robert Jervis, *Perception and Misperception in International Politics* (Princeton, N.J.: Princeton University Press, 1976), pp. 128–142; Irving Janis and Leon Mann, *Decision*

Making: A Psychological Analysis of Conflict, Choice, and Commitment (New York: Free Press, 1977).

4. Quoted in Nicholas Lemann, "Remember the Alamo," *New Yorker*, October 18, 2004: 157.

5. Kenneth Waltz, *The Spread of Nuclear Weapons: More May Be Better*, Adelphi Paper no. 171 (London: International Institute for Strategic Studies, 1981); Scott Sagan and Kenneth Waltz, *The Spread of Nuclear Weapons: A Debate Renewed*, 2nd ed.(New York: Norton, 2003). For a range of different views, also see Marc Trachtenberg, "Waltzing to Armageddon?" *National Interest*, no. 69 (Fall 2002): 144–155; Eric Herring, ed., *Preventing the Use of Weapons of Mass Destruction*, special issue of *Journal of Strategic Studies* 23 (March 2000); T.V. Paul, Richard Harknett, and James Wirtz, eds., *The Absolute Weapon Revisited: Nuclear Arms and the Emerging International Order* (Ann Arbor: University of Michigan Press, 1998); Victor Utgoff, ed., *The Coming Crisis: Nuclear Proliferation, U.S. Interests, and World Order* (Cambridge, Mass.: MIT Press, 2000). Also see Robert Litwak, "Non-proliferation and the Dilemmas of Regime Change," *Survival* 45 (Winter 2003–2004): 7–32; and Andrew Flibbert, "After Saddam: Regional Insecurity, Weapons of Mass Destruction, and Proliferation Pressures in Postwar Iraq," *Political Science Quarterly* 118 (Winter 2003–2004): 547–567.

6. Comprehensive Report of the Special Advisor to the DCI on Iraq's WMD (known as the Duelfer report), September 30, 2004, vol. 1, pp. 8, 31.

7. Quoted in Patrick Tyler, "Chief UN Inspector Expects Work on Iraq to Start Nov. 27," *New York Times*, November 16, 2002; Rice held a very different view before September 11: Condoleezza Rice, "Promoting the National Interest," *Foreign Affairs* 79 (January/February 2000): 52, 60.

8. The United States did diplomatically engage Iraq in the 1980s, but clumsily. See Bruce Jentleson, *With Friends like These: Reagan, Bush, and Saddam, 1982–1990* (New York: Norton, 1994); and Evan Resnick, "Engagement as a Tool of Foreign Policy," Ph.D. dissertation, Department of Political Science, Columbia University, 2005.

9. Thomas Schelling, *Arms and Influence* (New Haven, Conn.: Yale University Press, 1966).

10. George Quester, *Deterrence before Hiroshima: The Airpower Background of Modern Strategy* (New York: Wiley, 1966), discusses prenuclear deterrence; John Mearsheimer, *Conventional Deterrence* (Ithaca, N.Y.: Cornell University Press, 1983), analyzes deterrence without weapons of mass destruction.

11. Glenn Snyder, "The Balance of Power and the Balance of Terror," in Paul Seabury, ed., *The Balance of Power* (San Francisco: Chandler, 1965), pp. 184–201; also see Robert Jervis, *The Meaning of the Nuclear Revolution* (Ithaca, N.Y.: Cornell University Press, 1989), pp. 19–23. The Bush administration's national security strategy issued in the fall of 2002 made this as a general point, although obviously Iraq was the nation most in mind: WMD "may also allow these states to attempt to blackmail the United States and our allies to prevent us from deterring or repelling aggressive behavior of rogue states." White House, "The National Security Strategy of the United States" (Washington, D.C., September 2002), p. 15.

12. Senate Select Committee on Intelligence, "Report on the U.S. Intelligence Community's Prewar Intelligence Assessments on Iraq," (Washington, D.C.: U.S. Government Printing Office, July 7, 2004), pp. 371–393. It is also interesting that the Bush administration did worst-case analysis for Iraq, but best-case analysis for global climate change and other environmental issues. Although the realms, evidence, and causal mechanisms are very different, the obvious suspicion is that we cannot explain the positions by a general propensity toward risks or toward taking action as opposed to waiting, but rather that the perception of and attitude toward risk in each area is driven by the desired conclusion. Of course this also may be true of those who favored acting against global warming but not against Saddam.

13. The latter is the topic of Barry Posen's important counterfactual probing of how the United States might have responded to the Iraqi invasion of Kuwait in 1990 if Iraq had had nuclear weapons: "U.S. Security Policy in a Nuclear-Armed World, Or: What if Iraq Had Had Nuclear Weapons?" *Security Studies* 6 (Spring 1997): 1–31. Also see Dean Wilkening and Kenneth Waxman, *Nuclear Deterrence in a Regional Context* (Santa Monica, Calif.: RAND Corporation, 1995).

14. Richard Betts presciently noted this problem in "What Will It Take to Deter the United States?" *Parameters* 25 (Winter 1995–1996): 70–79. For the argument that with the American use of nuclear weapons deterred, Saddam could have used his conventional forces to attack his neighbors, see Edward Rhodes, "Can the United States Deter Iraqi Aggression? The Problem of Conventional Deterrence," unpublished paper, Rutgers University, 2003. For an analysis of the structurally similar problem of deterring a PRC attack on Taiwan that reaches a more optimistic conclusion, see Robert Ross, "Navigating the Taiwan Strait: Deterrence, Escalation, and U.S.–China Relations," *International Security* 27 (Fall 2002): 48–85; also see Thomas Christensen, "Posing Problems without Catching Up: China's Rise and the Challenges for U.S. Security Policy," *International Security* 25 (Spring 2001): 5–40. Elsewhere I have discussed what the actors expected from nuclear weapons and what effects they seem to have had in the 1999 Kargil crisis between India and Pakistan: Robert Jervis, "Kargil, Deterrence, and IR Theory," in Peter Lavoy, ed., *The Kargil Crisis* (forthcoming).

15. In Schelling's terms, the U.S. statements of deterrence against Iraq would have been warnings rather than threats: that is, explanations that American interests would require the United States to intervene rather than signals aimed at changing the U.S. interest by staking its reputation on acting, and so making intervention warranted where it would not have been in the absence of these statements. Thomas Schelling, *Strategy of Conflict* (Cambridge, Mass.: Harvard University Press, 1960), pp. 123–124. As I will discuss in the concluding chapter, however, it is noteworthy that not only in the case of this war, but in four other post–Cold War cases as well, the United States had to use brute force because its coercive threats, even though seemingly credible, proved not to be effective.

16. Betts, "What Will It Take to Deter the United States?"

17. Posen, "U.S. Security Policy in a Nuclear-Armed World."

18. For a fascinating study of information flows in Nazi Germany, see Zachary Shore, *What Hitler Knew: The Battle for Information in Nazi Foreign Policy* (New York: Oxford University Press, 2003).

19. The fullest exposition is Kenneth Pollack, *The Threatening Storm: The Case for Invading Iraq* (New York: Random House, 2002); also see Robert Lieber, "Foreign Policy 'Realists' Are Unrealistic on Iraq," *Chronicle of Higher Education*, October 18, 2002. For good discussions of Saddam's reasons for his wars, see Gregory Gause III, "Iraq's Decisions to Go to War, 1980 and 1990," *Middle East Journal* 56 (Winter 2002): 47–70; and Fred Lawson, "Rethinking the Iraqi Invasion of Kuwait," *Review of International Affairs* 1 (Autumn 2001): 1–20. In many other cases as well, what are generally referred to as failures of deterrence actually are cases in which no deterrent threats were issued; see Richard Ned Lebow and Janice Gross Stein, "When Does Deterrence Succeed and How Do We Know?" *Canadian Institute for International Peace and Security*, Occasional Paper no. 8 (February 1980).

20. For a fuller discussion, see John Mearsheimer and Stephen Walt, "An Unnecessary War," *Foreign Policy*, no. 134 (January/February 2003): 50–59; Chaim Kaufmann, "The Vulnerability of the Marketplace of Ideas: Threat Inflation and the Selling of the Iraq War," *International Security* 29 (Summer 2004): 11–16.

21. Richard Ned Lebow, *Between Peace and War: The Nature of International Crisis* (Baltimore: Johns Hopkins University Press, 1981); Robert Jervis, Richard Ned Lebow, and

Janice Gross Stein, *Psychology and Deterrence* (Baltimore: Johns Hopkins University Press, 1985).

22. Schelling, *Arms and Influence*, pp. 69–91, 99–105, 172–176; Jervis, *Meaning of the Nuclear Revolution*, pp. 29–35.

23. Transcript of press conference, *New York Times*, February 1, 2003; for a similar statement, see Richard Cheney, "Remarks by the Vice-President to the Heritage Foundation," October 9, 2003, available at http://www.whitehouse.gov/news/releases/2003/10/20031010-1.html.

24. David Sanger, "U.S. Plans to Pressure Iraq by Encouraging Scientists to Leak Data to Inspectors," *New York Times*, November 9, 2002; Felicity Barringer and David Sanger, "U.S. Says Hussein Must Cede Power to Head Off War," *New York Times*, March 1, 2003. Some of the inconsistencies in Bush's policy in this regard are reported in Bob Woodward, *Plan of Attack* (New York: Simon & Schuster, 2004), pp. 314–320. A related problem may have complicated Bush's attempt to induce Iraqis to defect and provide information about Saddam's WMD program, because they knew that doing so was likely to trigger an invasion of their country. The same phenomenon may be at work in North Korea: Kim Jung Il reportedly told the president of China "that he doubted that the United States would give North Korea security guarantees even if it agreed to forsake nuclear programs." Quoted in Jim Yardley, "Kim in Beijing: But Nowhere to Be Seen," *New York Times*, April 21, 2004.

25. Quoted in Julia Preston, "Security Council Votes, 15–0, for Tough Iraq Resolution; Bush Calls It a 'Final Test,'" *New York Times*, November 9, 2002; also quoted in Steven Weisman, "How Powell Lined Up Votes, Starting with His President's," *New York Times*, November 8, 2002.

26. According to Woodward, Bush believed that the French and German behavior led Saddam to believe that the United States would not carry out its threats: Woodward, *Plan of Attack*. p. 346.

27. Ibid., pp. 83–84.

28. This conclusion is consistent with the argument of Kenneth Schultz, *Democracy and Coercive Diplomacy* (New York: Cambridge University Press, 2001), although some of the steps of the reasoning are different.

29. The efforts needed to make the threat credible may also simultaneously undermine the credibility of the promise not to invade if Saddam disarms, as noted above.

30. For the psychological dynamics involved, see Daryl Bem, "Self-Perception Theory," in Leonard Berkowitz, ed., *Advances in Experimental Social Psychology*, vol. 6 (New York: Academic Press, 1972), pp. 1–62; Deborah Larson, *Origins of Containment: A Psychological Explanation* (Princeton, N.J.: Princeton University Press, 1985); and Joel Brockner and Jeffrey Rubin, *Entrapment in Escalating Conflicts: A Social Psychological Analysis* (New York: Springer-Verlag, 1985).

31. Duelfer Report, p. 32.

32. Richard Betts, "Suicide from Fear of Death?" *Foreign Affairs* 82 (January/February 2003): 1–10.

33. A similar motive operated during the Gulf War: Posen, "U.S. Security Policy in a Nuclear-Armed World," pp. 14–15.

34. See, for example, Thom Shanker and David Johnston, "U.S. Lists Iraqis to Punish, or to Work With," *New York Times*, February 26, 2003.

35. White House, "National Strategy to Combat Weapons of Mass Destruction" (Washington, D.C., December 2002), p. 3.

36. Brent Scowcroft later revealed that the president had decided not to respond in this way if Saddam had used chemical weapons but the attack had been ineffective: George Bush and Brent Scowcroft, *A World Transformed* (New York: Knopf, 1998), p. 463. I doubt whether Bush or anyone else could have predicted his own reaction to such developments, however. Posen's analysis of how the United States could have exercised

intrawar deterrence if Saddam had possessed nuclear weapons in 1991 assumed that the United States sensibly would have resisted the temptation to seek regime change.

37. Most of the world apparently believed the main American goal was to control Iraq's oil: Adam Clymer, "World Survey Says Negative Views of U.S. Are Rising," *New York Times*, December 5, 2002.

38. Quoted in Karen DeYoung, "U.S. Officials Say U.N. Future at Stake in Vote," *Washington Post*, February 25, 2003.

39. Anthony Shadid, "Arabs Fix Focus on Iraq after War," *Washington Post*, February 21, 2003.

40. Adam Nagourney and Janet Elder, "Public Says Bush Needs to Pay Heed to Weak Economy," *New York Times*, October 7, 2002.

41. John Mueller points out that the day after the bombing of the shelter, the percentage of Americans who believed that the United States was making enough efforts to avoid killing civilians increased from 60 to 67, however. "Public Support for Military Ventures Abroad: Evidence from the Polls," in John Norton Moore and Robert Turner, eds., *The Real Lessons of the Vietnam War: Reflections Twenty-five Years after the Fall of Saigon* (Durham, N.C.: Carolina Academic Press, 2002), p. 217.

42. Philip Green, *Deadly Logic: The Theory of Nuclear Deterrence* (Columbus: Ohio State University Press, 1966); Charles Osgood, *An Alternative to War or Surrender* (Urbana: University of Illinois Press, 1962); Anatol Rapoport, *Strategy and Conscience* (New York: Harper & Row, 1964); Robert Jervis, *Perception and Misperception in International Politics* (Princeton, N.J.: Princeton University Press, 1976), ch. 3; Paul Stern, Robert Axelrod, Robert Jervis, and Roy Radnor, eds., *Perspectives on Deterrence* (New York: Oxford University Press, 1989); Lebow, *Between Peace and War;* Jervis, Lebow, and Stein, *Psychology and Deterrence.* So Charles Krauthammer had a point in noting that those who argued for the efficacy of deterrence against Saddam had attacked the reliance on this instrument during the Cold War. "The Obsolescence of Deterrence," *Weekly Standard*, September 12, 2002, p. 8; also see Tod Lindberg, "Deterrence and Prevention," *Weekly Standard*, February 3, 2003, pp. 24–28.

43. Janice Gross Stein, "Deterrence and Reassurance," in Philip Tetlock, Jo Husbands, Robert Jervis, Paul Stern, and Charles Tilly, eds., *Behavior, Society, and Nuclear War*, vol. 2 (New York: Oxford University Press, 1991), pp. 8–72.

44. Supporters of the Bush administration believe that the renunciation was largely caused by the example of the war in Iraq; critics argue that it was largely driven by Qaddafi's desire to end his diplomatic isolation and that the accord of 2004 was only the culmination of a long and quiet process nurtured by the Clinton administration.

Notes to Chapter 4

1. For somewhat similar analyses, but with varying evaluations, see James Chace, "Imperial America and the Common Interest," *World Policy* 19 (Spring 2002): 1–9; Charles Krauthammer, "The Unipolar Moment Revisited," *National Interest*, no. 70 (Winter 2002/2003): 5–17; Stephen Peter Rosen, "An Empire, if You Can Keep It," *National Interest*, no. 71 (Spring 2003): 51–62; Robert Art, *A Grand Strategy for America* (Ithaca, N.Y.: Cornell University Press, 2003); Andrew Bacevich, *American Empire: The Realities and Consequences of U.S. Diplomacy* (Cambridge, Mass.: Harvard University Press, 2002); Zbigniew Brzezinski, *The Choice: Global Domination or Global Leadership* (New York: Basic Books, 2004); Walter Russell Mead, *Power, Terror, Peace, and War: America's Grand Strategy in a World at Risk* (New York: Knopf, 2004).

2. See Deborah Larson, *Origins of Containment: A Psychological Explanation* (Princeton, N.J.: Princeton University Press, 1985), which draws on Bem's theory of self-perception:

Daryl Bem, "Self-Perception Theory," in Leonard Berkowitz, ed., *Advances in Experimental Social Psychology*, vol. 6 (New York: Academic Press, 1972), pp. 1–62.

3. Paul Kennedy, *The Rise and Fall of the Great Powers: Economic Change and Military Conflict from 1500 to 2000* (New York: Random House, 1987); Robert Gilpin, *War and Change in World Politics* (New York: Cambridge University Press, 1981); Geoffrey Parker, *The Grand Strategy of Philip II* (New Haven, Conn.: Yale University Press, 1998), and *Empire, War, and Faith in Early Modern Europe* (London: Allen Lane, 2002); Paul Allen, *Philip III and the Pax Hispanica, 1598–1621: The Failure of Grand Strategy* (New Haven, Conn.: Yale University Press, 2000); James Tracy, *Emperor Charles V, Impresario of War: Campaign Strategy, International Finance, and Domestic Politics* (New York: Cambridge University Press, 2002).

4. White House, "The National Security Strategy of the United States" (Washington, D.C., September 2002), pp. i, 1. Bush's West Point speech similarly declared: "Moral truth is the same in every culture, in every time, and in every place. ... We are in a conflict between good and evil." and "When it comes to the common rights and needs of men and women, there is no clash of civilizations." "Remarks by the President at 2002 Graduation Exercise of the United States Military Academy," White House press release, June 1, 2002, p. 3. After a standard recitation of American values, Colin Powell similarly declaimed: "These ideals aren't ours alone. They are born of the experience of all mankind, and so they are the endowment of all mankind. These ideals are cherished on each and every continent. ... These ideals are a blueprint for the brotherhood of man." In an irony that he probably missed, he said this in a speech commemorating George Kennan's hundredth birthday, from which Kennan was fortunately absent. "Remarks on the Occasion of George Kennan's Centenary Birthday," Princeton, February 20, 2004, availabe at www.state.gov/secretary/rm/29683.htm.

5. "Remarks by the President at the United States Air Force Academy Graduation," White House press release, June 2, 2004. Also see "Doctor Condoleezza Rice Discusses President's National Security Strategy," White House Press Release, October 1, 2002, p. 3.

6. For the moralistic strain in American foreign policy, see Arnold Wolfers, *Discord and Collaboration* (Baltimore: Johns Hopkins University Press, 1962), ch. 15; Jon Western, "Bush Grand Strategy: The Doctrine of Moral Realism," unpublished MS, Dept. of Political Science, Mount Holyoke College, November 2003; Melvyn Leffler, "Bush's Foreign Policy," *Foreign Policy*, no. 144 (September/October 2004): 22–23. Also see Charles Krauthammer, "Democratic Realism: An American Foreign Policy for a Unipolar World," (Washington, D.C.: American Enterprise Institute, 2004).

7. Quoted in John Lewis Gaddis, *Strategies of Containment: A Critical Appraisal of Postwar American National Security Policy* (New York: Oxford University Press, 1982), p. 130. Of course this insight is a staple of sociology of knowledge. See, for example, Karl Mannheim, *Ideology and Utopia: An Introduction to the Sociology of Knowledge*, translated by Louis Wirth and Edward Shils (New York: Harcourt, Brace, 1936); and Hans Morgenthau, *Scientific Man vs. Power Politics* (Chicago: University of Chicago Press, 1946). Also see E.H. Carr, *The Twenty Years' Crisis, 1919–1939* (London: Macmillan, 1939).

8. Kenneth Waltz, *Man, the State, and War* (New York: Columbia University Press, 1959), chs. 4–5. It follows that it is particularly important to keep nuclear weapons out of the hands of dictatorial regimes or to replace the latter if they do get them. For critical discussions, see Robert Litwak, "Non-proliferation and the Dilemmas of Regime Change," *Survival* 45 (Winter 2003–2004): 7–32; and Andrew Flibbert, "After Saddam: Regional Insecurity, Weapons of Mass Destruction, and Proliferation Pressures in Postwar Iraq," *Political Science Quarterly* 118 (Winter 2003–2004): 547–567. Woodrow Wilson was not the first leader to be guided by a second-image theory: Continental statesmen in the post-Napoleonic era were committed to the idea that the establishment

of democracies would spread to their neighbors and disturb the peace, and they concluded that the autocracies had a common interest and duty to put down democratic revolutions.

9. Quoted in David Sanger, "U.S. to Withdraw from Arms Accord with North Korea," *New York Times*, October 20, 2002.

10. For a good discussion, see Stefan Halper and Jonathan Clarke, *America Alone: The Neo-Conservatives and the Global Order* (New York: Cambridge University Press, 2004). Halper and Clarke also show the great differences on these points between the current generation of the neo-conservatives and the founding fathers of the movement.

11. Quoted in Frank Bruni, "For President, a Mission and a Role in History," *New York Times*, September 22, 2001; "President Thanks World Coalition for Anti-terrorism Efforts," White House press release, March 11, 2002, pp. 3–4; also see "Remarks by the President at 2002 Graduation Exercise," pp. 4–5. For a discussion of the utopian strain in Bush's thinking, see Michael Boyle, "Utopianism and the Bush Foreign Policy," *Cambridge Review of International Affairs* 17 (April 2004): 81–103, and relatedly, Ron Suskind, "Without a Doubt," *New York Times Magazine*, October 17, 2004, pp. 44–.

12. "President Bush, Prime Minister Koizumi Hold Press Conference," White House press release, February 18, 2002, p. 6.

13. "President, Vice President Discuss the Middle East," White House press release, March 21, 2002, p. 2.

14. "President Discusses the Future of Iraq," speech to the American Enterprise Institute, February 26, 2003, White House press release. Bush apparently said similar things in private: Bob Woodward, *Plan of Attack* (New York: Simon & Schuster, 2004), p. 412. For a general discussion of the administration's optimism about the effects of overthrowing Saddam on the Middle East, see Philip Gordon, "Bush's Middle East Vision," *Survival* 45 (Spring 2003): 155–165.

15. Quoted in David Sanger and Thom Shanker, "Bush Says Regime in Iraq Is No More; Syria Is Penalized," *New York Times*, April 16, 2003. Most academics are skeptical of this version of the domino theory, but it should be noted that the overthrow of Saddam does seem to have contributed to the growth of protest movements in Syria. Neil MacFarquhar, "Hussein's Fall Leads Syrians to Test Government Limits," *New York Times*, March 20, 2004.

16. President's Radio Address, "War on Terror," White House Press Release, March 8, 2003; note the typical association of terrorists and "terrorist states."

17. Also see White House, "National Strategy to Combat Weapons of Mass Destruction" (Washington, D.C., December 2002), p. 1.

18. Quoted in James Risen, David Sanger, and Thom Shanker, "In Sketchy Data, Trying to Gauge Iraqi Threat," *New York Times*, July 20, 2003.

19. It is no accident that the leading theorist of this school of thought, Albert Wohlstetter, trained and sponsored many of the driving figures of the Bush administration, including Paul Wolfowitz and Richard Perle.

20. Letter accompanying "National Security Strategy of the United States," p. ii. Calling this aspect of the Bush Doctrine and our policy against Iraq "preemptive," as the Bush administration does, is to do violence to the English language. No one thought that Iraq was about to attack anyone; rather, the argument was that Iraq, and perhaps others, are terrible menaces that eventually would do the United States great harm, and had to be dealt with before they could do so and while prophylactic actions could be taken at reasonable cost. For a study of cases of the threat or use of force to prevent states from gaining WMD, see Robert Litwak, "The New Calculus of Pre-emption," *Survival* 44 (Winter 2002–2003): 53–79.

21. Dale Copeland, *The Origins of Major War* (Ithaca, N.Y.: Cornell University Press, 2000); also see John Mearsheimer, *The Tragedy of Great Power Politics* (New York: Norton, 2001). For important conceptual distinctions and propositions, see Jack Levy, "Declining Power and the Preventive Motivation for War," *World Politics* 40 (October 1987): 82–107; and, for a study that is skeptical of the general prevalence of preventive wars but presents one example, Jack Levy and Joseph Gochal, "Democracy and Preventive War: Israel and the 1956 Sinai Campaign," *Security Studies* 11 (Winter 2001/2002): 1–49. On the U.S. experience, see Art, *Grand Strategy for America*, pp. 181–197. Randall Schweller argues that democratic states fight preventively only under very restrictive circumstances in "Domestic Structure and Preventive War: Are Democracies More Pacific?" *World Politics* 44 (January 1992): 235–269, and notes the unusual nature of the Israeli cases. For the argument that states are generally well served by resisting the temptation to fight preventively, see Richard Betts, "Striking First: A History of Thankfully Lost Opportunities," *Ethics and International Affairs* 17, no. 1 (2003): 17–24. For a review of power transition theory, which in one interpretation is driven by preventive motivation, see Jacek Kugler and Douglas Lemke, eds., *Parity and War: Evaluations and Extensions of the War Ledger* (Ann Arbor: University of Michigan Press, 1996).

22. "World War One as Galloping Gertie," in Schroeder, *Systems, Stability, and Statecraft: Essays on the International History of Modern Europe*, David Wetzel, Robert Jervis, and Jack Levy, eds. (New York: Palgrave, 2004), p. 139.

23. Marc Trachtenberg, *History and Strategy* (Princeton, N.J.: Princeton University Press, 1991), ch. 3; William Burr and Jeffrey Richelson, "Whether to 'Strangle the Baby in the Cradle': The United States and the Chinese Nuclear Program, 1960–64," *International Security* 25 (Winter 2000/2001): 54–99. Gregory Mitrovich shows how much of America's early Cold War policy was driven by the fear that it could not sustain a prolonged confrontation: *Undermining the Kremlin: America's Strategy to Subvert the Soviet Bloc, 1947–1956* (Ithaca, N.Y.: Cornell University Press, 2000).

24. The American tradition of preventive actions is stressed in John Lewis Gaddis, *Surprise, Security, and the American Experience* (Cambridge, Mass.: Harvard University Press, 2004); and Marc Trachtenberg, "The Bush Strategy in Historical Perspective," in James Wirtz, ed., *Bush's Nuclear Posture Review* (New York: Palgrave Macmillan, forthcoming). In his radio address to the country 60 years to the day before the terrorist attacks, President Roosevelt justified his policy toward Nazi Germany (which in its manifestation of supporting British convoys in the Atlantic he described dishonestly) in terms of the legitimacy of preventive war. As this case reminds us, preventive war of course has always had its critics, partly regarding its implications for checks and balances within the American government. As Abraham Lincoln argued during the war with Mexico: "Allow the President to invade a neighboring nation whenever he shall deem it necessary to repel an invasion … and you allow him to make war at pleasure. … If today he should choose to say he thinks it necessary to invade Canada to prevent the British from invading us, how could you stop him? You may say to him, 'I see no probability of the British invading us'; but he will say to you, 'Be silent: I see it, if you don't.'" Quoted in Arthur Schlesinger, Jr., "Eyeless in Iraq," *New York Review of Books*, October 23, 2003, p. 24.

25. "National Security Strategy of the United States," pp. ii, 15; also see "In President's Words: Free People Will Keep the Peace of the World," *New York Times*, February 27, 2003; "Bush's Speech on Iraq: 'Saddam Hussein and His Sons Must Leave,'" *New York Times*, March 18, 2003; and Tony Blair's statement, quoted in Emma Daly, "Both Britain and Spain Dismiss Offer on Iraq Missiles," *New York Times*, March 1, 2003.

26. Quoted in Carl Hulse, "Senate Republicans Back Bush's Iraq Policy, as Democrats Call It Rash and Bullying," *New York Times*, March 8, 2003. Also see Rice, "Rice discusses President's National Security Strategy," p. 2.

27. *Meet the Press*, interview with Tim Russert, February 8, 2004, available at www.msnbc.msn.com/id/4179618; also see Bush interview with Diane Sawyer, "Ultimate Penalty," December 16, 2003, available at http://abcnews.go.com/sections/primetime/US/bush_sawyer_excerpts_1_031216.html.

28. One of those outside the government who helped formulate the Bush Doctrine denies that it is unilateralist: Philip Zelikow, "The Transformation of National Security," *National Interest*, no. 71 (Spring 2003): 24–25. The Bush administration has been much more multilateral in the area of trade. Although it has increased both agricultural subsidies and tariffs on steel, it has offered to reduce the former if the EU does, accepted the WTO decision ruling the latter illegal, and generally supported strengthening the WTO.

29. "Gladstone as Bismarck," in Schroeder, *Systems, Stability, and Statecraft*, p. 102; also see pp. 103, 115–117.

30. Quoted in Steven Erlanger, "Bush's Move on ABM Pact Gives Pause to Europeans," *New York Times*, December 13, 2001; French foreign minister De Villepin similarly said, "We feel that Europe needs the United States, but the United States also needs Europe. You just cannot go out and do things alone," *New York Times*, September 22, 2002. Also see Suzanne Daley, "Many in Europe Voice Worry That U.S. Will Not Consult Them," *New York Times*, January 31, 2002; Steven Erlanger, "Protests, and Friends Too, Await Bush in Europe," *New York Times*, May 22, 2002; and Elizabeth Becker, "U.S. Unilateralism Worries Trade Officials," *New York Times*, March 17, 2003.

31. Quoted in Karen DeYoung, "Chirac Moves to Repair U.S. Ties," *Washington Post*, April 16, 2003; quoted in Robert Kagan, *Of Paradise and Power: America and Europe in the New World Order* (New York: Vintage, 2004), p. 119.

32. Ron Suskind, *The Price of Loyalty: George W. Bush, the White House, and the Education of Paul O'Neill* (New York: Simon & Schuster, 2004); quoted in Elizabeth Drew, "Bush: The Dream Campaign," *New York Review of Books*, June 10, 2004, p. 25.

33. Quoted in Bob Woodward, interview with Bush in *Washington Post*, November 19, 2002 (also see Woodward, *Bush at War*, p. 281); quoted in Somini Sengupta, "U.N. Forum Stalls on Sex Education and Abortion Rights," *New York Times*, May 10, 2002. For a similar remark by Secretary of Defense Rumsfeld, see Eric Schmitt, "Rumsfeld Says Allies Will Support U.S. on Iraq," *New York Times*, August 28, 2002.

34. Jacques Poos, foreign minister of Luxembourg, which at that point held the European Community presidency, quoted in David Gardner, "Crisis in Yugoslavia," *Financial Times*, July 1, 1991.

35. Patrick Tyler and Felicity Barringer, "Annan Says U.S. Will Violate Charter if It Acts Without Approval," *New York Times*, March 11, 2003. Before he joined the Bush administration as Undersecretary of State, John Bolton made it clear that the United States should be careful not to lend legitimacy to international law even when supporting it would reach short-run American goals. "Should We Take Global Governance Seriously?" *Chicago Journal of International Law* 1 (Fall 2000): 205–221.

36. Paul Schroeder sharply differentiates hegemony from empire, arguing that the former is much more benign and rests on a high degree of consent and respect for diverse interests. "The Mirage of Empire versus the Promise of Hegemony," in Schroeder, Robert Jervis, and Jack Levy, eds., *Systems, Stability, and Statecraft* pp. 297–305. Others run the two together: e.g., Frank Ninkovich, *The United States and Imperialism* (Oxford: Blackwell, 2001). I agree that distinctions are needed, but at this point both the terms and the developing American policy are unclear. I have a soft spot in my heart for primacy because it has the fewest connotations, and in the early 1990s I

argued that the United States did not need to seek primacy (at least I was sensible enough to avoid saying whether the United States would be sensible). Robert Jervis, "The Future of World Politics: Will It Resemble the Past?" *International Security* 16 (Winter 1991/1992): 39–73, and "International Primacy: Is the Game Worth the Candle?" *International Security* 17 (Spring 1993): 52–67. For discussions about what an empire means today, whether it necessarily involves territorial control, and how it can be maintained, see Rosen, "An Empire, if You Can Keep It." Also see James, Kurth, "Migration and the Dynamics of Empire," *National Interest*, no. 71 (Spring 2003): 5–16; Anna Simons, "The Death of Conquest," *National Interest*, no. 71 (Spring 2003): 41–49; Andrew Bacevich, ed., *The Imperial Tense: Prospects and Problems of American Empire* (Chicago: Ivan Dee, 2003); and Niall Ferguson, *Colossus: The Price of America's Empire* (New York: Penguin, 2004).

37. It was only after World War I that even lip service was paid to the concept that all states had equal rights; the current U.S. stance would be familiar to any nineteenth-century diplomat.

38. Excerpts are available at http://www.globalsecurity.org/wmd/library/policy/dod/npr.htm.

39. "Remarks by the President at 2002 Graduation Exercise," p. 4. The Wolfowitz draft is summarized in "Excerpts from Pentagon's Plan: Prevent the Re-Emergence of a New Rival," *New York Times*, March 8 and Patrick Tyler, "Pentagon Drops Goal of Blocking New Superpowers," *New York Times*, May 24, 1992. Also see Zalmay Khalilzad, *From Containment to Global Leadership? America and the World after the Cold War* (Santa Monica, Calif.: RAND Corporation, 1995); and Robert Kagan and William Kristol, eds., *Present Dangers: Crisis and Opportunity in American Foreign and Defense Policy* (San Francisco: Encounter Books, 2000). This stance gives others incentives to develop asymmetric responses, of which terrorism is only the most obvious example. For possible PRC options, see Thomas Christensen, "Posing Problems without Catching Up: China's Rise and the Challenges for U.S. Security Policy," *International Security* 25 (Spring 2001): 5–40.

40. The Roosevelt Corollary to the Monroe Doctrine was similarly based on the American commitment to take care of the interests of European nationals in the Western Hemisphere, thereby removing the need for European countries to meddle.

41. It is noteworthy that hegemonic stability theory comes in both a malign and a benign version: Duncan Snidal, "The Limits of Hegemonic Stability Theory," *International Organization* 25 (Autumn 1985): 579–614. For the applicability of these theories to the pre-Bush, post–Cold War world, see Michael Mastanduno, "Preserving the Unipolar Moment: Realist Theories and U.S. Grand Strategy after the Cold War," *International Security* 21 (Spring 1997): 49–88; the exchange between Mark Sheetz and Mastanduno, "Debating the Unipolar Moment," *International Security* 22 (Winter 1997/1998): 168–174; Ethan Kapstein and Michael Mastanduno, eds., *Unipolar Politics: Realism and State Strategies after the Cold War* (New York: Columbia University Press 1999); and G. John Ikenberry, ed., *America Unrivaled: The Future of the Balance of Power* (Ithaca, N.Y.: Cornell University Press, 2002).

42. See, for example, David Reynolds, *From Munich to Pearl Harbor: Roosevelt's America and the Origins of the Second World War* (Chicago: Ivan Dee, 2001); and Warren Kimball, *The Juggler: Franklin Roosevelt as Wartime Statesman* (Princeton, N.J.: Princeton University Press, 1991).

43. Melvyn Leffler, *A Preponderance of Power: National Security, the Truman Administration, and the Cold War* (Stanford, Calif.: Stanford University Press, 1992); Thomas Christensen, *Useful Adversaries: Grand Strategy, Domestic Mobilization, and Sino–American Conflict, 1947–1958* (Princeton, N.J.: Princeton University Press, 1996). For the domestically imposed limits on this process, see Aaron Friedberg, *In the Shadow of*

the Garrison State: America's Anti-Statism and Its Cold War Grand Strategy (Princeton, N.J.: Princeton University Press, 2000); and Michael Hogan, A Cross of Iron: Harry S. Truman and the Origins of the National Security State, 1945–1954 (New York: Cambridge University Press, 1998).

44. Geir Lunstestad, "Empire by Invitation? The United States and Western Europe, 1945–1952," Journal of Peace Research 23 (September 1986): 263–277; and James McAllister, No Exit: America and the German Problem, 1943–1954 (Ithaca, N.Y.: Cornell University Press, 2002).

45. Charles Maier, In Search of Stability: Explorations in Historical Political Economy (New York: Cambridge University Press, 1987), p. 148. Also see John Lewis Gaddis, We Now Know: Rethinking Cold War History (New York: Oxford University Press, 1997); and Thomas Risse-Kappen, Cooperation among Democracies: The European Influence on U.S. Foreign Policy (Princeton, N.J.: Princeton University Press, 1995). Others stress the degree to which consent was a product of American coercion: Mark Sheetz, "Continental Drift: Franco-German Relations and the Shifting Premises of European Security," unpublished dissertation, Department of Political Science, Columbia University, 2002; Marc Trachtenberg, ed., Between Empire and Alliance: America and Europe during the Cold War (Lanham, Md.: Rowman & Littlefield, 2003), esp. ch. 1.

46. William Wohlforth, "The Stability of a Unipolar World," International Security 24 (Summer 1999): 5–41; and William Odom and Robert Dujarric, America's Inadvertent Empire (New Haven, Conn.: Yale University Press, 2004). See also Kenneth Waltz, "Structural Realism after the Cold War," International Security 25 (Summer 2000): 5–41. For dissenting but unconvincing views, see Immanuel Wallerstein, "The Eagle Has Crash Landed," Foreign Policy, no. 131 (July/August 2002): 60–68; Emmanuel Todd, After the Empire: The Breakdown of the American Order, translated by C. Jon Delogu (New York: Columbia University Press, 2003); and Michael Mann, Incoherent Empire (New York: Verso, 2003). The well-crafted argument by Robert Kudrle that the United States does not always get its way even on some important issues is correct, but I think it does not contradict the basic structural point. "Hegemony Strikes Out: The U.S. Global Role in Anti-Trust, Tax Evasion, and Illegal Immigration," International Studies Perspectives 4 (February 2003): 52–71. Even in the military area, where U.S. dominance is most pronounced, it is not clear that America's capabilities are sufficient to reach its goals unaided, however. Barry Posen, "Command of the Commons: The Military Foundation of U.S. Hegemony," International Security 28 (Summer 2003): 5–46. Furthermore, as I will discuss at the end of this chapter, many American goals cannot be reached by military means.

47. See, for example, G. John Ikenberry, "After September 11: America's Grand Strategy and International Order in the Age of Terror," Survival 43 (Winter 2001–2002): 19–34, After Victory: Institutions, Strategic Restraint, and the Rebuilding of Order after Major War (Princeton, N.J.: Princeton University Press, 2001), and "Is American Multilateralism in Decline?" Perspectives on Politics 1 (September 2003): 533–550; John Gerard Ruggie, Winning the Peace: America in the New Era (New York: Columbia University Press, 1996); John Steinbruner, Principles of Global Security (Washington, D.C.: Brookings Institution Press, 2000); and Benjamin Barber, Fear's Empire: War, Terrorism, and Democracy (New York: Norton, 2003). More popular treatments are Clyde Prestowitz, Rogue Nation: American Unilateralism and the Failure of Good Intentions (New York: Basic Books, 2003); and Michael Hirsh, At War with Ourselves: Why America Is Squandering Its Chance to Build a Better World (New York: Oxford University Press, 2003). See Joseph Nye, The Paradox of American Power: Why the World's Only Superpower Can't Go It Alone (New York: Oxford University Press, 2002), pp. 154–163, for a good discussion of the different circumstances under which unilateralism and multilateralism are appropriate; also see John Van Oudenaren, "What Is 'Multilateral'?" Policy

Review no. 117 (February–March 2003): 33–47, and "Unipolar versus Unilateral," *Policy Review*, no. 124 (April–May 2004): 63–74. Randall Schweller's critique of Ikenberry is very relevant to my argument: "The Problem of International Order Revisited: A Review Essay," *International Security* 26 (Summer 2001): 161–186.

48. Richard Betts, "The Soft Underbelly of American Primacy: Tactical Advantages of Terror," *Political Science Quarterly* 117 (Spring 2002): 19–36. Also see Paul Pillar, *Terrorism and U.S. Foreign Policy* (Washington, D.C.: Brookings, 2001).

49. See, for example, Jesse Helms's defense of unilateralism as the only way consistent with American interests and traditions. "American Sovereignty and the UN," *National Interest*, no. 62 (Winter 2000/2001): 31–34. For a discussion of historical, sociological, and geographical sources of this outlook, see Louis Hartz, *The Liberal Tradition in America: An Interpretation of American Political Thought since the Revolution* (New York: Harcourt, Brace, 1955), ch. 11; Wolfers, *Discord and Collaboration*, ch. 15; also see Barry Buzan, *The United States and the Great Powers: World Politics in the Twenty-first Century* (London: Polity, 2004). For other historical analysis, see "Roundtable," *Diplomatic History* 26 (Fall 2002): 541–644. For a discussion of current U.S. policy in terms of America's self-image as an exceptional state, see Stanley Hoffmann, "The High and the Mighty," *American Prospect* 1 (January 2003): 28–31.

50. Thus it is not entirely surprising that many of the beliefs mustered in support of U.S. policy toward Iraq parallel those held by European expansionists in earlier eras. Jack Snyder, "Imperial Temptations," *National Interest*, no. 71 (Spring 2003): 29–40.

51. *The Peloponnesian War*, translated by Rex Warner (Harmondsworth: Penguin, 1954), p. 363. I should note that this generalization, although apparently secure, rests to a considerable extent on our searching on the dependent variable. That is, we are drawn to cases of such expansion because they are dramatic, especially when they come to grief, and because we lack a systematic way of looking for instances in which a state had the ability to expand its sphere of influence but declined to do so.

52. Quoted in Hans Morgenthau, *Politics among Nations: The Struggle for Power and Peace*, 5th ed., rev. (New York: Knopf, 1978), pp. 169–170; emphasis in the original. Also see Paul Sharp, "Virtue Unrestrained: Herbert Butterfield and the Problem of American Power," *International Studies Perspectives* 5 (August 2004): 300–15.

53. Kenneth Waltz, "America as a Model for the World? A Foreign Policy Perspective," *PS: Political Science and Politics* 24 (December 1991): 9; also see Waltz's discussion of the Gulf War: "A Necessary War?" in Harry Kriesler, ed., *Confrontation in the Gulf* (Berkeley, Calif.: Institute of International Studies, 1992), pp. 59–65. Charles Krauthammer also expected this kind of behavior, but believed that it will serve the world as well as the American interests: Krauthammer, "The Unipolar Moment," *Foreign Affairs, America and the World*, 70, no. 1 (1990–1991): 23–33; also see Krauthammer, "The Unipolar Moment Revisited." For a critical analysis, see Chace, "Imperial America and the Common Interest." As Waltz noted much earlier, even William Fulbright, while decrying the arrogance of American power, said that the United States could and should "lead the world in an effort to change the nature of its politics." Quoted in Waltz's *Theory of International Politics* (Reading, Mass.: Addison-Wesley, 1979), p. 201.

54. Alexander Wendt and, more persuasively, Paul Schroeder would disagree or at least modify this generalization, arguing that prevailing ideas can lead, and have led, to more moderate and consensual behavior. Wendt, *Social Theory of International Politics* (New York: Cambridge University Press, 1999); Schroeder, *The Transformation of European Politics, 1763–1848* (New York: Oxford University Press, 1994), and "Does the History of International Politics Go Anywhere?" in Schroeder, *Systems, Stability, and Statecraft* pp. 267–284. This is a central question of international politics and history that I cannot fully discuss here, but I believe that at least the mild statement that unbalanced power is dangerous can easily be sustained.

55. See, for example, Fareed Zakaria, "Realism and Domestic Politics: A Review Essay," *International Security* 17 (Summer 1992): 177–198; Robert Tucker, *The Radical Left and American Foreign Policy* (Baltimore: Johns Hopkins University Press, 1971), pp. 69–70, 74–77, 106–111; and Stephen Van Evera, *Causes of War: Power and the Roots of Conflict* (Ithaca, N.Y.: Cornell University Press, 1999), p. 86. This process is also fed by the psychological resistance to giving up any position once it is gained; see Jeffrey Taliaferro, *Balancing Risks: Great Power Intervention in the Periphery* (Ithaca, N.Y.: Cornell University Press, 2004). For a discussion of alternative possibilities suggested by American history, see Edward Rhodes, "The Imperial Logic of Bush's Liberal Agenda," *Survival* 45, no. 1 (Spring 2003): 131–154.

56. Wolfers, *Discord and Collaboration*, ch. 5.

57. *Plan of Attack*, p. 1; also see pp. 37–41, 50.

58. The process may also work in reverse. The Soviet foreign policy adviser Georgi Arbatov is reported to have said, "Our very poor military performance in Afghanistan saved Poland. If we had been able to achieve our goals in Afghanistan reasonably quickly, I have no doubt we would have invaded Poland too." Quoted in David Arbel and Ran Edelist, *Western Intelligence and the Collapse of the Soviet Union, 1980–1990* (London: Frank Cass, 2003), p. 89. The declassified records reveal other considerations (see the articles and records in *Cold War International History Project Bulletin* [Washington, D.C., Woodrow Wilson Center for Scholars], no. 11 (Winter 1998): 3–133), but this factor may have played a role as well. Similarly, both President Kennedy and his brother Robert said that had the Bay of Pigs not led him to mistrust military advice and military solutions, he probably would have used force in Laos. Nigel Ashton, *Kennedy, Macmillan, and the Cold War: The Irony of Interdependence* (New York: Palgrave Macmillan, 2002), p. 41; and Edwin Guthman and Jeffrey Shulman, eds., *Robert Kennedy, in His Own Words* (New York: Bantam, 1971), pp. 13, 247.

59. Wolfers, *Discord and Collaboration*, ch. 10.

60. John Mueller, "The Catastrophe Quota: Trouble after the Cold War," *Journal of Conflict Resolution* 38 (September 1994): 355–375; also see Frederick Hartmann, *The Conservation of Enemies: A Study in Enmity* (Westport, Conn.: Greenwood Press, 1982).

61. Waltz, *Theory of International Politics*, p. 200.

62. John S. Galbraith, "The 'Turbulent Frontier' as a Factor in British Expansion," *Comparative Studies in Society and History* 2 (January 1960): 34–48, and *Reluctant Empire: British Policy on the South African Frontier, 1834–1854* (Berkeley: University of California Press, 1963). Also see Ronald Robinson and John Gallagher with Alice Denny, *Africa and the Victorians: The Official Mind of Imperialism* (London: Macmillan, 1961); and John LeDonne, *The Grand Strategy of the Russian Empire, 1650–1831* (New York: Oxford University Press, 2004). Chalmers Johnson notes the great spread of American military bases throughout the world in *The Sorrows of Empire: Militarism, Secrecy, and the End of the Republic* (New York: Metropolitan Books, 2004). For the broader dynamics at work, see the literature cited in note 3, above. A related imperial dynamic that is likely to recur is that turning a previously recalcitrant state into a client usually weakens it internally and requires further intervention.

63. Craig Smith, "U.S. Training African Forces to Uproot Terrorists," *New York Times*, May 11, 2004.

64. See especially Copeland, *Origins of Major War*; and Mearsheimer, *Tragedy of Great Power Politics*.

65. Waltz sees this behavior as often self-defeating; Mearsheimer implies that it is not; Copeland's position is somewhere in between.

66. Bush would endorse Wilson's claim that America's goal must be "the destruction of every arbitrary power anywhere in the world that can separately, secretly, and of its single choice disturb the peace of the world," just as he would join Wilson in calling

for "the spread of his revolt [i.e., the American revolution], this liberation, to the great stage of the world itself." "An Address at Mount Vernon," July 4, 1918, in Arthur Link et al., eds., *The Papers of Woodrow Wilson*, vol. 48, *May 13–July 17, 1918* (Princeton, N.J.: Princeton University Press, 1985), pp. 516–517.

67. Robert Jervis, "Was the Cold War a Security Dilemma?" *Journal of Cold War History* 3 (Winter 2001): 36–60; also see Paul Roe, "Former Yugoslavia: The Security Dilemma That Never Was? *European Journal of International Relations* 6 (September 2000): 373–393. For accounts of Bush's decision to overthrow Saddam that are consistent with these arguments, see Douglas Jehl and David Sanger, "Prewar Assessment of Iraq Showed Chance of Strong Divisions," *New York Times*, September 28, 2004; Nicholas Lemann, "Remember the Alamo," *New Yorker*, October 18, 2004: 157.The current combination of fear and hope that produces offensive actions for defensive motives resembles the combination that produced the pursuit of preponderance in the aftermath of World War II. Melvyn Leffler, *A Preponderance of Power: National Security, the Truman Administration, and the Cold War* (Stanford, Calif.: Stanford University Press, 1992), especially pp. 50–52.

68. A good account is Philip Gordon and Jeremy Shapiro, *Allies at War: America, Europe, and the Crisis over Iraq* (New York: McGraw-Hill, 2004). Also see Antje Winner, "Contested Compliance: Interventions on the Normative Structure of World Politics," *European Journal of International Relations* 10 (June 2004): 208–14. More extreme but not entirely different were the sentiments voiced in the first months of World War I by Helmut von Moltke, the chief of the German General Staff: "The spiritual progress of mankind is only possible through Germany. This is why Germany will not lose this war; it is the only nation that can, at the present moment, take charge of leading mankind towards a higher destiny," in Annika Mombauer, *Helmut von Moltke and the Origins of the First World War* [New York: Cambridge University Press, 2001], p. 283.

69. The best-known statement of this position is Kagan, *Of Paradise and Power*; also see Jed Rubenfeld, "The Two World Orders," *Wilson Quarterly* 27 (Autumn 2003): 22–36. For interesting perspectives, see Wesley Clark, *Waging Modern War: Bosnia, Kosovo, and the Future of Combat* (New York: Public Affairs, 2002), pp. 444–450; and Van Oudenaren, "What Is 'Multilateral?'" pp. 44–47.

70. Adam Clymer, "European Poll Faults U.S. for Its Policy in the Mid East," *New York Times*, April 19, 2002.

71. Quoted in David Sanger, "Witness to Auschwitz Evil, Bush Draws a Lesson," *New York Times*, June 1, 2003.

72. Quoted in John Tagliabue, "France and Russia Ready to Use Veto against Iraq War," *New York Times*, March 6, 2003.

73. This is a version of Stephen Walt's argument that states balance against threat, not power: *The Origins of Alliances* (Ithaca, N.Y.: Cornell University Press, 1987). For some of the fears of France and Germany held by their European partners, see Elaine Sciolino, "France and Germany Flex Muscles on Charter," *New York Times*, December 10, 2003.

74. Secretary of the Treasury Paul O'Neill's reaction in an NSC meeting at the start of the Bush administration that gave Iraq much more attention than he thought it deserved is instructive: "O'Neill thought about Rumsfeld's memo [calling for radical defense reforms]. It described how everything fit together. The focus on Saddam Hussein made sense only if the broader ideology—of a need to 'dissuade' others from creating asymmetric threats—were to be embraced." Suskind, *Price of Loyalty*, pp. 85–86.

75. Kenneth Waltz, *The Spread of Nuclear Weapons: More May Be Better*, Adelphi Paper no. 171 (London: International Institute for Strategic Studies, 1981); Scott Sagan and Kenneth Waltz, *The Spread of Nuclear Weapons: A Debate Renewed*, 2nd ed. (New York: Norton, 2003). For a range of views, see Marc Trachtenberg, "Waltzing to Armageddon?" *National Interest*, no. 69 (Fall 2002): 144–155; Eric Herring, ed.,

Preventing the Use of Weapons of Mass Destruction, special issue of *Journal of Strategic Studies* 23 (March 2000); and T. V. Paul, Richard Harknett, and James Wirtz, eds., *The Absolute Weapon Revisited: Nuclear Arms and the Emerging International Order* (Ann Arbor: University of Michigan Press, 1998).

76. For the question of how the Europeans will respond, see ch. 1, pp. 31–34.

77. See David Calleo, *The German Problem Reconsidered: Germany and the World Order, 1870 to the Present* (New York: Cambridge University Press, 1978); for a summary of relevant laboratory experiments, see Robert Goodin, "How Amoral *Is* Hegemon?" *Perspectives on Politics* (March 1 2003): 123–126.

78. "A Luncheon Address to the St. Louis Chamber of Commerce," September 5, 1919, in Arthur Link et al., eds., *The Papers of Woodrow Wilson*, vol. 63, *September 4–November 5, 1919* (Princeton, N.J.: Princeton University Press, 1990), p. 33.

79. Quoted in David Sanger, "A New View of Where America Fits in the World," *New York Times*, February 18, 2001.

Notes to Chapter 5

1. Good on this point are Giulio Gallarotti, "Nice Guys Finish First: American Unilateralism and Power Illusion," in Graham Walker, ed., *Independence in an Age of Empire: Assessing Unilateralism and Multilateralism* (Halifax, N.S.: Dalhousie University Centre for Foreign Policy Studies, 2004), pp. 225–236; and G. John Ikenberry, "The End of the Neo-Conservative Moment," *Survival* 46 (Spring 2004): 7–22; Ikenberry, "Why Bush Foreign Policy Fails," unpublished manuscript; Melvyn Leffler, "Bush's Foreign Policy," *Foreign Policy*, no. 144 (September/October 2004): 22–28. For some parallel tensions in American strategy during World War II see Paul Schroeder, *Systems, Stability, and Statecraft: Essays on the International History of Modern Europe*, edited by David Wetzel, Robert Jervis, and Jack Levy (New York: Palgrave, 2004), p. 220, and Warren Kimball, *The Juggler: Franklin Roosevelt as Wartime Statesman* (Princeton, N.J.: Princeton University Press, 1991).

2. "Remarks by the President at the United States Air Force Academy Graduation," White House press release, June 2, 2004; also see Bush's speech to the Army War College in May 2004: "President Outlines Steps to Help Iraq Achieve Democracy and Freedom," White House press release, May 24, 2004.

3. Douglas Frantz, et al., "The New Face of Al Qaeda," *Los Angeles Times*, September 26, 2004; cnn.com, "Musharraf 'Reasonably Sure' bin Laden is Alive," September 25, 2004 (http://www.cnn.com/2004/WORLD/asiapcf/09/25/musharraf/); Craig Smith, "Chirac Says War in Iraq Spreads Terrorism," *New York Times*, November 18, 2004.

4. Jim Miklaszewski, "Avoiding Attacking Suspected Terrorist Mastermind," *NBC News*, March 2, 2004, available at http://www.msnbc.msn.com/id/4431869/. Scot Paltrow, "Questions Mount Over Failure to Hit Zarqawi's Camp," *Wall Street Journal*, October 25, 2004.

5. Susan Sachs, "Poll Finds Hostility Hardening toward U.S. Policies," *New York Times*, March 17, 2004; "Bush vs. bin Laden (and Other Popularity Contests)," *New York Times*, March 21, 2004; Alan Cowell, "Bush Visit Spurs Protests against U.S. in Europe," *New York Times*, November 16, 2003.

6. For a related argument, see Richard Betts, "The Soft Underbelly of American Primacy: Tactical Advantages of Terror," *Political Science Quarterly* 117 (Spring 2002): 19–36; Paul Pillar, *Terrorism and U.S. Foreign Policy* (Washington, D.C.: Brookings, 2003).

7. Winston Churchill, *The Second World War*, vol. 3, *The Grand Alliance* (Boston: Houghton Mifflin, 1950), p. 370; also see p. 372. When explaining why the Allies had to work with Admiral Darlan, a German sympathizer, in North Africa, Franklin Roosevelt used a Balkan proverb to make the same point: "My children, it is permitted you in time of great danger to walk with the devil until you have crossed the bridge." Warren Kimball, ed., *Churchill and Roosevelt: The Complete Correspondence*, vol. 2, *The Alliance Forged* (Princeton, N.J.: Princeton University Press, 1984), p. 22.

8. The term is taken from Paul Kennedy, *The Rise and Fall of the Great Powers: Economic Change and Military Conflict from 1500 to 2000* (New York: Random House, 1987). A parallel argument was made earlier by Robert Gilpin, *War and Change in World Politics* (New York: Cambridge University Press, 1981).

9. War and finances were then inextricably linked, as is revealed by any number of fascinating studies. See, for example, John Brewer, *The Sinews of Power: War, Money, and the English State, 1688–1783* (New York: Knopf, 1989); James Tracy, *Emperor Charles V, Impresario of War: Campaign Strategy, International Finance, and Domestic Politics* (New York: Cambridge University Press, 2002); Geoffrey Parker, *The Grand Strategy of Philip II* (New Haven, Conn.: Yale University Press, 1998); Paul Allen, *Philip III and the Pax Hispanica, 1598–1621: The Failure of Grand Strategy* (New Haven, Conn.: Yale University Press, 2000).

10. H.M. Scott, "The Decline of France and the Transformation of the European States System, 1756–1792," in Peter Krüger and Paul Schroeder, eds., *The Transformation of European Politics, 1763–1848: Episode or Model in Modern History?* (Münster: Lit Verlag, 2002), pp. 105–128.

11. For an account that stresses these factors, see Niall Ferguson, *Colossus: The Price of America's Empire* (New York: Penguin, 2004), ch. 8. Also see Immanuel Wallerstein, *The Decline of American Power* (New York: New Press, 2004), and Peter Peterson, "Riding for a Fall," *Foreign Affairs*, 83 (September/October 2004): 111–125, which does a better job of recognizing the centrality of political will.

12. Quoted in Marc Trachtenberg, *A Constructed Peace: The Making* of the European Settlement, 1845–1963 (Princeton, N.J.: Princeton University Press, 1999), p. 244. The long-serving Soviet ambassador to the United States, Anatoly Dobrynin, concludes his memoirs by saying: "All great powers from the Roman to the British Empire have disintegrated because of internal strife and not from pressures from abroad," although I would add that the latter can contribute to the former: *In Confidence: Moscow's Ambassador to America's Six Cold War Presidents* (New York: Times Books, 1995), p. 618.

13. For criticisms of pluralism both normative and descriptive, see Theodore Lowi, *The End of Liberalism: Ideology, Policy, and the Crisis of Public Authority* (New York: Norton, 1969; 2nd ed., 1979); C. Wright Mills, *The Power Elite* (New York: Oxford University Press, 1956); Grant McConnell, *The Decline of Agrarian Democracy* (Berkeley: University of California Press, 1953). On pluralism in general see Andrew McFarland, *Power and Leadership in Pluralist Systems* (Stanford, Calif.: Stanford University Press, 1969), and McFarland, *Neopluralism: The Evolution of Political Process Theory* (Lawrence: University Press of Kansas, 2004). Also see David Sadler, "Defining the West: Ideology and U.S. Foreign Policy during the Cold War," in Philip John Davies, ed., *Representing and Imagining America* (Keele, U.K.: Keele University Press, 1996), pp. 210–219.

14. This claim was most commonly made by students of security, but was affirmed by some of those analyzing foreign economic policy as well. See Stephen Krasner, *Defending the National Interest: Raw Materials, Investments, and U.S. Foreign Policy* (Princeton, N.J.: Princeton University Press, 1978); and Robert Gilpin, "No One Loves a Political Realist," *Security Studies* 5 (Spring 1996): 3–26.

15. Keith Bradshear, "Pakistanis Fume as Clothing Sales to U.S. Tumble," *New York Times*, June 23, 2002.

16. James Burk, "Public Support for Peacekeeping in Lebanon and Somalia: Assessing the Casualties Hypothesis," *Political Science Quarterly* 114 (Spring 1999): 53–78.

17. Supporters of President Bush believe that such weapons were found, however: see the survey by the Program on International Policy Attitudes, University of Maryland,

"The Separate Realities of Bush and Kerry Supporters," October 21, 2004 (http://www.pipa.org/OnlineReports/Pres_Election_04/Report10_21_04.pdf).

18. See, for example, Douglas Jehl, "Tenet Says Dangers to U.S. Are at Least as Great as a Year Ago," *New York Times*, February 25, 2004.

19. An excellent study of FDR's strategy for dealing with the public is Steven Casey, *Cautious Crusade: Franklin D. Roosevelt, American Public Opinion, and the War against Nazi Germany* (New York: Oxford University Press, 2001).

20. Richard Benedetto, "Poll: Support for War Is Steady, but Many Minds Not Made Up," *USA Today*, February 28, 2003; an even larger effect was reported in Michael Tackett, "Polls Find Support for War Follows Party Lines," *Chicago Tribune*, March 7, 2003. Some findings indicate that what was seen as crucial was support from allies, not necessarily the United Nations. Gary Younge, "Threat of War: Americans Want UN Backing before War," *The Guardian* (Manchester), February 26, 2003. For data and analysis that shows continued American support for multilateralism, see the Chicago Council on Foreign Relations 2004 public opinion survey, at http://www.ccfr.org/globalviews2004/main.html and Ole Holsti, *Public Opinion and American Foreign Policy*, rev. ed. (Ann Arbor: University of Michigan Press, 2004), especially ch. 6.

21. I believe the victorious Spanish leader exaggerated, however, when he declared, "Now that the Socialist government in Spain has taken power [it] will have a great impact in the November elections in North America." Quoted in Elaine Sciolino, "Spain Will Loosen Its Alliance with U.S., Premier-Elect Says," *New York Times*, March 16, 2004.

22. In defending the idea of preventive war, Condoleezza Rice said that it "has to be used carefully. One would want to have very good intelligence." Online NewsHour, "Rice on Iraq, War and Politics," September 25, 2002, available at www.pbs.org/newshour/bb/international/july-dec02/rice_9-25.html.

23. The official American and British postmortems not only provide a good deal of information, but exemplify, and indeed parody, the conventional wisdom about the two countries' political cultures. The Senate Select Committee on Intelligence (SSCI) report, "US Intelligence Community's Prewar Intelligence Assessments on Iraq" (July 7, 2004) is more than just critical of the CIA, it is both a brief for the prosecution and quite partisan. It is also extremely long and detailed. It exemplifies the American penchant for as much information as possible and an adversarial approach to public policy questions. The British report of a committee of Privy Counselors chaired by the Rt Hon The Lord Butler of Brockwell KG GCB CVO, "Review of Intelligence on Weapons of Mass Destruction" (July 14, 2004), is shorter, displays a good understanding of the problems of intelligence, is embarrassingly exculpatory, and provides little help in thinking about how errors like this could be avoided. Also see Philip H. J. Davies, "Intelligence Culture and Intelligence Failure in Britain and the United States," *Cambridge Review of Internal Affairs*, 17 (October 2004): 495–520. For a strong argument that the administration knew the truth and lied about it, see David Sirota and Christy Harvey, "They Knew," August 4, 2004, www.inthesetimes.com. A similar view is implied in James Bamford, *A Pretext for War: 9/11, Iraq, and the Abuse of America's Intelligence Agencies* (New York: Doubleday, 2004) and John Prados, *Hoodwinked: The Documents That Reveal How Bush Sold Us a War* (New York: New Press, 2004). But neither of these books systematically explores the question of whether administration leaders believed what they were saying.

24. Indeed, during parts of World War II and the early Cold War Stalin's spies were able to provide information almost this good, and the dictator's reaction was to discount it because he could not believe that his adversaries could have been so incompetent as to permit this.

25. On politicization in general, see H. Bradford Westerfield, "Inside Ivory Bunkers: CIA Analysts Resist Managers' 'Pandering'—Part I," *International Journal of Intelligence and Counterintelligence* 9 (Winter 1996/1997): 407–424, and "Inside Ivory Bunkers: CIA Analysts Resist Managers' 'Pandering'—Part II," Jack Davis, "Analytic

Professionalism and the Policymaking Process" Sherman Kent for Intelligence Analysis Occasional Papers, vol. 2, October 2003 (Washington, D.C.: CIA). 10 (Spring 1997): 19-56; and Richard Betts, "Politicization of Intelligence: Costs and Benefits," in Richard Betts and Thomas Mahnken, eds., *Paradoxes of Strategic Intelligence: Essays in Honor of Michael I. Handel* (London: Cass, 2003), pp. 59–79. My analysis assumes that the administration believed that Saddam had WMD. Although no evidence has been produced to the contrary, one significant bit of behavior raises doubts: the failure of U.S. forces to launch a careful search for WMD as they moved through Iraq. Had there been stockpiles of WMD materials, there would have been a grave danger that these would have fallen into the hands of America's enemies, perhaps including terrorists. I cannot explain the U.S. failure, but the conduct of much of the U.S. occupation points to incompetence.

26. Douglas Jehl, "C.I.A. Chief Says He's Corrected Cheney Privately," *New York Times*, March 10, 2004. A devastating analysis of the way in which the administration distorted and misstated intelligence is Senator Carl Levin, "Report of an Inquiry into the Alternative Analysis of the Issue of an Iraq–al Qaeda Relationship," October 21, 2004, www. Levin.senate.gov.

27. SCCI, pp. 449–464; 479–488.

28. SCCI, pp. 272–285; 357–365; also see Richard Stevenson and Thom Shanker, "Ex-Arms Monitor Urges an Inquiry on Iraqi Threat," *New York Times*, January 29, 2004; Kenneth Pollack, "Spies, Lies, and Weapons: What Went Wrong," *Atlantic Monthly*, January–February 2004, pp. 88–90. For a first-hand account of the pressures in the Defense Department, see Karen Kwiatkowski, "The New Pentagon Papers," *Salon*, March 10, 2002, available at http://archive.salon.com/opinion/feature/2004/03/10. For a rebuttal, see SSCI, 282–283. For a case that provides an interesting parallel to Iraq, see Doug Stokes, "Countering the Soviet Threat? An Analysis of the Justifications for US Military Assistance to El Salvador, 1979–92," *Cold War History* 3 (April 2003): 79–102.

29. Jessica Mathews and Jeff Miller, "A Tale of Two Intelligence Estimates," *Carnegie Endowment for International Peace*, (March 31, 2004); Donald Kennedy, "Intelligence Science: Reverse Peer Review?" *Science* 303 (March 26, 2004); Center for American Progress, "Neglecting Intelligence, Ignoring Warnings," January 28, 2004, available at http://www.americanprogress.org/site/pp.asp?c=biJRJ8OVF&b=24889; Prados, *Hoodwinked*, pp. 77–93; SSCI, pp. 286–297.

30. This is a common pattern: see Jervis, *Perception and Misperception*, ch. 6; Ernest May, *"Lessons" of the Past: The Use and Misuse of History in American Foreign Policy* (New York: Oxford University Press, 1973); Yuen Foong Khong, *Analogies at War: Korean, Munich, and the Vietnam Decisions of 1973* (Princeton, N.J.: Princeton University Press, 1992).

31. Wesley Wark, *The Ultimate Enemy: British Intelligence and Nazi Germany, 1933–1939* (Ithaca, N.Y.: Cornell University Press, 1985). The literature on motivated bias is discussed and applied to international politics in Robert Jervis, Richard Ned Lebow, and Janice Gross Stein, *Psychology and Deterrence* (Baltimore: Johns Hopkins University Press, 1985). Lord Hutton's report clearing the Blair government of the BBC's charges that it distorted intelligence notes the possibility that analysts were "sub-consciously influenced" by their knowledge of what the government wanted to hear. Quoted in Brian Urquhart, "Hidden Truths," *New York Review of Books*, March 25, 2004, p. 44.

32. David Reynolds, "Churchill and the British 'Decision' to Fight on in 1940: Right Policy, Wrong Reasons," in Richard Langhorne, ed., *Diplomacy and Intelligence during the Second World War: Essays in Honour of F. H. Hinsley* (Cambridge: Cambridge University Press, 1985), pp. 147–167; Deborah Larson, "Truman and the Berlin Blockade: The Role of Intuition and Experience in Good Foreign Policy Judgment," in Stanley

Renshon and Deborah Larson, eds., *Good Judgment in Foreign Policy: Theory and Application* (Lanham, Md.: Rowman & Littlefield, 2003), pp. 127–152.

33. The best analysis is Joseph Cirincione et al., *WMD in Iraq: Evidence and Implications* (Washington, D.C.: Carnegie Endowment for International Peace, January 2004); for an update, see Alexis Orton, "Intelligence Patterns and Problems," *Carnegie Analysis*, July 19, 2004 http://www.ceip.org/files/nonprofit/templates/article.asp?NewsID=6591; also see David Isenberg and Ian Davis, "Unravelling the Known Unknowns: Why No Weapons of Mass Destruction Have Been Found in Iraq," British American Security Information Council Special Report 2004.1 (January 2004); David Cortright, Alistair Millar, George Lopez, and Linda Gerber, "The Flawed Case for the War in Iraq," Fourth Freedom Forum and Kroc Institute for International Peace Studies, University of Notre Dame, Policy Brief F12 (June 2003); "Opening Statement of Senator Carl Levin at Senate Armed Services Committee Hearing with DCI Tenet and DIA Director Jacoby," March 9, 2004, available at http://www.fas.org/irp/congress/2004_hr/levin030904.html.

34. A specific question is why the Clinton administration distorted what Saddam's son-in-law, Kamel Hussein, said after he defected. It was widely reported that he claimed that Saddam had retained a large WMD program; in fact, what he said was that while Saddam had a large program before the Gulf War, he destroyed it in its aftermath. John Barry, "The Defector's Secret," *Newsweek*, March 3, 2003, p. 6. For many observers, Kamel's report was a large part of the reason to believe that Saddam had chemical and biological weapons. Perhaps the Clinton administration spread, or at least did not correct, this version in order to maintain support for sanctions.

35. The four investigations of Pearl Harbor conducted in the five years after the attack failed to settle the basic questions, as shown by Martin Melosi, *The Shadow of Pearl Harbor: Political Controversy over the Surprise Attack, 1941–46* (College Station: Texas A&M University Press, 1977). It took an unofficial (but government-sponsored) study much later to shed real light on the problems in an analysis that remains central to our understanding not only of this case but of surprise attacks in general: Roberta Wohlstetter, *Pearl Harbor: Warning and Decision* (Stanford, Calif.: Stanford University Press, 1962).

36. I draw on the large literature on intelligence, intelligence failures, and surprise attack. In addition to Wohlstetter, *Pearl Harbor*, see especially Richard Betts, *Surprise Attack: Lessons for Defense Planning* (Washington, D.C.: Brookings Institution Press, 1982); Barton Whaley, *Codeword BARBAROSSA* (Cambridge, Mass.: MIT Press, 1973); James Wirtz, *The Tet Offensive: Intelligence Failure in War* (Ithaca, N.Y.: Cornell University Press, 1991). Much of this work rests on analysis of how individuals process information and see the world, as I have discussed in Robert Jervis, *Perception and Misperception in International Politics* (Princeton, N.J.: Princeton University Press, 1976). On the basis of doing a postmortem on why the CIA was slow to see that the Shah of Iran might fall, I came to the conclusion that many of the problems centered on organizational habits, culture, and incentives, however. A much sanitized version of my study is Robert Jervis, "What's Wrong with the Intelligence Process?" *International Journal of Intelligence and Counterintelligence* 1 (Spring 1986): 28–41. For a detailed study of the failure of American, Dutch, and U.N. intelligence to anticipate the capture of Srebrenica and the massacre of the men captured there, see Cees Wiebes, *Intelligence and the War in Bosnia, 1992–1995* (Münster: Lit Verlag, 2003). For all their weaknesses in this area, democracies probably do a better job of assessing their adversaries than do nondemocracies. See Ralph White, "Why Aggressors Lose," *Political Psychology* 11 (June 1990): 227–242; and Dan Reiter and Allan Stam, *Democracies at War* (Princeton, N.J.: Princeton University Press, 2002).

A fuller analysis of this case would compare the judgments reached by different countries and by different agencies within the American government. It is striking that in the cases of the aluminum tubes and unmanned aerial vehicles, the dissents from the alarmist and incorrect majority view were registered by the agencies with special expertise. It would also be useful to know more about why the media were not more critical of the intelligence reports before the war: a good start is Michael Massing, "Now They Tell Us," *New York Review of Books*, February 26, 2004, pp. 43–49. The similar role of the media in enabling the corporate corruption and false claims in the 1990s is examined in Maggie Mahar, *Bull! A History of the Boom, 1982–1999* (New York: HarperBusiness, 2003).

37. *On War*, edited and translated by Michael Howard and Peter Paret (Princeton, N.J.: Princeton University Press, 1976), p. 117. As I noted in the introduction, anyone who sees intelligence errors in terms of the failure to "connect the dots" does not understand the problem.

38. SSCI, p. 65.

39. Douglas Jehl, "Reading Satellite Photos, Then and Now," *New York Times*, February 8, 2004; also see the interview with former State Department intelligence official Greg Thielman on "The Man Who Knew," 60 Minutes II February 4, 2004, available at http:www.cbsnews.com/stories/2003/10/14/60II/main577975.shtml, and for a slightly different version, SSCI, p. 20.

40. This is a common pattern: see Jervis, *Perception and Misperception*, ch. 6; Ernest May, *"Lessons" of the Past: The Use and Misuse of History in American Foreign Policy* (New York: Oxford University Press, 1973); Yuen Foong Khong, *Analogies at War: Korean, Munich, and the Vietnam Decisions of 1973* (Princeton, N.J.: Princeton University Press, 1992).

41. The basic phenomenon is discussed in Jervis, *Perception and Misperception*, ch. 4; for the Iraq case, see Douglas Jehl, "U.S., Certain That Iraq Had Illicit Arms, Reportedly Ignored Contrary Reports," *New York Times*, March 6, 2004. Among the few who doubted that Iraq had WMD were former arms inspector Scott Ritter, Glens Rangwala, a lecturer in politics at Cambridge University (http://middleeastreference.org.uk/iraqncbfurther.html), and France's President Jacques Chirac, who told Hans Blix, the chief of U.N. inspections, that he thought the previous inspections and sanctions had effectively disarmed Iraq, and that the common belief to the contrary was a product of the tendency of intelligence services to "intoxicate each other:" Hans Blix, *Disarming Iraq* (New York: Pantheon, 2004), p. 129. The only person I know who doubted that Saddam had a stockpile of chemical weapons is my colleague Warner Schilling, who pointed out that such weapons have a short shelf life unless they are extremely sophisticated.

42. Here and throughout this section I am indebted to Chaim Kaufmann, "Threat Inflation and the failure of the Marketplace of Ideas: The Selling of the War," *International Security* 29 (Summer 2004).

43. A good illustration of this is Secretary of State Powell's reaction to his preparation for his January 2003 UN speech: "The more Powell dug [into the intelligence] the more he realized that the human sources were few and far between on Iraq's WMD. It was not a pretty picture. Still, like Bush and the other war cabinet members, he was much influenced by Saddam's past behavior. The dictator had used WMD in the 1980s, and then in the 1990s, and if he wasn't hiding anything now, all he had to do was to come clean. Powell agreed when Cheney argued, "Why in the world would he subject himself for all those years to UN sanctions and forgo an estimated $100 billion in oil revenue. It makes no sense!" (Bob Woodward, *Plan of Attack* [Simon & Schuster, 2004], p. 298.) It is also not surprising that when Bush was presented with the specific evidence supporting the conclusion that Iraq had WMD, he is reported to have said "Is that all?" (Ibid., p. 249.)

44. "Comprehensive Report of the Special Advisor to the DCI on Iraq's WMD," September 30, 2004 (Duelfer report), pp. 29, 55, 62, 64. John Mueller had earlier speculated that Saddam's limitations on the inspectors were motivated by his fear of assassination:

"Letters to the Editor: Understanding Saddam," *Foreign Affairs*, 83 (July/August 2004): 151.

45. Duelfer report, p. 34, also see p. 57. Ending economic sanctions and ending inspections would not necessarily have coincided and it is not clear which of them was viewed as most troublesome, and why. The UN resolutions provided for the latter to continue even after the former ended, and Saddam had terminated inspections in 1998. This presents a puzzle because if inspections had been the main barrier, Saddam should have resumed his programs at that point, as most observers expected. But it is hard to see how the sanctions were inhibiting him because after the institution of the Oil for Food program, the regime had access to sufficient cash to procure much of what it needed.

46. White House, "The National Security Strategy of the United States" (Washington, D.C.: September 2002), p. 16.

47. Kenneth Waltz, *Man, the State, and War* (New York: Columbia University Press, 1959). For a statement of the second-image argument by nongovernment supporters of the Bush doctrine, see Robert Kagan and William Kristol, "The Right War for the Right Reasons," *The Weekly Standard*, February 23, 2004, pp. 20–28. From this it follows, as they say, that "the key question...was not only what weapons Saddam had but what weapons he was trying to obtain, and how long it might be before containment failed and he was able to obtain them." For a similar second-image argument from scholars at the other end of the political spectrum, see Mary Caprioli and Peter Trumbore, "Identifying 'Rogue' States and Testing Their Interstate Conflict Behavior," *European Journal of International Relations* 9 (September 2003): 377–406. At times Bush stresses the pernicious role of Saddam and his personality: "I don't think America can stand by and hope for the best from a madman. ... You can't rely upon a madman, and he was a madman." *Meet the Press* interview with Tim Russert, February 8, 2004, available at http://www.msnbc.msn.com/id/4179618. Consistent with this, a former White House official reports that "Bush appears to have a simple test for evaluating his fellow leaders: Good people or bad people? Do they have a vision for their countries or not?" Glenn Kessler, "How Bush Interacts with World Leaders," *Washington Post*, June 8, 2004.

48. *Meet the Press* interview with Russert; also see Bush interview with Diane Sawyer, "Ultimate Penalty," December 16, 2003, available at http://abcnews.go.com/sections/primetime/US/bush_sawyer_excerpts_1_031216.html; "President Bush Discusses Progress in the War on Terror," address at Oak Ridge National Laboratory, White House press release, July 12, 2004. Colin Powell said something similar in "Remarks on the Occasion of George Kennan's Centenary Birthday," February 20, 2004, available at http://www.state.gov/secretary/rm/29683pf.htm, despite having taken a somewhat different position the week before: Glenn Kessler, "Powell: Arms Doubts Might Have Affected View of War," *Washington Post*, February 3, 2004.

49. For evidence for reasoning along these lines, see Duelfer report, pp. 11, 66–67.

50. The interrogations of Saddam and his associates yield scattered evidence that he was thinking along these lines: ibid., p. 66.

51. Ibid., p. 32. It is also possible that Saddam believed that the United States actually knew he did not have WMD and this too would have reduced the pressures on the United States to invade: Bob Drogin, "Through Hussein's Looking Glass," *Los Angeles Times*, October 12, 2004. For another attempt to re-create Saddam's views, see David Kay, "Iraq's Weapons of Mass Destruction: Lessons Learned and Unlearned," *Miller Center Report*, 20 (Spring/Summer 2004): 7–14. Also see Blix, *Disarming Iraq*, pp. 265–66.

52. Thomas Schelling, *Strategy of Conflict* (Cambridge, Mass.: Harvard University Press, 1960).

53. Indeed, shortly before the war the Bush administration returned to the position that to avoid invasion, Saddam would not only have to disarm but also to step down. Felicity Barringer and David Sanger, "U.S. Says Hussein Must Cede Power to Head Off War," *New York Times*, March 1, 2003.

54. For excellent studies of when coercion does and does not succeed in changing behavior, see Alexander George, David Hall, and William Simons, *The Limits of Coercive Diplomacy: Laos, Cuba, Vietnam* (Boston: Little, Brown, 1971); Alexander George and William Simons, eds., *The Limits of Coercive Diplomacy*, 2nd ed. (Boulder, Colo.: Westview, 1994); and Robert Art and Patrick Cronin, eds., *The United States and Coercive Diplomacy* (Washington, D.C.: United States Institute of Peace Press, 2003). For a discussion of failures of coercion that cannot be explained by standard theories, see Richard Ned Lebow and Janis Gross Stein, "Deterrence: The Elusive Dependent Variable," *World Politics* 42 (April 1990): 336–369; and Lebow and Stein, "Beyond Deterrence," *Journal of Social Issues* 43, no. 4 (1987): 5–72.

55. Gregory Gause III, "Iraq's Decisions to Go to War, 1980 and 1990," *Middle East Journal* 56 (Winter 2002): 47–70; and Fred Lawson, "Rethinking the Iraqi Invasion of Kuwait," *Review of International Affairs* 1 (Autumn 2001): 1–20.

56. For the argument that this extreme military pressure made a political settlement more difficult to reach, see Robert Pastor, "The Delicate Balance between Coercion and Diplomacy: The Case of Haiti, 1994," in Art and Cronin, eds., *The United States and Coercive Diplomacy*, pp. 119–156.

57. For further discussion, see Robert Jervis, *System Effects: Complexity in Political and Social Life* (Princeton, N.J.: Princeton University Press, 1997), pp. 44–45.

58. The literature on intelligence is obviously too large to cite here, but a good starting place is Ernest May, ed., *Knowing One's Enemies: Intelligence Assessment before the Two World Wars* (Princeton, N.J.: Princeton University Press, 1984); and my review-essay on this book: Robert Jervis, "Intelligence and Foreign Policy," *International Security* 11 (Winter 1986–1987): 141–161.

59. In addition to the Duelfor report, see, for example, Steve Coll, "Hussein Was Sure of Own Survival," *Washington Post*, November 3, 2003; James Risen, "CIA Had Only Very Little Data on Iraqi Arms, Ex-Inspector Says," *New York Times*, January 26, 2004; Thom Shanker, "Regime Thought War Unlikely, Iraqis Tell U.S." *New York Times*, February 12, 2004; Stanley Meisler, "American Policy Gave Hussein Reason to Deceive," *Los Angeles Times*, February 8, 2004; Brian Bennett, "Notes from Saddam in Custody," *Time*, December 14, 2003; and Pollack, "Spies, Lies, and Weapons." My own thoughts on why Saddam did not respond to American coercion are sketched in Robert Jervis, "The Credibility of U.S. Threats against Iraq," *SIPA News*, June 2003, pp. 3–5.

60. Quoted in Arthur Schlesinger, Jr., *A Thousand Days: John F. Kennedy in the White House* (Boston: Houghton Mifflin, 1965), p. 769.

61. Quoted in Barbara Slavin, "U.S. Softens Stance on Mideast Democratic Reforms," *USA Today*, April 12, 2004; for later developments, see Slavin, "U.S. Toning Down Goals for Mideast," *USA Today*, May 27, 2004. For a general discussion of the prospects for liberalization in the Middle East and the American efforts, see Tamara Cofman Wittes, "The Promise of American Liberalism," *Policy Review*, no. 125 (June/July 2004): 61–76. There is something to the argument that Carter's policy toward the Shah's regime in Iran was an exception, but policy-making was chaotic here, and the consequences of the policy are more apparent in retrospect than they were at the time. The United States did support democratization in South Korea and, with some reluctance, in the Philippines, but in these cases the alternative appeared even less likely to bring stability.

The administration's stress on the importance of democracy increased after the invasion of Iraq. The obvious explanation is the failure to find WMD and the concomitant weakening of the argument that the war was necessary to protect the United States and its regional allies, which meant that greater emphasis had to be placed on the value of liberating Iraq. One might think that claims for the importance and feasibility of democracy would have fallen away as the problems in Iraq mounted. But the psychological need to reduce cognitive dissonance leads us to expect exactly what happened. Just as the members of the cult studied by Leon Festinger reacted to the fact that the world did not end as they had predicted, not by abandoning their faith but by redoubling their commitment (Leon Festinger, Henry Riecken, and Stanley Schachter, *When Prophecy Fails: A Social and Psychological Study of a Modern Group That Predicted the Destruction of the World* [New York: Harper & Row, 1964]), the fact that things did not turn out as the administration expected means that the decision could be justified only by stressing that democracy was both possible in Iraq and a central American objective. The alternative would be to admit that the policy was incorrect, and this would have been very difficult for psychological as well as political reasons.

62. "President Bush Discusses Freedom in Iraq and Middle East," White House press release, November 6, 2003; also see "Remarks by President at the United States Air Force Academy Graduation."

63. For the argument that ideological affinity often plays a large role in one state's stance toward another, see Mark Haas, *Ideology, Threat Perception, and Great Power Politics* (Ithaca, N.Y.: Cornell University Press, 2005).

64. "U.S. Recognizes New Leader for Turkish Cypriots," *New York Times*, May 27, 2004.

65. A cautionary tale is provided by the memoirs of the British commander in the newly created Iraq after World War I: Sir Arnold Wilson, *Mesopotamia 1917–1920: A Clash of Loyalties* (London: Oxford University Press, 1931), especially pp. 259, 268–272, 311–312.

66. For a good comparison of the resources that occupying powers have been willing to devote to democratic reconstruction since World War II, see James Dobbins et al., *America's Role in Nation-Building: From Germany to Iraq* (Santa Monica, Calif.: RAND Corporation, 2003).

67. See Mark Peceny, *Democracy at the Point of Bayonets* (University Park: Penn State University Press, 1999); Tony Smith, *America's Mission: The United States and the Worldwide Struggle for Democracy in the Twentieth Century* (Princeton, N.J.: Princeton University Press, 1994). For discussions of the attempts at rebuilding war-torn states after the Cold War, see Roland Paris, "Peacebuilding and the Limits of Liberal Internationalism," *International Security* 22 (Fall 1997): 54–89; and Chester Crocker, Fen Osler Hampson, and Pamela Aall, eds., *Turbulent Peace: The Challenges of Managing International Conflict* (Washington, D.C.: United States Institute of Peace Press, 2001). Stephen Knack gives a negative answer to the question "Does Foreign Aid Promote Democracy?" *International Studies Quarterly* 48 (March 2004): 251–266. The effects of the U.S. sponsorship of economic development during the Cold War, as well as the motives and worldview that produced it, have been the subject of a large and largely ideological literature.

68. For the concept of natural order see Stephen Toulmin, *Foresight and Understanding: An Enquiry into the Aims of Science* (Bloomington: Indiana University Press, 1961). For an intriguing argument that democracy will indeed flourish in the absence of imposed obstacles, see John Mueller, *Capitalism, Democracy, and Ralph's Pretty Good Grocery* (Princeton, N.J.: Princeton University Press, 1999); for an excellent analysis that is skeptical of the ease of democratic transitions, see Thomas Carothers, "The End of the Transition Paradigm" *Journal of Democracy* 13 (January 2002): 5–21.

69. "President Bush Discusses Freedom in Iraq and Middle East," p. 3; also see "President Discusses the Future of Iraq," speech to the American Enterprise Institute, White House press release, February 26, 2003.

70. See Ian Shapiro, "The State of Democratic Theory," in Ira Katznelson and Helen Milner, eds., *Political Science: The State of the Discipline* (New York: Norton, 2002), pp. 235–265; Barbara Geddes, "The Great Transformation in the Study of Politics in Developing Countries," in Katznelson and Milner eds., *Political Science*, pp. 342–370; Adam Przeworski, Michael Alvaraz, Jose Antonio Cheibub, and Fernando Limongi, *Democracy and Development: Political Institutions and Well-Being in the World, 1950–1990* (Cambridge: Cambridge University Press, 2000). For a critique see Charles Boix and Susan Stokes, "Endogenous Democratization," *World Politics* 55 (July 2003): 517–549.

71. Quoted in Steven Weisman, "U.S. Muffles Sweeping Call to Democracy in Mideast," *New York Times*, March 12, 2004.

72. Michael Doyle, "Kant, Liberal Legacies, and Foreign Affairs, Part 1," *Philosophy and Public Affairs* 12 (Summer 1983): 205–235, and "Kant, Liberal Legacies, and Foreign Affairs, part 2," *Philosophy and Public Affairs* 12 (Autumn 1983): 323–353; also see Erik Gartzke, Preferences and the Democratic Peace," *International Studies Quarterly* 44 (June 2000): 191–210, and "The Futility of War: Capitalism and Common Interests as Determinants of the Democratic Peace," unpublished MS, Columbia University.

73. Edward Mansfield and Jack Snyder, *Electing to Fight: Why Emerging Democracies Go to War* (Cambridge, Mass.: MIT Press, 2005).

74. Quoted in Douglas Jehl, "U.S. Says It Will Move Gingerly Against Sadr," *New York Times*, April 7, 2004. Similarly, in the run-up to the war in Kosovo, General Wesley Clark endorsed the view that the problem was caused by the fact that the Belgrade regime was not democratic: *Waging Modern War: Bosnia, Kosovo, and the Future of Combat* (New York: Public Affairs, 2001), p. 128.

75. Public opinion data in the spring of 2004 were ambivalent but not encouraging: while most Iraqis were glad that Saddam was ousted, said their own lives were better because of the invasion, and thought that their country would be less safe if Coalition forces left, they viewed those forces as occupiers rather than liberators, thought they should leave immediately, and viewed George Bush unfavorably. Available at http://www.cnn.com/2004/world/meast/04/28/iraq.poll/iraq/poll/index.html

76. Robert Art, "Why Western Europe Needs the United States and NATO," *Political Science Quarterly* 111 (Spring 1996): 1–39.

77. In addition to the discussion in chapter 1, see David Frum and Richard Perle, *An End to Evil: How to Win the War on Terror* (New York: Random House, 2003), pp. 238–253.

78. For further discussion, see Seth Jones, "The European Union and the Security Dilemma," *Security Studies* 12 (Spring 2003): 114–157.

79. See the discussion in chapter 4, and the literature cited there.

80. Walter Lippmann, *Public Opinion* (New York: Macmillan, 1922).

81. Ibid., P. 95. It is also worth noting that Lippmann's chapter on intelligence argues: "It is no accident that the best diplomatic service in the world is the one in which the divorce between the assembling of knowledge and the control of policy is most perfect" (*Public Opinion*, pp. 381–382).

INDEX